Liberté, Égalité and *Fraternité* at Work

Liberté, Égalité and *Fraternité* at Work

Changing French Employment Relations and Management

Steve Jefferys

palgrave
macmillan

First published 2003 by
PALGRAVE MACMILLAN
Houndmills, Basingstoke, Hampshire RG21 6XS and
175 Fifth Avenue, New York, N.Y. 10010
Companies and representatives throughout the world

PALGRAVE MACMILLAN is the global academic imprint of the Palgrave
Macmillan division of St. Martin's Press, LLC and of Palgrave Macmillan Ltd.
Macmillan® is a registered trademark in the United States, United Kingdom and
other countries. Palgrave is a registered trademark in the European
Union and other countries.

ISBN 0–333–74137–4

This book is printed on paper suitable for recycling and made from fully
managed and sustained forest sources.

A catalogue record for this book is available from the British Library.

Library of Congress Cataloging-in-Publication Data
Jefferys, Steve.
        Liberté, égalité, and fraternité at work: changing French employment relations
    and management / Steve Jefferys.
            p. cm.
        Includes bibliographical references and index.
        ISBN 0–333–74137–4
            1. Industrial relations – France – History. 2. Labor unions – France – History.
    3. Industrial policy – France – History. 4. France – Social policy – 19th century.
    5. France – Social policy – 20th century. I. Title.

    HD8430 .J44 2003
    331'.0944–dc21   2002035833

10 9 8 7 6 5 4 3 2 1

Printed and bound in Great Britain by
Antony Rowe Ltd, Chippenham and Eastbourne

For Stam, James and Margot

Contents

List of Tables

List of Figures

List of Acronyms

AAH	*Allocation adulte handicapé*	Disability benefit
ACOSS	*Agence centrale des organismes de sécurité sociale*	Central agency for social security
AFEP	*Association française des entreprises privées*	Privately-owned (very large) employers' association
AGFF	*Association pour la gestion des fonds de financement*	Investment fund management agency
AGIRC	*Association générale des institutions de retraite des cadres*	Supplementary pension scheme for managers
ALF	*Allocation de logement à caractère familial*	Family housing benefit
API	*Allocation de parent isolé*	Single parent benefit
APL	*Aide personalisée au logement*	Individual housing benefit
ANPE	*Agence nationale pour l'emploi*	National Employment Agency
APM	*Association progrès du management*	Union of Clubs for Management Progress
ARPE	*Allocation de remplacement pour l'emploi*	Early retirement benefit
ARRCO	*Association des regimes de retraite complémentaire*	Supplementary pension scheme for non-managerial workers
ASF	*Association pour la structure financière*	Financial structure association (financing early retirement)
CA	*Conseil d'administration*	Company board
CAP	*Commission administrative paritaire*	Joint administrative advisory committee (public sector only)
CCI	*Chambre de Commerce et de l'industrie*	Chamber of Commerce and Industry
CE	*Comités d'entreprise*	Works councils
CF	*Complément familial*	Family supplement

CFTC	Confédération française des travailleurs chrétiens	National Christian Workers' Union
CFDT	Confédération française démocratique du travail	National Democratic Workers' Union
CGC	Confédération générale des cadres	National Managers' Union
CGPF	Confédération générale de la production française	National manufacturing confederation
CGPME	Confédération générale des petites et moyennes entreprises	National Association of small and medium-sized firms
CGT	Confédération générale du travail	General Workers' Union
CGTU	Confédération générale du travail unitaire	United General Workers Union
CID-UNATI	Confédération Intersyndicale de Défense et d'Union Nationale d'Action des Travailleurs Indépendants	Self-employed Defence and Action Association
CJD	Centre des jeunes dirigeants	Young executives' centre
CMU	Couverture maladie universelle	Universal health cover
CNAF	Caisse nationale d'allocations familiales	National family allowance agency
CNAM	Caisse nationale d'assurance-maladie	Health service agency
CNAMTS	Caisse nationale d'assurance-maladie des travailleurs salariés	Workers' health service agency
CNAVTS	Caisse nationale de l'assurance-vieillesse des travailleurs salaries	Workers' old age pension agency
CNPF (Patronat)	Conseil national du patronat français	French Bosses Council
CSG	Contribution sociale généralisée	National social insurance deduction
CSL	Confédération des syndicats libres	Free trade union confederation
EDC	Entrepreneurs et Dirigeants Chrétiens	Christian entrepreneurs and executives
ENA (énarque)	École nationale d'administration	School of National Administration/ graduate

Ethic	*Entreprises de taille humaine indépendentes et de croissance*	Club for growing, independent medium-sized firms
FEN	*Fédération de l'éducation nationale*	National Teachers Union
FN	*Front national*	National Front party
FNB	*Fédération nationale du bâtiment*	Building employers' association
FNSEA	*Fédération nationale des syndicats d'exploitants agricoles*	National farmers' Union
FO	*CGT–Force Ouvrière*	Workers' Power – CGT
HEC	*École des Hautes Études Commerciales*	Advanced Business School
ICT	*Ingénieurs, cadres et techniciens*	Managers, engineers and technical workers
Medef	*Mouvement des entreprises de France*	French Business Movement
MNR	*Mouvement national républicain*	National Republican Front
MRP	*Mouvement républicain populaire*	Popular Republican Party
MV	*Minimum vieillesse*	Guaranteed minimum old age pension
OPACIF	*Organisme paritaire agréé dans le cadre du congé individuel de formation*	Individual training leave joint management body
PARE	*Plan d'aide au retour a l'emploi*	Back to Work plan
PCF	*Partie communiste française*	French Communist Party
PDP	*Partie démocrate populaire*	Popular Democratic Party
PME	*Petites et moyennes entreprises*	SME – small and medium-sized firms
PS	*Parti socialiste*	Socialist Party
RPR	*Rassemblement pour la République*	All for the Republic
SMIC	*Salaire minimum interprofessionnel de croissance*	National growth minimum wage
SMIG	*Salaire minimum interprofessionnel garanti*	National guaranteed minimum wage
SNPMI	*Syndicat national du patronat moderne et indépendant*	Independent modern employers' association
SNUI	*Syndicat national unifié des impôts*	Tax staffs' united national trade union

SUD	*Solidaires unitaires et démocratiques*	Together United and Democratic trade union
UCANSS	*Union des caisses nationales de sécurité sociale*	National social security agency
UDF	*Union pour la démocratie française*	Union for French Democracy
UIMM	*Union des industries métallurgiques et minières*	Engineering and mining employers' association
UMP	*Union pour la majorité présidentielle*	Union for a Presidential Majority
UNAPL	*Union nationale des professions liberals*	Liberal professions' association
UNEDIC	*Union nationale interprofessionnelle pour l'emploi dans l'industrie et le commerce*	Unemployment insurance for industry and commerce
UNSA	*Union nationale des syndicats autonomes*	National Union of Independent Unions
UPA	*Union professionnelle artisanale*	Skilled Crafts Association

Preface

The research for this book began in 1998 when I combined a European Union teaching fellowship at the University of Évry organised by Jean-Pierre Durand with a sabbatical semester generously provided by Keele University. Since then, writing has continued in fits and starts, most often when I have been able to look out on the Roc d'Enfer in the Haute-Savoie. Macmillan, in its current incarnation as Palgrave Macmillan, has been most understanding as successive deadlines swept by, most often on a tide of other contractural research commitments. As these were often linked to Anglo-French or wider European comparisions, however, they frequently contributed both directly and indirectly to this book. To my friends and research colleagues Thérèse Beaupain, Mick Carpenter, Sylvie Contrepois, Peter Cooper, Frederik Mispelblom, Birger Simonson, Carole Thornley and Christer Thornqvist, with whom I have collaborated on European research and writing projects over recent years I owe much for having made me think more laterally than I once did. Frank Burchill and the other believers at the Keele University school of 'real industrial relations' also helped enormously in providing the space to think, research and write. At my current university, the London Metropolitan University, where I am Professor of European Employment Studies and Director of the Working Lives Research Institute, new colleagues and friends have been genuinely welcoming.

The book's mistakes are entirely mine. But many friends and colleagues have helped me avoid making more serious ones. Among those who have kindly and helpfully commented on one or more of the chapters or articles I have written recently on France are Yochanan Altman, Christian Dufour, Jacques Freyssinet, Daniel Furjot, Janine Goetschy, Guy Groux, Phillippe Marlière, Mike Newman, Jacques Rojot, Jean Vincent and Guy Vernon. Sylvie Contrepois, Gérard Duménil, John Grahl, Richard Hyman, Bernie Moss and Jens Thoemmes were all especially helpful, either in providing very detailed comments on particular chapters or in offering challenging overview comments. To Sue Milner, who brought her own expertise selflessly to a detailed critical reading of the whole text, I owe a special debt. I would also like to specifically thank my friends in Paris, Anne-Christine, Bruno and Nicole from whom I learned much, and those in Bellevaux, Haute Savoie, where Corinne and Daniel (now in Brittany) helped to give me the space and stimulation to get it done.

Finally, I would like to thank my family. It is not just that Michael, the 10-year-old, who lived with me in France when I began this book, spending a year at local primary schools in Paris and the Haute-Savoie, was terrific company. He also continuously asked relevant and nearly unanswerable questions like, 'Why are there so many strikes in France, Dad?' To Joan and Kerry I owe solid support, toleration of my optimism and real friendship. From Stam, my alter-father John Saville, there has always been constant encouragement. Finally, I also owe my actual parents, James and Margot, to whom this book is also dedicated, and who both died too soon. Having two of the brightest of the 1930s generation of LSE leftists as parents was not always easy: but it was always interesting. Thanks.

Introduction

With 58.4 million inhabitants recorded in the 1999 census, metropolitan France has the same-sized population as the United Kingdom, although the French are spread over more than twice the land surface. At the beginning of the twenty-first century France is still, narrowly, and depending on how you measure it, the world's fourth or fifth biggest economy. Although its national output was more than six times smaller than that of the United States, two and a quarter times smaller than Japan's and a third smaller than Germany's, in 1996 its 22-million 'active' population produced slightly more 'purchasing power parities' than did the United Kingdom's 26 million, and slightly fewer by 2001. The current economic strength of France is largely built upon annual increases in productivity averaging 3 per cent per year between 1960 and 1994, measured by real GDP per employed person, nearly double the rate in the United Kingdom over the same period (OECD 1996a: 53).

Although concerned with how a huge wealth-creating society is organised, about the strength of capital and how it is managed, this book is also about the lives of ordinary people. Our adult lives start when much is shared. There are, of course, initial critical differences in gender, ethnic origins and social class that frame our degree of choice. Yet, along with the two other key life-time contracts over partnering and housing, life experiences are shaped overwhelmingly by work (or its absence), and by the employment relations it engenders.

What do I understand by the key terms used in this study? *Work* provides (or denies) income and the opportunity to exercise choice over consumption, and it situates individuals within a certain social organisation of labour, giving or denying them status in front of their peers. *Management*, an American term that only became global during the second half of the twentieth century (Carpenter and Jefferys 2000), is about shaping the relationships of subordination that occur within the social organisation of production. It embraces both the loci of economic and social power (generally capital, land or the state apparatus) and the detailed individual hierarchical relationships that flow from that power. *Employment relations* are concerned with the wide range of

1

elements that create different work experiences. This term, for me, includes both what has become known as human resource management (HRM) (management strategies aimed at securing the maximum co-operation possible from workers) and industrial or labour relations – 'encompassing not only the relations between unions and management and the regulation of wages and employment conditions, but also the public policies towards labour markets and labour market organisations, and the legal and institutional framework within which these organisations interact' (Visser 1999: 1).

The book is primarily about France, a country introduced to me by my economist and labour historian absentee father, who made Paris his home for 41 years. But I hope that the book is not only about one country. It may be read more broadly as being about work everywhere and the kinds of political, economic and social factors that lead to or enable particular kinds of experiences and particular kinds of lives. It is thus offered to three discrete but overlapping audiences. To all interested in such issues, it attempts to add to our understanding of the interactions between work and society in a world now dominated by global capitalism. In particular, it points to the continued relevance of ideology in shaping collective human behaviours. To those interested in the culture and politics of France, it introduces the histories and realities of French employment relations and management. To those more directly concerned with management, HRM and industrial relations, it aspires also to provide an (inevitably brief) introduction to France.

One of France's greatest twentieth century historians, Braudel (1991: 666), once asked rhetorically: 'Is it perhaps both France's tragedy and the secret of its charm that it has never really been won over to capitalism?' This observation is at the theoretical heart of this book. I will argue that the continuing tensions between the ideologies of *liberté, fraternité* (better known today as *solidarité*) and *égalité* (translated as being between 'freedom, social solidarity and equality') are reflected in the tensions within employment relations between ideologies of subordination, mediation and resistance.

Why place such an emphasis on ideology? The reason is that it holds the key to understanding why on certain occasions people mobilise with others to assert their collective interests. If people have the same interpretation of a certain situation ('our glasses are clearly half empty'), then this makes it much more probable that they will act to try and bridge the strategic gap between their collective expectations and their actual situation. In the real world it is very rare for all participant–observers of such a strategic gap to either share the same analysis or to view the world around them only from one perspective. Much more often people's perceptions are coloured by a wide range of views making decisive collective action difficult to mobilise. These muddled thoughts – mixing elements from different perspectives – usually dominate until some decisive external event provides sufficient clarity of view among a large enough social group to mobilise them to common action.

Consider the case of the Normandy-based Moulinex company, one of France's most successful paternalistic firms between its founding in 1936 and the 1980s. In 2000, it was merged with the Italian-owned Brandt organisation, whose new top managers were now totally remote from the local workforce, and who viewed the world as being essentially a marketplace in which the new owners of the firm had total freedom to dispose of the company's factories and labour force if that was in their interests. They expected a certain level of profitability from the organisation and when it was not forthcoming believed in their right to act to bridge the strategic gap. This world view, the common, market one, rooted in the primacy of individual *liberté*, was undoubtedly shared by many of the 5,600 French-based employees who in March 2001 learned that their new 'owners' intended to close three factories and make 2,800 workers redundant. But there were also competing world views present among the workforce. One conceded management had the right to take unpleasant decisions, but believed that on the grounds of social solidarity, of a common *fraternité* between the owners and the employees, that the workers' views and interests should be taken into account. Since management had often proved mistaken in the past, the Moulinex group works council commissioned an accountancy consultants' report to show them that there was a realistic alternative. This was another world view derived from a much more vigorous assumption of a real equality of rights between employees and employers. The consistent critical *égalité* perspective in contrast denied altogether that the 'owners' had any absolute right to dispose of the socially constructed factories the workers had created and the jobs they provided. Those who saw the world through this perspective believed that the closure and redundancies could be stopped by occupying the factories and building a broad-based political campaign to force the owners to retreat.

The mobilisations around these different world views led, by November 2001, to the declaration of the company's bankruptcy, the subsequent cherry-picking by its principal competitor of a third of the firm and to government intervention to end a three-month factory occupation by its agreeing to pay each of the sacked 3,700 French workers an additional £5,000 redundancy 'bonus'. At the 2002 presidential elections in the commune of one of the closed factories, one after-effect was that they also contributed to one of the highest (16.2 per cent) votes for the combined Trotskyist candidates – the same proportion as for Jacques Chirac.

The choices that different collectives of people made in the Moulinex example were made within clear economic and technological environment restraints. Yet the processes of human decision-making in modern capitalist societies are not predetermined by those restraints. Of course, those who exercise power in capitalist societies are driven by an embedded social requirement to realise profit. This necessitates continuous expansion and periodic transformations of the means of production, of management and of employment relations to realise new means of making profits. Social relations are therefore continually being reconfigured to extract labour from workers to service a system in which, while they reap some benefits, they are far from being the chief beneficiaries. This essentially conflictual requirement constrains many of the political and cultural features of modern societies, including work, management, employment relations and patterns of state welfare.

Yet, how those who exercise power and those who are subordinate to it, actually view the world and then mobilise to take specific choices is an inherently uncertain process that leads to a wide variety of social forms and power relations. These are influenced by factors such as national traditions and institutions as well as by the strength and direction of mobilisations by employers or workers. While largely following the outcomes of direct power struggles between (and within) ruling elites and the ruled, the actual terms of resource allocation in contemporary society also reflect the political skills and the mobilising capability (including access to the state) of the contending parties.

In this book, the results of my own theoretical approach are seen in the selection of evidence from the political and social contexts to explain the collective processes leading to conflict and co-operation at work, and to particular patterns of management and employment relations. While I focus on the workplace and its regulation, I also use a wide lens to refer to the wider terrain of French politics and French society. This is not just because changes in French welfare (the level of sickness or unemployment benefit, for example) have consequences for the French labour market. They also have institutional effects and hence consequences on mobilising capacity. For example, the 1946 law running state welfare through jointly managed committees of employers and unions actually encouraged the emergence of managerial trade unionism.

A wider lens is needed also because political developments such as the internal conflicts within the French political right in 1981 and 1995, for example, were important for the evolution of the room to manoeuvre of French management. A model of the approach taken in this book to the interrelationships between politics, management, work and state welfare is represented in Figure 0.1.

In taking this book beyond the traditional narrow limits of academic employment relations I am building on the convincing suggestions made by Esping-Andersen (1990; 1992) that it is impossible to properly consider how labour markets function without taking into account the various ways in which the state structures entry into and exit from the labour market. One key function the state performs is to create a minimum basis of trust (or predictability) necessary to stabilise labour markets. Esping-Andersen's image of welfare as institutionalised protection afforded to workers, freeing them from having to rely exclusively upon their own individual resources is

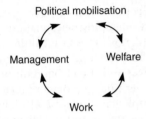

Figure 0.1 The linkages between politics, management, work and state welfare

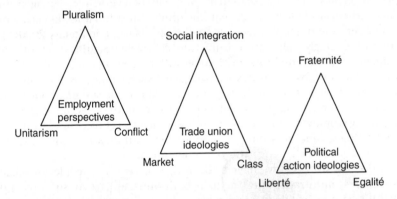

Figure 0.2 Conceptual models of employment relations, trade union ideologies and political action

Source: With acknowledgement to Richard Hyman (1996).

illuminating. He calls this 'decommodification', interventions restricting the extent to which human labour is reduced to a pure commodity. In this book, I trace not only the 'protections' offered through state education and training, through state social housing and state health services, but also the 'protective' measures that establish limits to the legal working week and minimum wages, and place obligations on employers to 'protect' their workers' health and safety and to give their employees certain rights to information and consultation concerning their working lives.

Employment relations can only be fully understood, then, through also examining the political choices that govern the direction and extent of state interventions, and that help shape actors' world views. My approach in attempting to both simplify and clarify a highly complex process involving the evolution of political, managerial and trade union thought and behaviour leans on the three discrete triangular models graphically illustrated in Figure 0.2.

The first triangle is based on Fox's (1966) analytical distinction between three major ideological frameworks in employment relations, those of pluralism, unitarism and conflict. *Pluralist* ideology recognises the existence and legitimacy of conflict in employment relations between employers and employees, and structures choices towards minimising its consequences on production and society. Pluralist choices are concerned with the recognition of employee representatives and the elaboration of law-based or collective agreement-based rules governing employment relations that are acceptable to both workers and employers. *Unitarist* ideology tends to see conflict within the enterprise as illegitimate and as deviant behaviour. From the legal act of ownership comes a form of divine right to manage. From this perspective comes the view shared by four out of every five managers in France's 1999 workplace survey that 'the firm's senior and line management best understand the problems of its employees' (Malan and Zouary 2000: 6). Unitarist strategies aim at securing the complete identification of the employee with the employer, whose rules will then become acceptable to all. *Conflict* ideology, by contrast, sees struggle between employers and employees as permanent and inevitable under capitalism, a system it views as incapable over the long term of devising continuously acceptable rules governing employment relations. Conflict-influenced choices tend to aim at maximising the mobilisation capability present in the evolving processes of rule creation, rule challenge and rule amendment.

In the real world, as we have already argued, very few people (or social classes or administrative elites) actually both think and act consistently and logically within a single ideological optic. But the analytical exercise of trying to assess which are the dominant influences and how they change over time is helpful in allowing us to understand much of the behaviour of French employment relations actors.

A second helpful model of the complexity of ideological influences has been drawn by Hyman (1996; 2001). He is concerned with sketching the ways in which the principal European trade union movements are inspired by different ideological influences. He sees three contrasting ideological poles: one is around social integration, where a major object of trade union action was to achieve the acceptance by society of a legitimate place and pluralistic role for the unions; a second lies around the dominance of market ideology, where trade union aims were strictly business, about maximising the price of the particular occupational or enterprise-based labour collective being bargained over; and a third pole lies around class conflict and the idea that trade union action is a part of a wider struggle with more general goals seeking to transform society as a whole. The point here again is not that any single trade union movement may be mapped wholly or purely on to one or other of these concepts: trade union consciousness is always an amalgam of ideas from all three poles. But Hyman goes on to argue that what distinguishes national traditions between different countries is that each country tends to be more exposed to influence from two of these poles at the expense of the third.

The third helpful framework in mapping and modelling the ideological choices made in French management and employment relations derives directly from French history. The revolutionary tryptique, *liberté*, *égalité* and *fraternité*, adorns the front of every town hall in France. But these words also symbolise patterns of thought and choices that have helped shape French welfare and that continue to inspire different forms of political mobilisation. Arguably they are still useful in analysing the ways in which cooperation or conflict over resource allocations in the workplace is mobilised and justified.

The third term in the tryptique, *fraternité* (fraternity, brotherhood), first appeared in the French language in the twelfth century when it was one of the key words in the Christian discourse. By the time of the French Revolution it was common to use it in both its technical sense of a family relationship and its figurative sense of an attitude or behaviour where, without being related, people treat each other with love or close friendship. After the short-lived Second Republic of 1848 when it was officially added to *liberté* and *égalité*, it slowly dropped out of common usage, being at first used interchangeably with, and after the emergence of socialism in the 1890s being largely replaced by, the somewhat more secular term *solidarité*. This has less of the moral sense of closeness and identification that distinguishes *fraternité* (Borgetto 1993: 3–7). *Solidarité* is now commonly associated with the principle that the French Republic should be anti-racist. But it is also a much more *active* concept than *fratnernité*. By the 1970s and 1980s, *solidarité* dominated the trade union discourse. Its gender neutrality and narrower meaning appeared more appropriate to the times, with the term 'fraternally' being almost exclusively reserved for formal trade union correspondence (Hetzel *et al.* 1998). The concepts *fraternité–solidarité* are both closely linked with the notions of *inclusion*, the organisation of society in the interests of all, with the *sharing* of common values, and with a moral obligation to *act collectively* in pursuit of these values, all of which have been identified both with a critique of free market capitalism and with the justification of collective struggles (Friot 1998). They also remain a key part of Social Catholic discourse suggesting that societal rules should be modelled on the family rather than on the market or on the prosecution of an inherently divisive class struggle (Frey 1995: 131).

Liberté (liberty), although always implying a form of 'non-constraint', combines two meanings. There is the sense of 'freedom' that inspired Voltaire to write a pamphlet campaigning for 'freedom of thought' in 1763. For the following two hundred years, *liberation struggles* involved revolutionary overtones, whether for the suffrage or national independence. Yet, beginning in 1791, with the banning of trade unions in Revolutionary France as an affront to individual *liberté*, throughout the nineteenth century, and again increasingly since the 1970s, *liberté* has also meant *economic liberalism*, 'free trade', and what is now often called *neo-liberalism*. Thus, although freedom has always been the cry of the oppressed, 'liberty' has always also embraced the freedom *to* oppress, closely associated both the idea of the 'free' market (in which capital is 'free' to seek the lowest possible price for labour) and with the unitarist argument that the individual liberty of an employer entitles him or her to dispose of their assets and any labour they buy in whichever way they want.

Égalité or 'equality' also combines two related meanings: of being fair and just to all people (equity), and the idea of treating all people as if they were your friends. From Jean-Jacques Rousseau's 1754 essay on the origins of inequality to the Paris Commune of 1870, it was thus a highly radical term, giving rise to 'egalitarian' revolutionary groups (Hetzel *et al.* 1998: 100). Through most of the twentieth century it has remained a radical term, proposing that every human being is in most ways equal with every other, and that all have a 'right' to be treated in the same way by the law. It is still used today by those who experience gender, racial, income, class or other forms of inequality and discrimination, and is at the core of the legal sense of injustice.

Each of these analytical three-cornered models throws some light upon the related areas of employment relations, trade union consciousness and political action. Juxtaposing these three distinct models makes it possible to see that some of the tensions between the poles in each of these models are similar. While each of them captures a distinct area of thought and different issues, the choices taken and behaviours may originate in what, from this analytical perspective, appear to be overlapping ideologies. Thus, a pluralist employment perspective may be associated with the prioritisation of trade union goals of social integration and Social Catholic political goals of *fraternité* and *solidarité*; unitarism may be stronger when political liberalism is entrenched, and this may be associated with an ideology of market unionism; and where conflict perspectives on employment relations are influential there will almost certainly be greater emphasis on class struggle within the trade union movement, as well as on a more radical interpretation of *égalité* that extends as far as 'common ownership' of societal wealth.

Yet, there is never complete domination by any of the ideological poles: people's consciousness is usually contradictory, embracing elements from all of the poles and with their respective weights varying through life and in relation to their life experiences. Thus, the importance of each group of coherent ideas to people and to the collective organisations they form will change over time along with the political and social terrain. I refer to them in the narrative of this book not because they have a real existence in and of themselves, but because they constitute a helpful analytical framework for suggesting how patterns of thought and behaviour change over time.

Ideas about rights and justice in employment relations do not exist in a vacuum. They emerge and develop in relation to people's material experiences of the distribution of resources. I see the choices that affect this distribution as reflecting employers' and workers' degrees of social cohesion, their awareness of the balance of power at any given moment, and their mobilisation capacity, both in terms of the state and at work. The strength of the state and the degree of inertia of its institutions also play key roles. The resulting employment relations profile is not dominated by a single ideology, nor is it necessarily consistent over time. It is essentially open to choice rather than the result of some mechanical determinism. These choices are made according to the dominant world views of the collectives who make them and in the light of their different mobilising capacities. What the book argues is that what is new at the start of the twenty-first century is not the existence of different class interests, but their reconfigured degrees of influence. The ideologies of *liberté*, *unitarism* and the *market* are still being challenged as ways of seeing the world, but they are more in the ascendant in work in France today at the start of the third millennium than 20 or 30 years ago, arguably nearly as dominant as they were one hundred years ago.

The book is loosely organised in three parts. Those who only wish to consider issues about the present should start reading from Chapter 4. But this would mean missing Chapter 1, which deals with French theoretical attempts to understand the dynamic of French employment relations, and Chapters 2 and 3, which ground what follows in historical reality. Indeed, a key object of the book is to embody what the late French philosopher and left activist, Pierre Bourdieu, called a 'united social science, where history becomes historical sociology of the past, and sociology becomes a social history of the present'.

The first chapter considers how many French academics approach and theorise their country's employment relations. This brief overview is not an optional extra. French intellectuals continue to attempt to use their ideas to influence events. Thus, several of those cited in this book (including Luc Boltanski, Robert Castel, Thomas Coutrot, Alain Lipietz, Philippe Marlière and Gérard Noiriel) signed an appeal published in *Le Monde* on 30 June 2000 calling (unsuccessfully as it turned out) for the government to refuse to ratify the new UNEDIC agreement on unemployment insurance. To understand where these and others are coming from is part of the process of getting to know France. The book next provides a historical and contemporary overview of the evolution and patterns of management, work and welfare that structure contemporary French employment relations. Chapter 2 offers an overview of the evolution of France as one of the world's major industrial powers. Chapter 3 examines the construction of the patterns of management, work and welfare forming the background to French employment relations up to the 1980s.

I then turn to exploring the contemporary social and economic reality. Chapter 4 sketches the recent evolution of the key structures of population, industry and finance, social class and politics that make up the background to today's social organisation of production. Chapter 5 considers how the

French state continues to structure business, the labour market and welfare at the start of the twenty-first century. Chapter 6 considers the evolution of French capitalism and management. Chapter 7 turns to French employers' organisations and their strategies, while Chapter 8 looks at employee representation and trade unions. The book's conclusion (Chapter 9) brings together some of the comparative themes suggested elsewhere in the book.

1
Theorising French Employment Relations

Theory cannot be avoided in writing a book on France. The slow pace of French nineteenth century industrialisation left a strong legacy of Enlightenment thought to the twentieth century. Even at the start of the twenty-first century ideas and ideology remain important, sustained not least by the obligation on 600,000 French 18-year-olds who take the *baccalauréat* each year to sit a compulsory examination in philosophy. Unlike their pragmatic cross-channel neighbours, 'intellectuals' and 'theory' in France are still viewed as making a valid contribution. Government, employers and trade unions continue to look to them for advice on current practice. Thomas Coutrot, the industrial relations section head at the Ministry of Labour's statistics and research division, DARES, puts it like this:

> Theory is not a luxury. Empirical analysis, in reality, is not sufficient on its own. To create a view of reality, it is necessary to have access to theoretical models that structure the questions, select the dimensions judged relevant, order the variables, and organise the causalities. (Coutrot 1998: 9)

What is this 'theorising' that is still alive and kicking in France? Theory may be seen as a method for reliably solving second-hand jigsaw puzzles where the box lid with the original picture has gone missing. Theory should help explain why certain pieces lock together, what the missing pieces (there are always several) would have looked like, and even why they are missing. What is important in developing such explanations is to know the 'principles of inclusion and selection (that are) linked to (explicit or implicit) criteria of significance' (Hyman 1994: 167). How do you decide to make certain deductions on the basis of only very partial knowledge? The more useful a theory is, the more you should be able to successfully apply the same general approach when you look at the next puzzle – or in our case at another set of work experiences or pattern of employment relations. Theorising that is not so useful selects data in ways that mean it is of little use in other contexts, and in some instances, does not even explain clearly the evidence or context around which it was conceived. Good theorising helps create a view of reality and patterns of causalities that may be useful in other contexts.

This chapter starts by looking at some of the main 'criteria of significance' used by three French academic disciplines concerned with employment relations. As will become apparent in the narrative of the book, the state has played a particularly important part in shaping French empoyment relations. Understanding the interface between employers and employees has often, therefore, started from a legal perspective, from a sociological or from an historical one (or all three). The chapter then critically discusses three of the many theories connecting the different economic, political and social elements underlying employment relations.

1.1   Academic approaches to employment relations

Legal

Within arms reach of every French human resource manager is an up-to-date copy of the *Code du Travail*. Access to the weighty French Labour Code – my version has 1,776 pages of 8 pt print including annotations commenting on recent court decisions – is absolutely indispensable for all French managers concerned with personnel policy. Little wonder that lawyers constitute one of the main groups of academic commentators upon French employment relations, nor that prospective personnel managers often study law at university. One of the first specialist employment relations journals was a legal one, *Droit Social*, founded in 1938 (Caire 1996: 37). Lawyers are often called on to give advice on the implementation of sectoral collective agreements that are also never far from French personnel managers' elbows. This is because once agreements are signed between the employers' association representing firms within a particular industry and (one or more of) the unions present in that sector, its terms may be extended by the Ministry of Labour to become the legal basis of all employment conditions in the sector.

Whose interests are served by the presence of extensive labour law restraining the 'liberty' of action between employer and employees? A standard explanation is that the law and judiciary are 'neutral' elements, acting disinterestedly between the contending parties in the interests of the 'greater good' of the whole society. But others argue that the steady accumulation of labour law shows that the law can reform capitalism for the better, undermining its most negative aspects. Then there are those who argue that the expansion of French labour law, far from undermining capitalism, has tended to legitimate it. A third group rejects both the 'forward march of labour law' argument and the 'legitimating' theory. This group sees labour law much like other law within capitalist society, as fundamentally a conservative force designed to protect existing resource inequalities. However, it also sees it as being capable of changing rapidly in response to wider changes in the economic, political and social fabric, and, occasionally, in response to the technical quality of a legal case (Collin *et al.* 1980). Gérard Lyon-Caen describes labour law as 'born within a capitalist system that needed a free and mobile labour force; grown up through workers' struggles, it represents at the same time both the demands of waged workers and those of an economy founded on the private company and on profit'. For him labour law 'by going beyond (without ignoring) legal technicalities raises the most fundamental problems of civilisation and provides an understanding of how they change... it has become a major science' (Lyon-Caen *et al.* 1994: 4).

In the 1990s, several appeal court judgements decided that the individually established work contract had a higher priority than collectively negotiated agreements. Lyon-Caen (1998) argues that this legal upgrading of the individual contract reflects the changing balance of forces in the 1980s and 1990s with employers increasingly gaining the upper hand in the labour market. It has helped weaken the force of collective contracts and, as a result, once the Jospin government of 1997–2002 decided to encourage collective bargaining over working time reductions, it had to leave many 'shadowy areas' to be sketched in by the participating parties. Another of France's leading labour lawyers, Alain Supiot, theorises that this 'contracturalisation of society' is obscuring both individual liberty and social equality by requiring individuals to contractually subordinate themselves to someone else's power. 'Marrying liberty and slavery, equality and hierarchy, they turn upside down labour law and laws shaping responsibilities and open the way to new forms of power over men.' Contracturalisation, he concludes, is a symptom of 'a renewal of feudal methods of structuring the social fabric' (Supiot 2001: 6). The law and the judiciary create the context within which rules establish workers' degrees of liberty and equality in exchange for their subordination. To this extent they therefore feature powerfully among the industrial relations 'actors' who help to shape the spaces within society where employers and employees circle each other.

Sociological

The importance of contractural collective agreements in France also provides scope for another group of academics to enter the frame: those sociologists of work who specialise in *relations professionnelles* (literally 'occupational relationships'), the area closest to the Anglo-Saxon idea of 'industrial' or 'labour' relations. While French legal academics tend to approach their employment relations through tight textual analysis, French work sociologists are much more holistic, seeing the construction of work rules as a process influenced by a wide number of actors and societal factors. Caire (1996) identifies three particular features of French industrial relations academics. First, he suggests that because most are themselves strongly influenced either by Marxism or by Social Catholicism, they are particularly sensitive to ideology, giving it a key role as an explanatory factor. Second, they tend to see conflict (its presence or absence) as central to industrial relations. Third, their view of the scope of industrial relations is very wide, indeed. Never narrowly interested in the fairly feeble institutions of employment relations, they always took a very broad view.

From its beginnings in the 1950s, French work sociology was initially associated with Georges Friedmann's Marxist critique of Taylorism. The studies he and his followers carried out tended to focus on those sectors most exposed to it, particularly the car industry. *Sociologie du Travail*, the key academic journal in the field, founded in 1959, reflected this emphasis. Until at least the end of the 1970s, work sociology therefore tended to focus on male physical work rather than on the wider labour process. This started to change after 1968, when it became much clearer that the working class was highly fragmented. Increasingly work sociologists then looked at the work experiences of women, clerical workers and immigrants as well as the classic male breadwinner.

Several French work sociologists found the broad industrial relations systems framework charted in by Dunlop's (1958) Cold War study helpful at a very basic level in identifying the different social entities – the state, the employers and the unions – and rule-making processes that make up the French industrial relations 'system'. Few of them share Dunlop's technological functionalism, although, as we shall see below, the 'regulation school' gets close, and many others are criticised by Linhart for endorsing the 'consensualism' present in Dunlop (Linhart 1996: 136). Most, however, stress the dynamics of change and choice available to the actors that were largely absent from Dunlop, and suggest a possible plurality of 'industrial relations systems' (Crozier 1990).

Jean-Daniel Reynaud, one of the leading figures in French industrial relations, criticises Dunlop for implying a kind of equality between actors, pointing out that in negotiating the Grenelle Agreement at the end of the 1968 mass strike the right-wing French prime minister was very far from simply being an actor on equal terms with the unions and the employers. Jean Saglio reinforces this critique of Dunlop's concept of the determinants of an industrial relations system arising from the interplay of the economic, politico-legal and technological contexts. He argues that the contexts that limit the behaviours of the different actors are all themselves socially and politically determined, and should be understood as arising in turn from 'strategic choices', rather than as absolute restraints (Saglio 1990).

For Reynaud the political system cannot be reduced to a 'context' within which an autonomous industrial relations system takes shape. He argues there is no 'stable frontier between the political and the industrial relations systems', that industrial relations have 'their own logic' and autonomy, and he rejects all 'global societal determinism' (Reynaud 1990: 281–2). What he draws from Dunlop, therefore, is the concept that the plurality of existing work rules are neither a consequence of a particular economic structure nor of some inner-determination of the system. In a complex book first published in 1989, '*The Rules of the Game: collective action and social regulation*', Reynaud develops this argument further. Building on the Roy-Burrawoy studies of how American mid-West machinists established elaborate social rules for organising production by making a 'game' out of the labour process, he argues that 'society' does not exist other than as the intersection of rules. Rules may be created 'jointly' or 'autonomously'. But

> ...the creation, maintenance and transformation of rules, the activity itself of rule-making (*régulation*), are at the centre of social life. They are even what gives it is distinctive character. If we agree to define rule-making as that kind of moral obligation that imposes itself on the social actors even when they are its authors, to which they submit at least partially even if they are negotiating it.... It is it (rule-making) that defines the real social constraints of the games in which social actors take part. (Reynaud 1993: 270)

Reynaud goes on to suggest that 'creating rules for relationships, is to give a sense to social space, allowing distinctions between the top and the bottom, initiative and discipline, order and obedience' (*ibid.*: 280). For Reynaud, it is therefore by understanding the rule-making process through creating a 'science of rules' that sociologists like him can either 'help make better' rules or at least 'help make them more coherent' (*ibid.*: 297). His starting point is that of a classical pluralist: he believes consensus between capital and labour can be achieved if only the right rules are constructed.

From the 1980s, when the world economic slowdown prompted firms to develop more distinctive managerial strategies, work sociologists have shifted focus to organisational sociology and 'the firm', investigating how and why individuals with different interests cooperate together. Linhart (1996) suggests this follows a distinction increasingly drawn between the nature of work and the local and national labour market. By the early 1990s, this division had led to the erection of a new 'sociology of the firm' (see Segrestin 1992) that Linhart criticises for suggesting that firm values and cultures can be analysed separately from the wider society and world of work. But the pioneer of post-war organisational sociology was Michel Crozier. He stressed the limited rationality of individual goals and behaviours, the presence of spoken and non-spoken objectives and the fact that all human relations are an exchange. Organisational behaviour, for Crozier, cannot be deduced from macro-level phenomena or from functionalist assumptions: it can only be understood by examining 'the use people make of their margins of freedom' and through 'analysing the constraints operating on the actors seen through their behaviours and especially through the feelings they express' (Crozier 1990: 313). This approach privileged observation of individual behaviours in trying intuitively to identify what he sees as several 'systems' of possible 'concrete action' that can overlap, separate and come back together.

The acceleration of French trends towards company-based negotiations and management-based human resource strategies aimed at encouraging employee commitment to the firm meant that from the early 1980s, the firm has also been viewed as a key organising context within which society evolves. Thus, while recognising the historical socialising constraints of external law and internal employee actions, Denis Segrestin (1992: 201) argues that 'the firm has become a beacon social institution. It is now seen – even more than politics – as the determining arena in which social transformation is likely to occur'. From roots going back to the corporations of pre-capitalist France, he sees the modern firm as having finally taken over at the end of the twentieth century as the key locus of social change. This view is close to that of the French employers' organisation, the *Medef*, whose president Ernest-Antoine Seillière argued in the 2002 elections that the firm is central to change and 'there is no hiatus between the success of the firm and the general interest of the country' (*Le Monde*, 15 January 2002).

Historical

Rather than use the comparative method between two or more contemporary sets of laws, outcomes, rules or individual behaviours, the historical method contrasts employment institutions and structures over time. Groux (1990) thus sought to understand changing patterns of employment relations through a study of managerial trade unionism in post-war France. By the late 1980s, this had grown to become markedly 'stronger' than manual worker trade unionism (14 per cent compared to 8 per cent density). His research involved constructing a factual account of the changing patterns, strategies and practices of managerial unionism, and then testing his findings against theories concerning the rise of the working middle classes and the evolution of trade unionism. Groux shows that the emergence of managerial unionism was largely the result of the post-war *institutionalisation* of employee representation, whereby the state insisted, despite the opposition of large numbers of managers, that they elect delegates to represent their occupational group at company level and that their union appoint delegates to help run parts of the national welfare state. While borrowing liberally from the discourses and practices of existing trade unionism, the *Confédération générale des cadres* (CGC) then fashioned its own identity and demands, particularly around management issues of modernisation and expertise. In this the CGC reflected a continuity with the earlier associations of professional engineers that had stressed 'harmonious class collaboration' (from the Catholic engineers' association) and 'a third way' between 'the dictatorship of the proletariat' and the 'dictatorship of the boss' (from the secular engineers' association) (Groux 1996: 55). In showing how an industrial relations 'actor' was shaped, Groux contributes to debates both about how legal frameworks can stimulate collective behaviours, and how these behaviours are constructed out of particular combinations of political and occupational interest.

One of the most prolific of academic observers of French industrial relations, René Mouriaux, collaborated with Groux on a series of institutional studies of the three main French trade union confederations, the *Confédération française démocratique du travail* (CFDT) (Groux and Mouriaux 1989), the *Confédération générale du travail* (CGT) (Groux and Mouriaux 1992) and the *CGT–Force Ouvriére* (FO) (forthcoming). Mouriaux has also participated over the last 30 years in a fascinating on-going study of the evolution of trade union discourse (Hetzel *et al.* 1998). The entire resolutionary output of each of the four principal French union confederations (excluding the CGC) was entered into a huge data base and subjected to computerised textual analysis. This shows how the official language of each confederation changed between the 1970s and the 1980s, and how some parts of the discourse (on struggle and conflict) were shared by the CGT and CFDT and other parts (on the family and the third world) were shared by confederations with a common roots in Catholic trade unionism, the CFDT and *Confédération française des travailleurs chrétiens* (CFTC).

Mouriaux has always been ready to use his historical insights to help explain the present. Thus, after the French mass public sector strike of 1995 and high levels of participation in the unemployment, anti-racist and ecology movements of the 1990s (see Chapter 3), he shows how the FO has been 'frozen' in immobility, the CGT is in a process of 'prudent evolution', while the CFDT is going for 'realism at any price' (Béroud *et al.* 1998: 150). His approach is interesting because in emphasising that the trade union institutions he studies are more than the sum of its individual members, he points to the role of choice and human energy in shaping the future. Thus, after reviewing what in the mid-1990s appeared to him to be the three principal possible futures of French trade unionism – 'bargaining pure and simple', 'social pacts' or 'a re-energised struggle trade unionism' – he cites Heraclitus: 'We live in a confusing period where those who will carry the day are those who act the most rationally while believing the unbelievable' (Mouriaux 1994: 119).

1.2   Selected theories

The intensity of continuing academic interest in employment relations reflects both the continuing strong Marxist influence within French social science and the fact that it remains identified as a 'problem' awaiting 'solution' by the French ruling elite. This interest ensures there is no shortage of French theorising (much of it highly polemical) on the working class, the trade unions, labour law, welfare and the labour process. Here I can only flag up what appear to me to be the main theoretical trends in thinking about employment relations that have stood the test of time. I find it helpful to group the main contributions under the four main theoretical headings shown in the middle of Figure 1.1: neo-liberal, regulation, social movement and societal effect theories.

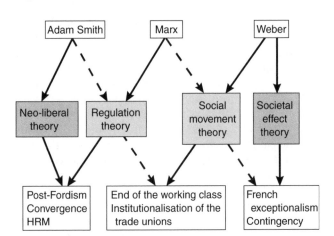

Figure 1.1   Conceptual map of French theories of work

Overall, and not unsurprisingly, the most influential of these four is neo-liberalism. Boyer (1995: 21) describes it well as 'methodological individualism'. Built on the philosophical foundations created by Frederik Hayek and Milton Friedman it suggests that the 'free market' for goods and for labour are inherently the most democratic way of organising what are inevitably going to be unequal societies. It and the American managerialism with which it is closely associated have had a major theoretical influence on all the other theories of employment relations during the last quarter of the twentieth century (Carpenter and Jefferys 2000). Nonetheless, its influence has, arguably, been more constrained in France than in some other industrial societies. This is certainly the view of the French employers' organisation, the *Medef*, which in 2002 congratulated France's conservative-dominated Constitutional Council for declaring unconstitutional a law limiting the circumstances in which firms could declare redundancies on the grounds that it infringed the 1789 Declaration of the Rights of Man recognising economic freedom (*Le Monde*, 15 January 2002). I will not discuss this dominant model further here because readers are more likely to be familiar with it than the other theories I examine that originate in France.

To a greater or lesser extent the three other theories in Figure 1.1 are critical of neo-liberalism. 'Regulation' theory is equally ambitious in seeking global explanations of the changing relationships between economic and social trends. 'Social movement' theory focuses on the importance of highly politically aware movements for change in explaining historical transformations of society. 'Societal effect' theory, by contrast, sets out a less ambitious stall, seeking to explain societal differences rather than establish a universal process. At the top of Figure 1.1 there are possible sources of inspiration (not always acknowledged) for the theoretical models. At the bottom of the figure are some of the key conclusions for employment relations derived by those working within each framework. These range from the conclusion that economic pressures on France are leading to the widespread adoption of a global labour process dominated by HRM methods and American managerialism, through assumptions that a class analysis of France is no longer appropriate (because the working class has been entirely fragmented and even individualised or because French trade unions have become institutionalised and dependent on the state), to the view that French employment relations remain exceptional to a considerable extent and that distinctive national cultural and historical contingencies strongly overdetermine any globalising pressures. We will return in the main body of the book to discuss how far these general conclusions are valid. Here, I shall merely summarise how these three important French theories understand employment relations, indicate who it is that I am pressing into my admittedly crude conceptual map, and suggest what I find helpful and unhelpful in them.

Regulation theory

The regulation school adapted John Dunlop's 'systems' theory to take account of crisis and change. Dunlop's (1958) American view was of fairly stable national 'systems' or sets of rules being created by the interaction of three main groups of actors, the state, management and unions, who shared common ideological assumptions. The directly derivative British 'Oxford School' of Flanders and Clegg also focused on rule-making processes and institutions within a stable society. By contrast the regulation school in France was born in the social turmoil of '1968'. A group of young economists emerged who were influenced by Marx, the Annales School of French economic historians and by the neo-Keynesian economist Kalecki. They tried to theorise the way in which the economic system *changes*, and in so doing how it *regulates* 'the dynamic process by which production adapts to new social demands at particular economic conjunctures and from within certain institutional forms' (Boyer 1987: 17). They were highly critical of conventional classical economic theory: 'A theory of social regulation is a universal alternative to the theory of equilibrium,' wrote Aglietta (cited in Boyer 1995: 548–9). He continued: '... it is the study of the transformation in social relations that creates new forms that are both economic and non-economic, and which are organised structurally to reproduce a determining mode of production'. This introduction of the idea that non-economic institutions and movements play an important part in shaping economic outcomes blew a huge hole in the narrow mechanics of classical economics.

The 'regulationists' went on to argue that different 'modes of regulation' arise with changing 'regimes of accumulation' where the balance between capital growth and consumption is altered. Their key idea is that the patterns of employment relations correspond to the kind of accumulation dominant at any one time and to the forms of technology being used. But when the accumulation regime changes, when it moves from stability into crisis, then the 'structural or institutional form' of the mode of regulation – the mix of institutions (firms, credit system, state, welfare) and behaviours (employment relations, consumption, training) that supported the old system – also change, albeit at different rhythms that may also effect the 'regime of accumulation'. Thus, for example, both capital and labour may take more or less out of national income.

'Fordism' is the name the regulationists give the post-war regime of accumulation and mode of regulation from roughly 1945 to 1973. This period, they suggest, saw a rising share of national wealth going to workers, and a falling share to profits. They argue that the subsequent crisis introduced a transition period marked by 'post-Fordist' or 'neo-Fordist' regimes, where 'mass' forms of production and consumption, and of workers' organisation and struggle were significantly less important than before. Jean-Pierre Durand, although critical of the idea that Taylorism has been displaced, nonetheless calls the outcome a 'new production model' (Durand 1996), while Boyer now emphasises the possibility of system 'hybridisation' (Boyer 1998).

Boyer's schematic approach summarising the principal French employment relations factors during the period 1973–1985 is shown in Table 1.1. Its categories reveal how closely the regulationists followed Dunlop as

Table 1.1   Regulation school view of employment relations, 1973–1985

	Principal characteristics
Trade unions	Low union density
	Multi-unionism
	Loose coordination
Employers	Divided
	Light structure
State	All present
	Tripartite
	Law crucial in changes
Collective bargaining	
Importance of:	
Productivity	Government makes declarations
Cost of living	CoL Index common
Labour market	Little influence
Regularity	Yearly
Level	Sector
Welfare	
Extent	Wide coverage
Level of benefits	At EEC average
How financed	By firms, individuals and the state

Source: Boyer 1987: 22.

well as their additional concern with productivity, inflation and welfare. For Boyer, France up to the 1970s successfully adapted the Fordist model in a rather exceptional way. He points to growing trade union effectiveness in the post-war period as an independent variable boosting consumer demand and in turn giving France an average GNP growth rate of 5.6 per cent a year between 1960 and 1973 (compared to 4.5 per cent in West Germany and 4.1 per cent in the United Kingdom). He also emphasises the role of the French state. In this period it was a major actor in employment relations. It gave legal force to the results of collective bargaining, and created a strong institutional framework that enabled workers' organisations to achieve a growing share of the fruits of France's economic growth (Boyer 1987: 25, 29).

Boyer maintains that the sociological method of the regulation school is close to that of the leftwing 'constructivist structuralist' French philosopher, Pierre Bourdieu who died in 2001 (Boyer 1995: 25). For Boyer, Bourdieu's two core concepts of *'habitus'* and *'champ'* provide a mechanism for satisfactorily interpreting the passage of methods of regulation from the society to the individual, as well as the interpenetration of both. By *habitus* Bourdieu means the 'collective' baggage that 'is deposited in each individual as lasting measures, as mental structuring' (cited in Boyer *ibid.*); by *champ* or 'field' he means 'the totality of objective relations between social actors or institutions' (Béroud *et al.* 1998: 48). Bourdieu sees the relations between *habitus* and *champ* as generating individual or collective action. 'Constructivist structuralism' is thus a way of arguing that the dominant and determining economic, cultural and political *structures* are *constructed* essentially by individuals. Bourdieu's resolution of the 'structure–process debate' can be criticised, however, for denying the relevance of social class and of any intrinsic social antagonism within capitalism (Béroud *et al.* 1998: 49).

Regulation theory itself has been subjected to many important criticisms within France: for the assumption behind 'Fordism' that it is possible to think of a period in which capitalism was stable; for ignoring the reality that 'Fordism' was never the principal production process in any single national capitalism; and for the theory's Parsonian functionalism (Reynaud 1990: 282; Linhart 1996: 140–1). It has been argued that regulation theory underestimated the extent to which the Taylorist–Fordist system was capable of responding to pressures for change and that it imposes the category of 'radical change' on top of that of 'progressive transformation' (Maurice 1993). Coutrot's (1998: 8–9) objections include the strong continuity in France of 'Taylorist and Fordist work organisational methods' into the 1990s; the appearance in firms most exposed to competition of major organisational changes that 'reflect more the evolution of Taylor–Fordist methods than their disappearance'; and the absence of any traces of a 'new post-Fordist compromise' in the practices of French or American employers. Here I am more concerned with the implications of the regulationist approach for French employment relations.

While the regulationists have clearly described the 'French' version of pre-1980 'Fordism', they are much less clear about how to characterise French society today. Thus, one of them notes that a weakness of the 'French model' is that it has still not created the 'micro-consistencies *required* for a passage towards "post-Fordism" where a good distribution of innovation and activity take place between large companies and SMEs' (Coriat 1995: 394–6) (my emphasis). France is told off because it does not appear to be doing what it is supposed (by regulation theory) to be doing! Coriat also admits it is difficult to decide whether the structures he sees are 'provisional, only describing the transition from Fordism to post-Fordism', 'Or, on the contrary, do they actually correspond to the new structures of post-Fordism?' Either little has changed fundamentally in the 'mode of accumulation', or much has changed and has not been fully 'passed on' through the effect of the new *champ* on the *habitus* of the social actors. In both cases the contemporary experience of the 'French model' sits uneasily within regulation theory. This is for three main reasons: first, what the regulationists thought was likely to be a relatively short period of transition or crisis followed by a new stability around a new mode of regulation and regime of accumulation has turned out to be on-going; second, they have seen that the current mode of regulation continues to involve significant elements of 'Taylorism–Fordism'; and third, they have witnessed at close hand a much stronger political dimension to employment relations than their model allows. For all except two years in the period between 1981 and 2002, there was either a French centre-left president or prime minister or both, and this has had, as we shall see, an important impact on the French 'mode of social regulation' while changing comparatively little in its 'regime of accumulation'.

Regulation theory is, therefore, unhelpful where it posits some kind of automatic reflex action by which its defined 'accumulation regime' *requires* certain responses from the 'regulation mode'. Its labels, 'Fordism', 'post-Fordism' or 'new production model' also create an unhelpful sense of determinism, when the forms of human behaviour they are trying to describe are actually full of inconsistencies, contradictions and challenges, any of which could significantly alter the future. They give a false impression of system stability in a highly unstable world.

Regulation theory remains helpful, however, where it reminds us that there is a close relationship between the processes and results of the division of the cake under capitalism and the forms of employment relations and of welfare that ensue. In this book, we therefore contextualize our discussion of French management and employment relations within considerations of profitability, finance and firm organisation and, of course, of the role played by the state.

Social movement theory

Social movement theory and 'the sociology of action' in France is closely associated with the work of Alain Touraine. He analysed the 1968 events (see

Chapter 2) as both confirming the importance of a particular definition of 'social movements' in changing society, and as demonstrating the emergence of a post-industrial society in which new social actors such as students and anti-nuclear movements would in future shape history. Sociology, he claims, 'can only be built out of a study of social movements which, alone, can deliver us from the vain search for the nature or essence of society, and lead us towards a vision of society as the sum of action systems, as in a drama where social movements play the principal roles' (Touraine 1993: 48). By the 1980s he estimated that the working class movement had been so thoroughly institutionalised that it no longer rose 'above demands and negotiations and call(ed) into question the mode of social management of industry'. It could no longer be seen as a 'social movement of central importance in industrial society' (Touraine *et al.* 1987: xv). For Touraine social classes, defined through people's relationships to the means of production and to property, do not exist. He recognises the presence of domination and conflict giving rise to power relationships that can change over time, but these are without any sense of purpose or direction. For Touraine broad categories such as 'the citizen' or 'the worker' are not central to explaining change. His critics argue that all that counts in his theory 'is the desire of each individual or of each collective group for self-expression' (Béroud *et al.* 1998: 35–41).

What conclusions can be drawn from Touraine's focus on social movements and rather general philosophical position to help explain trends in employment relations? I will first summarise his general approach and then look at his analysis of the mass strike movement of 1995. Touraine argues that French employment relations cannot be seen as a distinct academic area of study such as law or politics. He identifies three ways of describing the sets of rules and relationships that make up the 'action systems' concerned. First, there are those involved with what are often considered to be fundamental conflicts of interest; second there are those rules and relationships related to the workings of the labour market; and third those arising from the evolution of training and skills and more broadly from the process of change in working conditions. During most of the post-war period, Touraine suggests, the first two elements were largely integrated or subordinated within the third. Since 1975, 'a long historical cycle has ended' and the market now plays a predominant role. Most crucially there is 'the appearance of new fields and actors within conflicts that have been displaced from the arena of the production of goods to that of the production and distribution of symbols, and to cultural sectors'. In the context of this much more open economy, 'the national system of industrial relations has been replaced by company-level techno-human resource mobilisation strategies' while 'the unions, whose energies are being increasingly taken up by joint and partnership committees (with the employers – SJ), are being placed in a situation where they have neither influence based on involvement in power nor on oppositional action'. Thus, French 'trade unionism is no longer a social movement and at the same time it has failed to become a political actor of the first rank'. The result, he argues, is that the dynamic underlying industrial relations has shifted to 'a bipolarised situation where market constraints and new human resource management methods on the one side, and the creation of new social movements on the other, are exercising more and more initiative' (Touraine 1990: 375–7).

Touraine's model of a post-industrial world in which the workers' movement has effectively disappeared and where, although the shell of an earlier system of employment relations still exists, outcomes are increasingly shaped by the actions of new social movements that lack general or generalising politics or goals, is a bleak one. While it structures several components of contemporary France into an understandable pattern, it discards too much. Thus, it was unhelpful in predicting or explaining the French mass strike movement of December 1995. 'This can't be happening' was the Tourainian reaction. Touraine and his colleagues tried to 'prove' that despite all the evidence to the contrary, the strike was not actually a 'movement' but 'its shadow' or at best a 'quasi-movement' (Touraine 1996: 11, 213). In an extraordinary work of sociological rationalisation, Touraine first sets up what the movement should really have been about: how to save France from bureaucracy, corporatism and clientelism and to achieve the twin goals of 'combining efficiency with solidarity, internationalisation and national integration' (*ibid.*: 29). Then he argues that the strike could not have been a 'social movement' because it did not have these wider aims, and was also based on government employees, whose 'situation, interests, the goals of their action belong to a category the furthest removed from the savage confrontation of slave and master, of colonised and coloniser' (*ibid.*: 57). This last argument is highly questionable. Thus, while Touraine (*ibid.*: 13) asserts that 'the mobilisation showed a complete absence of perspectives, programme and even of analysis', Cours-Salies (1998) observes that among the inconvenienced public 'all agreed that jobs for all was the principal issue, even though this was not the objective of the strike and though the trade unions did not formulate any demands on this'. Béroud *et al.* conclude their review of Touraine's theory and his explanations for 1995 in these harsh terms:

> Forged over nearly thirty years, the concept of social movement becomes incapable of grasping the depth of a collective mobilisation: empty concept or concept emptied by an excess of historical requirements or by the abuse of definitions trying to impose a mould onto a real movement rather than to decipher it, from now on it only serves as a polemical statement of a reformist vision of social management that is at the heart of an economy subjected to capitalist rationality. (Béroud *et al.* 1998: 43)

Touraine may have established an unhelpful *theory* of social movements, but let us not throw the baby out with the bath water. For the purposes of this book what we will retain from Touraine, then, is his earlier focus on a broad approach to the manifestation of conflict within society. Besides the mass strike and street mobilisations of 1995, other nationally experienced French social movements in the second half of the 1990s – of students, of the unemployed, of the Greens, of 'illegal' immigrants, of 17–18-year-old school students and of anti-racists on 1 May 2002, as well as, of several public transport worker movements protesting acts of violence against their colleagues – also point to the need to integrate an understanding of conflict, passivity and mobilisation *outside* the workplace into our analysis of conflict, co-operation and organisation *within* the workplace.

Societal effect theory

Those theorists who emphasise most strongly the significance of nationally derived factors shaping management and employment relations are the 'societal effect' school originating in the University of Aix-en-Provence and the culturalists associated with Geert Hosfstede. While the former are closer to Weber and the latter to inidividual psychology, and as a consequence often lose sight of the relationship of social class to the economic structure in which people live their lives, they both offer important and useful insights into the nature of the employer–employee interface.

Societal effect theory does not claim to present a macro-level theory explaining employment relations, but by posing 'connections' and 'relationships' between different factors rather than as a hierarchical causal chain, it does in the end present quite a distinct model. Arndt Sorge, a German collaborator with the Aix school, defines the theory in these terms:

> The societal effect approach is based on one central proposition: whatever happens in one sector of society is always connected to events or to structures in other sectors. This means that social institutions such as industrial relations are related to other institutions such as vocational training, education, work organization, organizational structures, the legal system, politics, social stratification, and so on. (Sorge 1995: 243)

For example, in discussing whether it is possible to conceive of a system of stable rules governing industrial relations, the late François Sellier (1990) showed that in 1936 the French government prioritised collective bargaining to deal with low wage levels, while in 1950 it opted for a minimum wage fixed at about 10 per cent below the unskilled male workers' average in Paris engineering factories, a minimum level, which in 1952, it linked to price rises. In 1968, it was forced to order a massive catching up towards average wage levels, and in 1970, it established a system where the government could, if circumstances required, tweak the minimum rate upwards. Sellier's argument is that while both the system of rules and the underlying economic realities continuously changed, what remained constant was interrelationship of events in one sector with those in another. Throughout these 40 years, industrial conflict about low wages was transferred to political institutions and processes. Thus, although some rules governing wage determination, such as the core system of job classification, remained unchanged for most of the post-war period, overall he concludes it would be wrong to speak of a single shared Dunlopian French employment relations 'ideology'. Instead what dominates is 'heterogeneity' and a sense of the importance of French social institutions.

Lane (1989: 34) is a strong critic of the looseness of this formulation:

> ... the theoretical framework offered by the Aix group remains somewhat vague and ambiguous. There is, in fact, no theory in the conventional sense, i.e. the explanatory variables are never specified nor is the exact relation between culture as institutionalised patterns of action and the business organisation ever explicated.

Yet, they do suggest a methodological approach to change. This embraces the study of the firm, its work organisation and industrial relations, in the context of the influences on it of a range of significant nationally based social *institutions* (such as the political system, general education, training, employment measures and labour law, etc.). It is herein that lies the theory's punch. For if the most significant aspects of an employment relations system may be understood best with reference to *national* history and culture – and not by reference to the *general* evolution of capitalist accumulation (regulation theory) or to the eclipse of the centrality of the working class by individually constructed new social movements (Touraine) – then the implication is that societal institutions have a relative autonomy from both the underlying economy and from individual actions.

This collective 'cultural' argument was partially supported by Renaud Sainsaulieu who died in 2002. A student of Crozier, his observations and surveys of workers in the mid to late 1960s led him to suggest that employees take on one of four different kinds of psycho-social identities at work: group bonding, negotiating, identifying or withdrawal. Crucially, however, these identities were not predetermined. Individuals would take them on through dialectical interaction between their personality and the work environment and culture, and as they did so a whole social system of employment relations would evolve according to the relative strengths of the different identities present. In a postscript 11 years after his major study first appeared Sainsaulieu (1988) summarised his argument: 'Firm culture should then be understood as the result of the types of collective identities which get on, fall out, dominate each other or ally with one another at the heart of the organisation.' Each firm, like each country, he concluded can take on a distinct culture and 'sociological dynamic of human resources'.

Sainsaulieu (1988: 445) sees the societal effect school, the Dutch culturalist Hoftsede (1984) and Philippe d'Iribarne as broadly working within the same psycho-socio-cultural perspective as himself. d'Iribarne's perspective in *La logique de l'honneur* (1989) was to emphasise the historical significance of national tradition in shaping contemporary expressions of authority in the workplace. He identified enduring continuities between Tocqueville's observations of Franco-American differences two centuries ago and his own observations of Franco-American-Dutch life, government and management. Taking up Montesquieu's analysis of 'a logic of honour', d'Iribarne sees French group behaviour as being essentially distinguished by a common adherence to a series of historically shaped duties. The French chief executive's authority, d'Iribarne suggests, is rarely limited by laws or genuine contractural obligations; instead, his subordinates are protected by the rights and duties handed down by custom and practice (d'Iribarne 1989: 62).

These culturally specific approaches provide mid-range theories that often successfully explain observed national differences through the history of their institutions – an approach we attempt to integrate within the rest of this book. However, they are arguably less helpful in explaining the evolution of power imbalances within capitalist society and their major influence on how we all live out our collective, social lives.

1.3 Conclusion

This chapter argued that theory is important to approaching French employment relations and management. This is partly because most French writers consciously locate themselves within a distinctive view of the world when they discuss the relations between managers and managed. It is also because, as I shall argue throughout the narrative of this book, the ideas that people have collectively about the justice or injustice of their situation take on considerable force in shaping what they actually do. The presence or absence of conflict and change in employment relations is not just the result of a certain mix of structural social and economic factors. It is also the result of how people perceive that mix of socio-economic reality. And people's political and ideological perceptions and values are shaped by the explicit or implicit theories they have about the world and their situation in it.

The chapter sketched three of the main approaches taken to employment relations – legal, sociological and historical – and then briefly introduced three of the more influential theories that try to explain and offer predictions about the future course of employment relations, regulation theory, social movement theory and societal effect theory. While attempting to present these theories and to discuss their helpful and less helpful components as fairly as possible, my own theoretical approach cannot be ignored. Summarised in the introduction and underlying the way in which I select and discuss the changes observed in this book, I tend to interpret changes in the world about us as flowing from tensions between collectives of individuals acting more or less in concert to maximise the resources at their disposal. The following chapter therefore moves on from these important attempts at understanding the whole picture, to looking at the building blocks of French social and economic power.

2
Social and Political Roots to 1980

This chapter provides an overview of French management and employment relations before 1980. The aim is to offer a reasoned explanation of the processes behind the transformation of France from a network of predominantly agricultural and artisanal regional economies in which employment relations in the modern sense barely existed, to the complex industrial society that is the focus of this book. It argues that conditions were broadly favourable to the domination of state-structured varieties of economic and political liberalism up until the 1930s. Under the banners of *égalité* and *fraternité* the workers' movement of France's 'long' nineteenth century was strong enough to stage major rebellions against authoritarian liberalism in 1830, 1848, 1871 and 1906, but was too weak to sustain them. The subsequent emergence of a more homogeneous working class, the military and political defeats of first economic liberalism and then authoritarian capitalism in 1940 and 1944, the following 30 years of nearly full employment and the explosion of 1968, however, forged a new relationship between capital, labour and the state.

The French state continued to represent the interests of those with political and economic power, as it had done from its origins in the political and military turmoil that followed the collapse of Roman rule. Before 1940 the state intervened occasionally to 'co-ordinate' societal actors and avoid market failures or betrayals of the French national interest or as in 1936 to contain damaging social conflict, but after 1940 it became a constant and key regulator of capital–labour relations. Under the Fourth Republic the state sought to impose *pluralism*. Yet it was only partially successful in integrating minorities of the still pervasively unitarist employers and of the class struggle trade unionists into the new pluralist institutions. *Liberté* only partially ceded ground in the shaping of resource allocation to the more interventionist ideologies of *égalité* and *fraternité*. To understand this evolution and its enduring impact, this chapter begins by looking at the French people and the course of French politics up to 1980. It then examines the process of industrialisation and the evolution of social class. These social classes express themselves through a variety of institutions and the chapter finally examines the evolution of trade unions.

2.1   French society and population

Everywhere, before the twentieth century, French society was regulated by highly local micro-economies, where the fortunes of proximity to trading routes, soil, weather and disease largely determined the age of marriage, the birth rate, infant mortality and the pressure for seasonal or permanent migration. The Black Death of 1347–1350 and the following Hundred Years' War alone cut France's population from 20–22 million in 1328 to just 10–12 million by 1450 (Braudel 1991: 161). This period of acute labour shortage launched a partial 'deconversion' of its fully fledged feudal society. A contemporary complained of the Black Death survivors that 'these wretched people have started to get restless, saying that we keep them in too great a state of servitude ... that they want to be one with their lords, and that if they work on their lords' estates, they want to be paid' (quoted in Castel 1995: 82). Until the revolution of 1789, these 'deconverting' rural micro-economies were governed by the local nobility, deriving their authority either from roots stretching right back to the disintegration of Roman slave-owning France, or from the fifteenth century to the growing centralised patronage of the King. Royal and state power became increasingly absolute in the sixteenth century, and deeply entwined with economic growth and finance. At the onset of a series of wars with Spain in 1522, after his defeat of the Swiss at Marignan, François I took out the first interest-bearing national loan; and in 1539, he allowed French to be substituted for Latin in all legal documents.

By the eighteenth century, the largest of France's thousand growing towns had partly broken free from their semi-feudal relations. These big towns increasingly organised 'trade' in corporations that embraced masters, tradesmen and apprentices and elected their own mayors rather than simply put up with those appointed by the local lord. Yet commerce and the towns remained subject to the authority of the Crown: it was the King who granted corporations their trading rights, who divided France into five different customs regions, who appointed chief regional administrator/tax collectors and certain town office-holders to ensure a proportion of the commercial and urban wealth arrived in Paris. It was thus the King and the King's often highly capable ministers who by force and cunning structured the small local administrations and complicit urban political elites 'whose self-perpetuating dynasties appropriated local government for themselves'. Braudel (1991: 422) goes on to argue persuasively that 'The foundations of France's future social and political development ... were often rooted in the submission, abdication, not to say treachery, of the urban authorities'. They were to become the basis of the self-perpetuating state administrators who assumed so much importance in the nineteenth and twentieth centuries. These local elites of tax-collectors, lawyers and administrators made effective use of the discretion allowed them by the Crown: they became wealthy and their personal wealth provided the major market that kept urban traders and skilled artisans in business, helping sustain strong artisanal economies in dozens of dispersed towns that acted as magnets for craftsmen and migrants.

While perhaps initiated by a food surplus caused by the major fifteenth-century depopulation, it was subsequently the growth of commerce, along with the bounty of shipments of silver from the New World up to 1650 and the irregular spread of the new American 'wonder' crops (maize, potatoes and buckwheat) into different parts of France, that enabled a steady surplus of births over deaths to take place over the three centuries before 1789. By that revolutionary year, France's population had recovered to over 26 million (compared to the eight million of its diminutive English neighbour), with 16.5 per cent living in settlements with more than 2,000 people, and 9 per cent living in the 76 concentrations with over 10,000 (*ibid.*: 177, 444). France's prime location, straddling both the old trade routes to Northern Europe from the Mediterranean and Middle East, and the new routes from Europe's Western rim to the Americas, its climate, permitting the production of both grape and grain, and its comparatively stable and extensive central national administrative network underwrote this growth and made France the central pivot within Europe. This size, power and influence at the end of the eighteenth century explains well the global shock waves that emanated from its 1789 revolution.

France's only real weakness was the comparatively poor location and smaller size of Paris, compared to the seaports of London and Amsterdam, whose greater weights within smaller geographical territories provided a stronger economic stimulus to the rest of their economies. Even after the great eighteenth century highway-building effort (usually using forced peasant labour, the hated *corvée*) and Turgot's launch of a national Mail-coach and Stage-coach system in 1775, it still took three days to reach Calais, four days to reach Strasbourg, six days to reach Bordeaux and eight to reach Marseille (*ibid.*: 472).

Migration and immigration

Until the twentieth century, France's population remained strongly rooted in its productive and abundant countryside. Even today France still boasts hundreds of local cheeses, thousands of different wines and 6,000 open air markets that do about 7 per cent of internal trade and provide work for about half a million people (Menanteau 1999). This legacy testifies to an agriculturally diverse and important pre-industrial France where 'each part of the territory of France tended to exist closed in on itself' (Braudel 1986: 55). The 1804 Napoleonic Code had confirmed the equal rights of all children to share the parental estate, thereby unwittingly underwriting the survival of subsistence-farming France. This enabled peasants to continue to work farms that were repeatedly divided up until as late as midway through the twentieth century, and it encouraged them to have small families. The French Revolution and the seizure and division of the church estates also created in about one-third of the peasantry an anti-clerical tradition that later became Republican and regularly voted 'red' up until the 1980s.

France's population grew by nine million between 1801 and 1860, but from then until 1913 it increased by only 2.5 million, significantly more slowly than its smaller and more industrially and agriculturally productive neighbours. In this period both peasants and workers increasingly practised birth control, slowing down migratory pressures, keeping the job market tighter and allowing greater social mobility (Cross 1983: 6–7). One element that facilitates migration is a common language. This spread only slowly out from the Paris region (the *Île de France*) after the first millennium, and as late as 1863 a quarter of French communes still did not speak French or one of its derivative patois languages (Charle 1991: 148). With comparatively low internal migration, immigrants entering France from outside its borders constituted a major source of labour and population renewal.

In the two centuries between 1800 and 1999, France's population roughly doubled, as graphed in Figure 2.1. Two distinct tendencies may be observed: first, France's 'natural' rate of population growth was slowed and even put

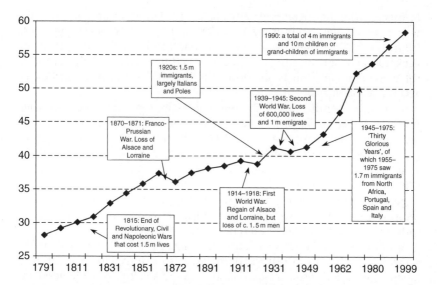

Figure 2.1 French population growth (millions), 1791–1999

Sources: Marchand and Thélot 1991: Table 1t; Schor 1996; for 1999, Besset 1999. The figure for 1941 is an average of the 1936 and 1946 data.

into reverse through the effects of war; second, immigration regularly made good those war losses, as after 1871, 1918 and belatedly after 1945.

France's central location on the world's major trade routes did not just mean most of the world's commodities crossed its territory: so too did a huge variety of the world's human beings. Immigrants were pushed by economic or political repression and pulled by labour shortages and the prospect of political and cultural *liberté*. And, as ever, these immigrants, among the most dynamic of their own generations, added enormously to France's already huge existing diversity of artistic, intellectual, economic and social life. Most were pulled towards Paris, the growing towns or to rurally located industries such as coal mining, iron and steel making and textiles with continuous labour shortages. To work they were obliged to take the worst jobs. A liberal economist complained in 1888:

> The French seldom are willing to be simple labourers or street sweepers, to do certain of the exhausting or painful jobs in the textile mills of the north, in the refineries or olive oil processing plants of the south … Belgians, Italians and sometimes Germans are needed for all the infinite and essential tasks of civilisation. The French people have become a kind of aristocracy among the more primitive peoples of Europe. (Paul Leroy-Beaulieu quoted in Cross 1983: 7–8)

First-generation immigrants already made up a significant proportion of the whole French population from the 1870s, and constituted a key ingredient from the 1920s. Table 2.1 shows how immigration occurred against the background of slowly rising urbanisation, and how as high a proportion of the working population as one-third still worked the land at the end of the Second World War.

In the nineteenth century the immigrants were primarily Belgian, then northern Italian or Spanish. Travelling relatively short distances they were more likely to be temporary. By the 1920s, the two million foreigners whose immigration the government actively encouraged came from further away, from Eastern and Southern Europe. By 1931, foreign workers made up 42 per cent of French miners, 30 per cent of building workers and 38 per cent of engineering workers, and it was they who bore the brunt of anti-immigrant reaction in the 1930s with the 1934 conservative government promising 'priority to French workers in the job market' (quoted in Cross 1983: 198).

After the Second World War France lost large parts of the colonial empire on which much of its wealth had been based. It was forced to turn to its own labour power and resources and, as these were lacking, it made good the labour shortages once more through immigration. In the 1960s and 1970s, Portuguese and Algerians entered France in roughly equal proportions, followed by Spaniards, Italians and Moroccans. Their rates of pay were less than 'French' workers even when doing the same work, since they could be

Table 2.1 Immigration, urbanisation and agriculture in France, 1851–1999

	Immigration as % of total pop.	Urbanisation (2000) as % of total pop.*	Working in agriculture as % of working pop.
1851	1.1	25.5	55.8
1866	1.7	30.5	50.5
1876	2.1	32.5	48.7
1881	2.6	34.8	46.3
1891	2.8	37.3	44.1
1901	2.6	41.0	41.0
1911	2.9	44.1	38.5
1921	3.9	46.3	36.2
1931	7.0	50.8	31.5
1946	4.3	53.2	31.6
1954	4.1	56.0	26.1
1962	4.7	61.6	20.1
1974	6.5	68.5	10.6
1982	7.5	68.9	8.6
1990	7.4	72.9*	4.5
1999	7.4	77.0*	2.7

* For 1990 and 1999 a new definition of 'urban area' has been used, defined as a geographical unity within which there are at least 5,000 jobs.

Sources: Schor 1996; Marchand and Thélot 1991: Tables 2, 3t; for 1990 and 1999 Boëldieu and Borrel 2000, Bessy-Pietri and Sicamois 2001, Amossé 2001.

put on a lower classification because of lack of 'training'. But almost always the jobs could be paid less because they were dirtier and harder, the jobs that the 'French' preferred not to take. Tens of thousands of immigrants, particularly North Africans, were obliged to live in primitive conditions on the outside of the major cities. In 1970, some 46,000 'foreigners' lived in 113 shanty towns around Paris (Schor 1996: 213–15). These immigrants entered a different France. It was not only urbanised, and recently heavily industrialised, it was also a France that had seen a significant post-Second World War compromise between the weakened political forces of the employers and the divided forces of the working class.

2.2   Political evolution

The conflict of interests over the allocation of France's huge natural resources between France's substantial peasantry, its slowly growing body of landless workers, and its tiny ruling elites could only be resolved through one of two forms of political regime: direct centralised control and dictatorship by the ruling elite, or government through a complex series of political alliances. No one class fragment could mobilise sufficient strength on its own. The key to holding power, or challenging for power, thus lay either in capturing power through the army (as did Napoleon I, Napoleon III and General de Gaulle), or in securing legitimation through allying otherwise irreconcilable interests in the National Assembly. In the nineteenth century these alliances were largely shaped by the direct legacy of the French Revolution.

One of the most important eighteenth century philosophers, Jean-Jacques Rousseau, argued that the 'general will', individual rights and the Nation were undermined by intermediate 'associations'. Chief among these he identified as the Catholic Church, whose property was confiscated by the Revolutionary Assembly on 2 November 1789. It was still in the name of *liberté* and to end socially divisive associations that in the Spring of 1791 the Constitutional Assembly passed the *Allarde* decree outlawing guilds (in very similar terms to the temporary ban introduced by Turgot in 1776). Shortly after this, while Parisian printers and carpenters agitated for higher wages, it passed the *Le Chapelier* law. This banned trade unions and any form of collective worker organisation such as 'discussions', 'posters', 'round Robins' and 'pressure against those who would work for a lower wage' (Soubiran-Paillet 1998). The *Le Chapelier* law was passed without discussion. The Jacobin left, led by Robespierre, did not protest. The only attack on it came from Jean-Paul Marat. In his newspaper, *L'Ami du peuple*, he attacked the law as 'usurping the sovereign rights of the people' (quoted in Robert 2000). This ban on trade unions and strikes was only finally removed in 1884.

We can see, then, that the birth of the French Republic spawned two parallel tensions: on the one hand between individualism and collectivism and on the other between modernism and corporatism, the latter being most strongly represented by the Catholic Church. This was not a simple right versus left cleavage. Sections of the local elites who supported the final overthrow of the Bourbons in 1830 or later opposed the Orleanist Monarchy in 1848 saw themselves firmly as individualists and modernisers. To secure change they had to create alliances with radical tradesmen who stressed *fraternité* and wanted socialism. Yet, when the dangers of socialism became too real these middle-class liberal reformers were ready to ally with more conservative forces.

Napoleon III's Second Empire, from 1852 to 1870 was the outcome of such an alliance between liberalism, the peasantry and the Catholic Church. It eventually collapsed not because of internal dissent, but as a result of the military defeat of Napoleon III. The Third Republic was subsequently baptised in the bloody suppression of the socialist 1871 Paris Commune. It was not, however, until 1877 in what Cobban (1981: 20–1) describes with some exaggeration as 'a more decisive social revolution than anything that had occurred in 1830, 1848 and 1871' that the Republicans finally secured an unshakeable majority ahead of the monarchists and Bonapartists in the Chamber of Deputies. They elected a President, appointed a Senate and undermined the strongly conservative influence of the competing sections of the Catholic landed gentry and urban *haute bourgeoisie* who wished to turn the clock back to either a Bourbon, or an Orleanist or a Bonapartist restoration.

Over the next 70 years a series of Republican governments balanced liberalism and the construction of a modern state with peasant protectionism and the emerging presence of working class socialism. Republicanism redefined itself as support for an elected head of state with limited powers, combined with strong elements of both nationalism and secularism (opposition to Catholic influence over government, education and social policy). This was understandable. It was finally only in 1892 that Pope Leon XIII asked French Catholics to recognise the reality of the Third Republic (Branciard 1990: 13). Gradually, left and right-wing Republican formations emerged. In the early twentieth century, the left Republicans increasingly faced competition for working class votes first from the Socialists and then from the Communists, while right Republicans competed for votes among the Catholic, peasant and small business electorates.

The experience of trade union illegality between 1791 and 1884, accompanied both by occasional counter-revolutionary repression and by more constant harassment of worker organisations and activities, emphasised divisions among the slowly cohering working classes. While most activists with the courage to conduct illegal organising activity were strongly anti-capitalist there was little unanimity about what this meant. Some rejected party political activity in favour of trade union militancy, but these were divided between those who wished to use it overthrow capitalism and those who used militancy to negotiate advantageous collective agreements with the employers. In 1906, the CGT called its first ever General Strike to try and impose an eight-hour day on the employers. Later the same year it adopted the Amiens Charter, a programme embodying the key elements of revolutionary syndicalism – the rejection of the political process as a means of advancing workers' conditions, and the embrace of the view that the trade union movement itself provides the organising framework for a new society. Among those who believed it was possible to capture political power for the workers, there were different divisions. There were those who wished to orchestrate a revolutionary seizure of power and those who believed in forming electorally oriented workers' political parties to represent their interests.

Several of these different strands were brought together after the First World War under the influence of the Bolshevik revolution. This coincided with the emergence of a mass working class and the eclipse of the peasant–worker economy. It also arrived at the moment when France was staggering under the loss of 1.25 million soldiers with half a million civilian casualties and three-quarters of a million permanently injured out of a total population of 39 million, and it provided new impetus to the still present ideas of class conflict and *fraternité*. As a result a Communist Party (PCF) was formed in December 1920 by the majority of delegates at the French Socialist

Party congress at Tours – although only 13 of the 68 Socialist deputies joined the new party. Despite being closely identified with the twists and turns of the Russian Communist Party, the PCF has remained a significant working class party until, arguably, the political debacle of 2002. It has, for example, been the only one to keep a mass membership continuously since 1944. Its broad base was created through its successful wartime marriage of nationalism and radical action, when from the May 1941 Northern coalminers' strike until the Liberation it played a major role within the resistance movement inside France. This cost it very dear: up to 75,000 of its members and sympathisers were shot during the war.

The Second World War also played an important role in preparing French capitalists for post-war state direction of the economy. The Vichy Government not only directly dictated wage rates through its local *préfets*, it also required all employers to join the 'family' corporatist trade organisation relevant to their sector. The government's Work Charter of October 1941 insisted further that in all workplaces with one hundred or more workers a Works Social Committee had to be established that would be presided over by the employer, but was formed of representatives of the manual and white collar workers along with managers (Robert 2001). This was the precedent for the *comités d'entreprise* decreed by De Gaulle in February 1945.

In October 1945, the PCF attracted 25 per cent of the vote for the First Constituent Assembly. This compared to 23 per cent for the Socialists and 24 per cent for a progressive Catholic party close to De Gaulle (Cobban 1981: 203–4). In the 1946 elections the Communists won 28 per cent of the first ballot vote, confirming it as France's largest political party (Price 1993: 226–8, 341). The presence of a substantial Communist party articulating a discourse of capital–labour conflict had important consequences for the post-war context of French employment relations. It made it more difficult for those sections of the employers who were looking for dialogue to find accommodating worker representatives, thereby reinforcing anti-trade union attitudes among the employers. But it also reinforced workers' sense of class identity and kept up pressure on the Socialists and progressive Republicans to promise significant reforms, while presenting a constant threat of strikes and street demonstrations if workers' interests were overlooked. The PCF's focus on extra-parliamentary pressure was reinforced by its exclusion from government between 1947 and 1981, despite it being the largest left party for all except the last few years of this period.

The constitution of the Fourth Republic was finally narrowly endorsed by a referendum in October 1946. Between 1946 and 1951, its first parliament saw repeated political divisions appear between the progressives and conservatives in the Catholic and Gaullist formations, and within the ranks of the Socialists. The exclusion of the Communists alongside repeated splits among the 'Third Force' of Socialists, Radicals and progressive Catholics over state support for Catholic schools, de-colonialisation and state intervention in industry combined to create significant political instability. The result was the creation of a series of temporary coalitions and by 1956, when the Fourth Republic's third and last parliament was elected, as many as 15 different governments had already held office (Cobban 1981: 207–13, 225).

The Fifth Republic

On 13 May 1958 the coalition-forging process among France's elected deputies ended. The Army staged a pre-emptive military coup in Algeria designed to prevent a new French government from negotiating French withdrawal from the colony that had been subjected to a nationalist liberation struggle since 1954. In the subsequent stalemate, when the Algerian-based officers were not sure enough of their conscripts to invade France and the French government lacked the authority to do anything about the military uprising, General de Gaulle announced he would respond to a 'legal' summons to return to power. He was voted Premier in the National Assembly on 1 June 1958 on the condition that he could rule by decree for six months. In September, he submitted the constitution of a new Fifth Republic to a referendum and against Socialist and Communist opposition won a 78-per cent referendum Yes vote. Effective legislative power was then transferred from the Assembly to a seven-year term President, who became responsible for nominating the Prime Minister. The National Assembly remained on a fixed five-year term, but it could be dissolved at any moment if the President so wished. Subsequent National Assembly elections on a two-round single constituency electoral system saw the left defeated – the Communists got 19 per cent of the vote and ten seats and the Socialists 15.5 per cent of the vote and 44 seats – while the new Gaullist party got four times as many. The Assembly then elected De Gaulle president. The old parties were largely destroyed and De Gaulle appointed several ministers from outside politics to help accelerate the technical modernisation of France to his first government. In 1963, bowing to the inevitable, he finally negotiated the Evian Agreement granting Algeria its independence (*ibid.*: 236–9) and shortly after winning the peace referendum he won another, introducing direct presidential elections (endorsed by a 62 per cent vote). Deputies to the National Assembly were also subjected to majority voting (with a second eliminating round) rather than the proportional representation system of the Fourth Republic, but they remained on five-year terms of office.

The establishment of the Fifth Republic partly represented the reassertion of the old state bureaucracy over the broader democratic political process. But De Gaulle's new governing alliance was not just between the right-wing generals, the senior civil service administrators and technocratic modernisers. It also embraced a significant part of the traditional Catholic conservative right. Thus, while initially receiving broad support as a way of ending the chaos of Fourth Republic politics, it was increasingly experienced as a mechanism for freezing French social relations at the very moment when economic growth was threatening to burst them apart. De Gaulle's Bonapartist presidential style of government was endorsed (with 55.2 per cent in the second round compared to Mitterrand's 44.8 per cent) in 1965 at the first Presidential election by universal suffrage, but his second term lasted only until 1969, when in the wake of the events of 1968 he resigned after being defeated in a referendum on a minor constitutional amendment.

De Gaulle's seizure of power had a profound effect on French management and employment relations. In taking over the political right he infused it with his own military conviction that leadership of the economy must come from the state. In his memoirs he wrote:

> The (economic) action needed directly shapes the nation's destiny and involves at every step labour relations. This implies an impetus, a harmonisation, rules that can only come from the state. In short, what is needed is *dirigisme* (centralised economic planning). (Quoted in Weber 1986: 125)

His *dirigiste* legacy was to make it very much more difficult after the 1970s than in other conservative political parties in advanced industrial countries for the political right to fully adopt neo-liberal deregulation policies.

May 1968 involved a massive challenge to De Gaulle and the bureaucratic, conservative and aloof Gaullist regime. It came particularly from students and younger workers, the sign that the first post-Second World War generation born and raised in an era of full employment and job security had reached maturity. Like their equivalents elsewhere in much of Western Europe, while the new generation of middle-class university students clashed with administrators used to dealing only with the children of the elite, the new generation of more educated young workers clashed with the authoritarianism and arrogance of their managers. But what created the difference in France was the combination of the spark created by the repression of student demonstrators with the presence of a discourse of class conflict that harked back to the achievements of the mass wave of factory occupations in 1936. In terms of the political balance between liberty, social solidarity (*fraternité*) and equality, the mass movement represented a major upswelling of struggle for the latter two, for social justice. At its peak some nine million workers were on strike and hundreds of thousands of 'new' manual and white-collar workers participated actively in workplace occupations and street demonstrations. Noiriel (1986: 267) argues that at each of the great twentieth century collective mobilisations (1906, 1936 and 1968) 'a new "generation" of only partially-rooted workers lacking in traditions, became the most radical in the heart of the struggle'.

The scale and violence of the May–June events also largely frightened Catholic and 'middle' France. The right subsequently made huge gains at the elections called by De Gaulle to end the social conflict. Thus, unlike elsewhere in Europe where the 30-year period of full employment ended with social democrat governments being elected to office nearly everywhere to defend and extend workers' rights, in France, where the workers' movement went furthest, the right held political power throughout the 1970s. May 1968 was both a major transforming and a profoundly conflictual social moment. For if De Gaulle's departure meant that Gaullism was technically dead, the conservative right held onto power. First, in the form of the prime minister and leader of the Gaullist political party, the *Union pour la Nouvelle République*, Georges Pompidou. He was elected De Gaulle's successor in 1969 in the wake of the Russian Communist invasion of Czechoslovakia and in face of an utterly divided left, but then died unexpectedly in 1974 (Northcutt 1992: 54–67). The direct Gaullist succession was then unclear and the *énarque* and former finance minister under De Gaulle and Pompidou, Giscard d'Estaing, profited from the confusion to establish his candidacy for President, narrowly winning it by 50.9 per cent to Mitterrand's 49.1 per cent in the second round. Giscard d'Estaing came from the same administrative elite that had supported De Gaulle in the 1960s. His election and attempts to break with Gaullism came at the moment that France was rocked by the onset of the 1973 oil crisis. Slower growth, rapid inflation and a huge escalation in strikes caused a new rift among the governing right-wing politicians. His party, the *Union pour la démocracie française* (UDF), grouped France's centre-right and economically liberal and European interests in contrast to the more protectionist Gaullists.

In 1976, Jacques Chirac (a youthful seller of the Communist newspaper, *L'Humanité* and subsequent elite *École nationale d'administration* (ENA) graduate who had been Giscard's first prime minister) refounded the Gaullist party in opposition to Giscard's centrist liberalism. Chirac's *Rassemblement pour la République* (RPR) party was an opportunistic ideological construct, embodying De Gaulle's political and social conservatism, *dirigisme* and nationalism. From the mid-1970s, therefore, the three major divisions on the right were between neo-liberal, Catholic corporatist and racist-nationalist (the National Front) conservatisms. While Giscard's economic response to the 1970s crisis differed little from that of most of the predominantly social democratic governments elsewhere in Europe at the time, it lacked their willingness to negotiate extensions of worker rights. Instead Giscard tried the improbable combination of supporting industries in crisis, extending social welfare to cushion the blow of rising unemployment, reviving the economy (through embracing elements of both neo-liberalism and incomes policy), and simultaneously tightening immigration controls. The policy mix was an uneasy one. After pushing Chirac into third position in the first round of the 1981 presidential election Giscard subsequently lost the second round to François Mitterrand, the Socialist Party candidate. France's new majority of industrial workers finally made its voice heard. Why did it take them so long to become a majority of the workforce?

2.3   Industrialising France

In 1946, nearly one-third of the working population were peasant farmers or farm labourers, and nearly half the French population lived in very small rural communities (see Table 2.1). Mid-way through the twentieth century France remained a worker–peasant society, even though it now had a large working class. For the wealthiest nineteenth century European country, whose eighteenth century Revolution had constructed a legal code that gave industry and trade complete *liberté*, this survival of rural and peasant France has been regarded as an anomaly. A 'revisionist' school of French economic historians, however, now argues that French economy and society were never permanently blocked, and that dynamic aspects repeatedly triumphed over inertia, with France continuously modernising in its own way since the eighteenth century (Bouvier 1987). Nonetheless, we still need to ask why industrialisation and urbanisation took so long by comparison with the British and German experiences?

Braudel (1991: 456–9) argues that the causes of the slow rate of French industrialisation were established well before 1789: the *ancien régime* was particularly effective in sucking in and spending capital from the towns in ways that did not feed back into the active parts of the economy; rural France failed to achieve an agricultural revolution to increase output and free labour for other tasks; and France failed to capitalise on the possibilities of a new world order created by the American War of Independence. Even after the 1789 Revolution many key things did not change. Thus, the wealthy town bourgeoisie used its capital to buy up confiscated Crown and Church lands but then did not farm them itself, preferring to rent them out on a traditional sharecropping basis; during the same period the revolutionary and Napoleonic wars cost France enormously in capital, men and lost trading opportunities. The national debt, whose interest charges alone had consumed half of all taxation in 1788, was just as unmanageable after the Revolution. The last technical bankruptcy of France occurred in 1797 and led to Napoleon establishing the Bank of France in 1800 and specifying in 1802 that interest payments to it had priority over all other state expenditure (Vaslin 2000).

Another continuity through the French Revolution lay in the state's attempts to control worker mobility. The worker's passbook or *livret ouvrier* was an attempt to discipline highly mobile artisans and early industrial workers so they would remain 'fixed' to their employer. It was first introduced in 1749, when workers were required to finish the job they had been hired to do and to give eight days' notice before leaving. Even then, they risked being fined or forced to go back to their former employer if they left without a written letter of permission signed by the employer. Other employers were forbidden to employ workers who did not have this necessary 'ticket', leading to a situation where anyone wishing to do paid work within a particular town had to first register with the town clerk. This system of temporary certificates was replaced in 1781 by the creation of a permanent passbook. This allowed the employer to insert both the dates between which he had employed the worker, and the outstanding debts that the worker still owed him. It would then become the responsibility of any new employer to pay these debts. The passbook method of controlling workers' mobility and their ability to lever up earnings ended temporarily during the Revolution but was reinstated in 1803 and 1813 under Napoleon I, when it was established that any worker without a passbook could be imprisoned for up to six months for *vagabondage*. This method of control was maintained until the 1890s for native French workers but retained for immigrant workers until the 1960s.

Noiriel (1986: 60) argues that the continued strength of rural France until at least the 1860s requires 'abandoning visions of the French Revolution as marking a clear break with the *ancien régime* and favouring the emergence of a modern working class'. While this is true it would be equally wrong to overlook one of the Revolution's lasting achievements. Its lawyers and intellectuals forged a radical alliance with the Parisian poor that created the *Jacobin* legacy of centralised, top-down reform. Moss (1994: 3) suggests this alliance first destroyed the old State–Church economic privileges in the name of economic liberalism and then 'pushed liberalism to the limits of socialism in 1792'. In so doing it made a deadly enemy of the Catholic Church, with its still considerable powers of mobilisation among the peasantry, yet without securing a permanent ally of equal weight among the rural workers or urban tradesmen. In the face of the 1799 military *coup* by Napoleon Bonaparte these middle-class Republicans recognised the inevitable. They allied themselves with the army generals and state administrators, the only elements capable of maintaining central control over the decentralised peasant–worker political economy of nineteenth century France. Many wealthy merchants who had loaned money to the *ancien régime* only to experience its many bankruptcies looked to the same source for stability of interest payments. One of the Revolution's enduring legacies was thus to create an anti-clerical, anti-absolute monarchist Republican tradition anchored around financial interests and the state administration. This tradition was embraced by those who stood to gain most: wealthy liberal modernisers, as well as, by many dispossessed urban workers, rural worker–peasants and peasants who now farmed Church land.

The role of the state remained critical after the 1815 Restoration. This is clear in the state's encouragement of railway building. Whereas England's early industrialisation and extensive network of private capital markets provided a synergy that boosted railway construction almost independently of the state, in France by 1835 only 560 kilometres of generally unprofitable track had been laid by companies quoted on the Stock Market. The 1842 economic crisis forced the government to intervene. It decided to introduce private–public finance partnerships. The state would put up about 15 per cent of the costs of construction and guarantee investors' money. The private companies would then build the track and operate it for fixed periods of time. In exchange the state would both decide how much the companies could charge their customers and the route of the line. Within eight years 3,000 kilometres of track had been laid, and during the 1848 Revolution when the only line being built to link Lyon and Paris went bankrupt, the state nationalised it to allow building to continue, offering continuing interest payments to the former shareholders. Between 1857 and 1883, a further 2,600 kilometres of track were nationalised as their companies hit financial difficulties. Finally, in 1938, as the private companies faced mounting losses, the state nationalised the rest (Vaslin 2001). For nearly a century the state consistently combined advancing France's infrastructure while supporting French investors.

Four forms of rural industry

Industrialisation in France was not synonymous with urbanisation. French industry did grow throughout the nineteenth century, but in the main this growth took place in the countryside, where the old traditional artisan sectors dominated until the 1880s. These were trades such as carpentry, upholstery, barrel-making, bookbinding, cabinet-making, printing, casting, leatherworking, marble masonry, glove-making, tanning, braiding, nail-making, mechanical work and shoe-making (Dewerpe 1989: 14). Some important artisanal industries like perfume-making, soap-making, hat-making and dress-making were often found in the towns. But the largest industrial employer in 1865, textiles and clothing with about half the industrial labour force outside the building trades, relied heavily on distributed production by a rural workforce.

Long *before* 1789 French industry already existed in its four essential forms: the travelling (contracting) artisan, the rooted artisanal family workshop, the dispersed cottage (proto-industrialisation – the domestic or putting-out system) and the compact-site factory. Long *after*, the first three continued to thrive (Braudel 1991: 505–9). They were based on multi-occupational flexibility within families, with seasonal and longer spells in industry alternating with work on the farm: a peasant–worker economy. These flexible industrial forms amply met the seasonal or fashion-driven home and overseas demand for their expensive hand-worked products. This demand for France's heterogeneous industrial output increased steadily as economic growth and more reliable transport made the world wealthier and while Paris enjoyed supremacy as the world's stylistic, cultural and intellectual capital.

It took the coming of the railways, putting the necessary infrastructure in place, to enable the *factory* form of industrialisation to accelerate its hesitating advance. In part this was because by the 1850s, the railways helped cheapen the price of France's quite rare coal supplies to one-sixth the price of France's abundant wood. This stimulated the production of boilers and steam engines, as well as the search for coal mines and coal miners. As this happened, the share of the fourth form of industrial organisation, the compact single-site 'factory', began to grow, especially near the coal-mining areas of Northern France where it could draw in Belgian immigrant workers. But outside textiles, firms were still small: in 1866 the average number of workers in engineering companies was 84, in mines and quarries just 24 and south of a line drawn across France between Geneva and Saint-Malo, not even this small advance had taken place (*ibid*.: 540–1). The importance of the North–South divide in France led Hervé le Bras to argue that the comparatively slow rate of French industrial growth in the fifty years before the First World War was due to excessive government investment (of the wealth of northern France) in the South by laying down a national education system, a railway network and an effective administration. 'By tempering the inequalities unleashed by the first wave of industrialisation, France (may have) limited its industrial growth, while succeeding in creating political unity' (le Bras, cited in *ibid*.: 542).

To grow faster still larger scale industry needed more capital investment and more risk-taking. Braudel (1991: 591–5) argues that the peasant's fear of 'bad times', and their regular occurrence in France over several centuries encouraged a widespread French mania for hoarding gold or silver coin that consistently deprived the economy of much-needed capital. Even those wealthy enough to invest some of their savings tended to plump for secure investments such as house or land rent or insurance that paid a guaranteed rate of return. And all preferred coin to bank notes. In 1856, the proportion of banknotes in France was just 20 per cent compared to 67 per cent in England, and even in 1999, when the Bank of England started to sell of its gold reserves in favour of more profitable (paper) investments, the Bank of France declared it would not be following suit. 'Gold is still firstly a question of confidence in the currency ... for psychological reasons' (Delhoummais 1999).

It was only, effectively, with the creation of provincial branches of the main banks after 1850 that French capitalism began to seriously tap the country's immense savings and investments began to flow more systematically into industry. Yet, even then French capitalism remained dominated by the narrow group of 20–25 high finance firms (*la haute banque*) comprising such family firms as Laffitte, Périer, Hentsch, Delessert and Rothschild, who between them had successively banked the Revolutionary Committee of Public Safety, Napoleon Bonaparte and King Louis-Philippe, and whose networks, expertise and interests were predominantly international. Not only did they continue to sit regularly on the board of the Bank of France throughout the nineteenth century, but in the 1850s and 1860s they also put up large amounts of capital to set up and sit on the boards of modern France's financial giants: Crédit Foncier, Crédit Industriel et Commercial, Crédit Lyonnais and the Société Générale (Braudel 1991: 654–61). Their international out-look and preference for 'low risk' loans to foreign governments continuously tweaked investment decisions away from industrial France: thus before the First World War, Tzarist Russia became a principal outlet for French foreign lending, with eventually disastrous results (Kemp 1979: 72). In the long run this 'external' view of banking's role dominated. So while French banks did loan short term to industry, they did not take a hands on approach and take shares in industry until the second half of the twentieth century. When wealthy French invested in stocks it was where there was little risk, as in the railway stocks guaranteed by the state.

Factory industrialisation

The cultural conservatism of the urban French middle and upper classes and their preferences for relatively high-priced manufactured goods were, per-haps, as important as the politics of bankers and governments in slowing factory industrialisation. Here, however, the 1860 Anglo-French Commercial Treaty was one key turning point. This liberal turn by Napoleon III reduced France's protective tariffs to 25 per cent. This rate was low enough to force French industry to modernise to defend its internal markets, so marking the beginning of the end of wide-scale domestic industry, but it was still high enough to avoid too rapid a change. By the 1890s, the harmonisation of a national railway network linked to steamships that could bring in cheap grain was another turning point: for the first time the peasant–worker econ-omy was exposed to the full force of competition (Noiriel 1986: 84). Between roughly 1860 and 1890 most of northern France was effectively industri-alised, a process that for many of those who entered the growing industrial cities was synonymous with pauperisation: in 1870, seven out of ten living in the workers' quarter of Saint Servan in Lille died before the age of 40 (*ibid.*: 27). Firm size grew more rapidly: by 1906, the average coal-mining firm employed 449 workers and two-thirds of the whole French workforce was employed in firms of more than ten workers, of whom 40 per cent worked in firms of more than 100. France even had major innovating industrial firms like Michelin, Schneider, Peugeot and Renault and its major cities had grown significantly: Paris up from one million in 1850 to 2.7 million by 1900; Marseilles and Lyon up from under 200,000 each to nearly half a million (Braudel 1991: 540; Noiriel 1986: 123).

Although the pace of change accelerated, the combination of a largely self-sufficient small peasantry who either did not need or did not have the cash to buy most manufactured goods with a very wealthy dispersed bour-geoisie who had clear preferences for hand-crafted products, meant there were many fewer domestic outlets for the mass produced goods that had fuelled British and were fuelling German industrialisation. Between 1841 and 1901, the population of England and Wales had doubled to 32 million, virtually catching up France, while London had grown from two million to five between 1841 and 1881, by when 40 per cent of the entire population of England and Wales lived in just six conurbations. In 1900, London was a marketplace of 6.5 million people, and Glasgow, Manchester and Birmingham each had between half a million and three-quarters of a million. Few of these Scots or English men and women had peasant or artisan parents or grandparents to supply them with food or household items. France, by contrast, remained relatively under-developed. It had fewer employers of very large numbers of workers and fewer heavily capitalised firms. Before the First World War there were just 21 large firms with a nominal capital equivalent to £2 million in France, compared to 45 in Germany and to 93 in Britain. And there were just ten firms with more than 10,000 employees, compared to 23 in Germany and to 17 in Britain (Cassis 1997).

The emergence of a French working class

The devastation wreaked on French peasant villages by the slaughter of 1914–1918 broke down the peasant–worker economy and helped establish a popular demand for mass-produced goods. The result was the domination of factory-industrialisation and the entrenching of a worker–peasant economy. By 1926, the combination of the post-First World War return of industrial Alsace (taken by Germany in 1870) with the massive immigration of Italian and Polish workers swelled the proportion of workers in industry and construction to the point where they finally exceeded the numbers working in agriculture. Inter-war industrialisation involved building large factories. No longer required to locate in rural areas close to raw materials or rivers, manufacturing now generally sought sites near potential sources of labour just outside the city centres: by 1931, half the industrial workforce worked in firms employing over 100, and 25 per cent were in firms with 500 or more employees. France's disparate nineteenth century 'workers' movement' gave way to a more homogeneous 'industrial working class' (Noiriel 1986: 123, 266). In the 1930s, a significant proportion of workers also began to be employed by the state. By 1939, the railways and parts of the arms and aeronautical industries had been nationalised (Bouvier 1987: 175).

After the Second World War French industry was largely restructured. Nationalisations, central economic co-ordination and a broad employment insurance-based welfare system were introduced. Economic recovery and unprecedented growth followed. Industrial production of half its 1938 level in 1945 had doubled by 1947 (Cochet 1997: 43). After the Communists left the government, France remained firmly on the American side in the Cold War and became a major recipient of Marshall Aid. Between 1948 and 1963 the French economy grew at an average rate of 4.6 per cent a year and a key indicator of national wealth, the proportion spent on food in household budgets fell from 44 per cent in 1949 to 28 per cent two decades later (Babeau 1991: 432). In part this growth reflected the efficiency and profitability of (and investment in) the new state industries. They included the coal industry, certain firms that had been penalised for their wartime collaboration (like the Renault car firm), the merchant marine fleet and leading aviation companies, the *Banque de France* and the four major deposit banks (including Crédit Lyonnais and Société Générale), 34 insurance companies and Paris' public transport system, the RATP (Cochet 1997: 36–9). French 'indicative' planning was more interventionist than Britain's. In theory free market-based, tripartite and politically accountable, *Le Plan* was in reality constructed around cordial relations between the top civil servants and major business leaders who had been fellow students at *les grandes écoles*, France's elite-forming post-graduate finishing schools.

Rapid economic growth saw the earlier 1926–1931 peak of over seven million industrial workers reached again in 1962, and an all-time high for industrial employment of 8.3 million workers in 1974, when 2.2 million worked in agriculture and 11 million were in the service sector (Marchand and Thélot 1991: 174). Across the whole economy these industrial workers tended to work in much larger concentrations than they had ever done before: by 1975 less than one in five worked in a firm with under ten employees, while just over one in five worked in units of 500 or more; in industry alone this last proportion was 35.6 per cent (Bordes and Gonzalez-Demichel 1998: 99). Perhaps the most remarkable testimony to the post-war 'thirty glorious years' is the 1970 poll that found that 88 per cent of workers had never been made redundant or fired (Noiriel 1986: 219). In that year 57 per cent of French households had a car, 69 per cent had a television, 79 per cent had a refrigerator and 56 per cent had a washing machine (Babeau 1991: 440). France had finally been transformed into an industrial society substantially structured around stable major manufacturing industries and the sale of their products, in which the many unstable and competing social classes of the nineteenth centuries had been narrowed down to a few.

Several elements explain the French productivity 'miracle' that contrasted a fall in the annual average value added by each active member of the labour force between 1896 and 1929 from a sluggish 1.6 per cent to just 1.3 per cent between 1929 and 1951, with the exceptional 5.2 per cent achieved between 1951 and 1973 (Marchand and Thélot 1991). In part this rebound was a reflection of the 'Malthusianism' of the French ruling class over the previous 150 years: the economy had suffered from underinvestment and was so far behind the British, German and American economies that the years after 1945 are, perhaps, better called the years of economic 'construction' rather than 'reconstruction'. Higher growth rates are always easier to achieve from an initially low base. In part higher productivity growth was due to the centralised direction of investment enabled by the finance available through the Marshall Plan, by the introduction of a centralised planning process, and by the nationalisation of a wide raft of industries that gave the state a significant economic policy weight in its own write. Another key element was the near-total reorganisation of working life in the factories where assembly lines became nearly universal. With France's participation in the European Economic Community (1957) and the establishment of the Fifth Republic (1958) came three other contributing factors: political stability, economic internationalisation (exports doubled from 10 to over 20 per cent of GNP between 1958 and 1973), and a pro-active industrial policy funding research and encouraging company mergers and the creation of 'national' champions (Stoffaës 1991: 445–51). It is also likely that the 'miracle' reflected the presence of a militant but minority trade union movement that was, nonetheless, largely excluded from any direct negotiations with the employer on issues within the workplace until 1969, when the law finally recognised workplace trade union organisation and union 'convenors' (*délégués syndicaux*).

The intensity of the transformation in which France dramatically 'caught up' with the mass production consumption levels that had been common for over 50 years in Britain probably helps explain (without justifying it) the French Regulation school's stress on the role of post-Second World War 'Fordist' mass consumption in driving 'Fordist' production and a 'Fordist' mode of employment regulation. However, few French academics have argued as mechanically as Chris Howell that 'as Fordism became better implanted in France, it set up intolerable strains on the dominant model of labor market regulation and ultimately resulted in the events of May 1968' (Howell 1992: 28). While industrial workers were working in larger workplaces in the 1960s and 1970s, and it is true they were among the most involved in the May–June 1968 occupations and strikes, a considerably smaller average workplace size had not prevented three million workers from striking and occupying their factories in 1936. Howell's mistake is to read too much directly from production characteristics. Hence his error in assuming that 'as seems likely, 1968 represented the last great challenge to the state the French labor movement was able to mount' (*ibid.*: 27). What he misses is an understanding of at least three political dimensions to class struggle all of which need to be present before normal 'strains' really do become 'intolerable' for more than a tiny minority. First, he ignores the leadership role played by key broad-based groups, with the students and younger workers being critical in 1968, and public sector workers (especially railway workers) in 1995 (Jefferys 1996). Second, Howell misses the significance of what Shorter and Tilly (1974) point to as a key element distinguishing mass strikes from other forms of mobilisation: the presence of labour movement actors prepared to offer a greater possibility of united action and co-ordination, what could be described as 'the confidence factor'. Finally, in both 1968 and 1995 it is also difficult to see the generalisation of struggle taking place on the mass scale that they did without their being provoked by the presence of right-wing governments that appeared to be highly remote and to have totally lost touch with the people. Class mobilisations can rarely be deduced simply or largely from changes in the production regime. The interplay of political and power relations between different social classes are crucial.

2.4   Social classes in France, 1870–1970

There is not the space here to provide more than a highly schematic view of the evolution of social classes from the nineteenth to the twentieth centuries. It is important to do so, though, because it is by reference to the opinions and behaviours of their peers that the various industrial relations actors we are interested in often made the choices they did. Class, however, is a complex concept to grasp, not least because while shaped out of people's experiences of family life, school, work and of their relative degree of control of their environment (their *social being* to use Marx's term), it is above all a living *relationship*. At any one moment history will be shaped both by the multitude of complex relationships that exist between social groups with different degrees of power, and by the range of societal institutions and ideologies which mediate between them and which over time have taken on an independence of their own. To do justice to the task would require several books and many excellent ones have been written. In French both Noiriel (1986) and Charle (1991) provide really interesting accounts, while I believe the best social history of the French working class written in English is the two volumes by Magraw (1992), the best historical treatment of industrial relations is by Shorter and Tilly (1974), and the best history of French socialism is by Moss (1976). Instead of attempting to synthesise their contributions, I try to create three pictures of social divisions at different periods of time based around people's mix of occupation and access to power. The first snapshot is taken at about the beginning of the factory industrialisation process, between 1865 and 1875, while the second comes at about its end, roughly one hundred years later. The third one, discussed later in the book, tries to capture contemporary reality. The first two pictures are bookended by the huge political–economic events of the 1871 Paris Commune and the 'events' of May 1968, and are separated by the systemic traumas of the First World War, the 1936 general strike and the German wartime occupation.

Social classes around 1870

Social class in France under the Second Empire (from 1852 to 1870) was brilliantly satirised in the 20 novels written by Emile Zola on the Rougon-Macquart family. The son of an Italian immigrant, Zola was brought up in provincial Aix-en-Provence before becoming acquainted with Parisian *salon* politics when he worked as press officer for the prestigious publisher Hachette. While the Imperial Court, some of the Nobility, a handful of the New Rich and *la haute banque* constituted a tiny interlocking network of extreme wealth and power at the centre of government, Zola shows how its rules on social status and formal behaviour and its disdain for trade and manufacturing, penetrated the much wider social class of urban-based landowners, whose wealth came largely from rents, as well as the upper-middle class professionals (the lawyers, magistrates, clergy, senior administrators, doctors, senior army officers and their wives) who effectively governed France. Exceptionally, where large rural employers dominated entire towns and had effectively appointed managers to carry out the day-to-day tasks, they too would be admitted to the local elite as indeed were a handful of new entrepreneurs to Napoleon III's Council of Ministers. Thus, Eugene Schneider, who employed 10,000 foundry workers at Le Creusot, was first Minister of Trade and Agriculture (1851) and then President of the Legislative Council (1867–1870). Schneider was a classic paternalist whose workshop rules included bans on reading newspapers or other publications, forming groups, singing, taking part in any kind of demonstrations or petitions, and organising any kind of collections or subscriptions (cited in Coutrot 1998). Napoleon III's Legislative Council comprised senior government administrators (one-third), landlords (one-fifth), inherited wealth (one-fifth) and businessmen (one-quarter). Determined to forge an elite supportive of his power, Napoleon III was pre-pared to pay: he introduced a single pension regime for all civil servants, raised their salaries and more than doubled their numbers to 265,000; he increased the size of the army, and within it particularly the officer corps, to around 450,000; and he subsidised a one-third expansion of the clergy to 164,000 in an attempt to neutralise Church opposition (Charle 1991: 76–86).

Just beyond the local governing circles came the merchants who organ-ised the putting out system, the shop owners and the artisan 'masters'. Each of these was rooted in a trade technically distant from other trades and hav-ing its own distinctive business cycle and markets. Beyond the 'masters' came a layer of skilled workers, the acquisition of whose trades came with elaborate initiation ceremonies after lengthy apprenticeships spent largely in observation, imitation and repetition. While they often aspired to become small masters themselves, the uncertainties of business meant that there was often a two-way movement between artisan employer and artisan tradesman. These tradesmen were literate, lived permanently within the community, and had traditions of craft solidarity. For these reasons they were the group who rallied most consistently throughout the nineteenth century to the revolutionary defence of *liberté* and who in 1848 had taken socialist ideas to poor peasants in rural France as well as to emerging factory concentrations (Moss 1994).

In rural areas there were at least further three overlapping sets of peasant interests. There were well-off peasants who through marriage or trade had been able to acquire enough land to produce a surplus, and who could afford to buy replacements so their sons could avoid conscription. There were poorer, subsistence-farming peasants who, occasionally, might work for a few days for a wealthier peasant or for local factories. And then there was the other group of poor peasants, the worker–peasants. They worked regu-larly for one or more merchants or factory owners and depended on money

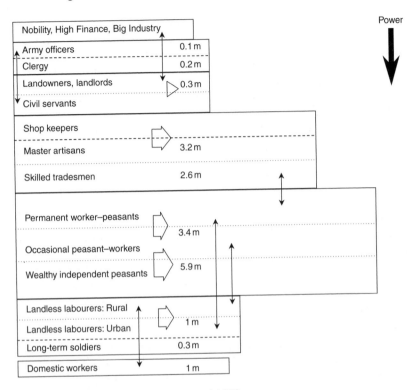

Figure 2.2   Occupational divisions around 1870

Sources: Adapted from data in Charle 1991; Marchand and Thélot 1991.

wages for survival. In addition, in both town and country there were large and growing numbers of (largely young) landless labourers who worked when they could get it, and survived by their wits when they could not. Finally, there were around one million domestic servants. Two-thirds of these were women. In 1866, women also comprised over a third of all workers with one million women working in one or another form of industry. The complex socio-occupational breakdown of France's approximately 18 million active workers is charted in Figure 2.2.

Individuals moved frequently in their own lifetimes inside each of the seven main occupational groupings divided by continuous horizontal lines in Figure 2.2. This mobility occurred between generations and within families, with close relatives commonly placed permanently or temporarily across all categories within each group (indicated by the dotted horizontal lines; the dashed lines separate the more distinctive occupational groups). Even more heterogeneity occurred, however, in the nineteenth century as a result of inter-class social mobility between these broad occupational groups (indicated by the narrow vertical two-way arrows). Class interests were constantly recomposing. Arguably only the peasantry achieved the degree of self-identity necessary to establish stable relationships with other classes (Charle 1991). Even that most classic of class relationships that was to develop strongly from the 1920s and 1930s, the antagonism and mistrust between manual factory workers and their employers, was mitigated before then by the relatively small numbers of available (i.e. landless) *French* workers.

While the working lives of at least half the population at that time was dominated by the weather, most of the rest experienced lives of job insecurity, job mobility and/or immigration. The migrants (from poverty-ridden rural areas) and immigrants (from Belgium, Italy and Germany) who found themselves in coal mining, factory work or in desperate urban poverty, alternated between moments of total passivity when they believed these experiences were only temporary, and violent rebellion when they realised they were trapped. Along with the more coherent and socialistic attitudes of the urban artisans, their responses to industrialisation made up what Noiriel (1986) terms the disparate and rebellious 'workers' movement' of what should be seen as a 'long' French nineteenth century that began in 1789 and only ended around 1918.

Among the ruling elite what was exceptional was that none of the distinct interest groups representing industrial, finance, agriculture or property was strong enough to permanently dominate the others or to single-handedly control what was already a 'bourgeois' state. The different weights of the key interest groups can be seen in estimates of the distribution of revenues in France in 1880. While incomes gained from profit and rent were twice those gained from wages, Figure 2.3 shows the relatively even distribution of profits from agriculture, industry (non-agriculture), land, shares and property.

In the political space created by the rivalries of the competing ruling elite interests, the state came to be partly controlled by an interlocking self-perpetuating group of top civil servants and senior army officers. These high state administrators formed alliances first with one dominant interest group and then with another. Their principal aim was survival and the passing on of their privileges to the next generation. In 1860, 56 per cent of tax inspectors were the sons of senior civil servants, as were 64 per cent of the civil engineering inspectorate (*Ponts et Chaussées*). Of the 220 *préfets* (the chief government police and civil authority in each *département* or county) appointed between 1852 and 1870, as many as 21 were the sons of *préfets* and another 30 were the sons or son-in-laws of generals (Charle 1991: 78). Power was administered by the state in the general interests of the wealthy and in order to preserve the privileges and power of France's semi-independent administrative elite. To do so it balanced the specific interests of various fragments of the ruling class rather than systematically privileging one or other of them.

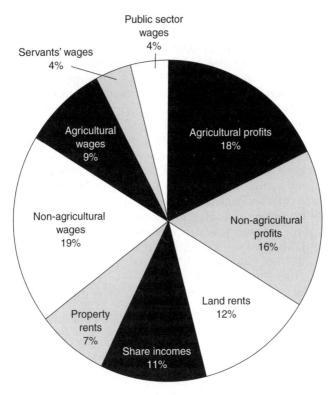

Figure 2.3   Distribution of revenues by type of profits and wages in France, 1880
Source: Morrisson 1991: 152–3.

Occupational divisions in the 1970s

One hundred years later the picture was very different. In 1979, industrial profits held up at 14.8 per cent of GNP but revenues from agriculture were below 5 per cent and profits had fallen as a per cent: shares were 5.5 per cent, property was 3.8 per cent, and profits from land were 0.8 per cent. Wages now took 71.1 per cent of GNP compared to half that share in 1880, of which public sector wages were 13.1 per cent compared to 4 per cent (Morrisson 1991: 152–3). The peasant–worker and the putting-out system had largely disappeared during and after the First World War. The contract worker and the artisan workshop were on the wane. Industry was no longer substantially artisanal, domestic or dominated by textiles. From the 1930s, cars, chemicals and household consumer goods were the major industrial employers. The French manual working class, too, had marked its arrival with the mass strike and occupations of 1936 (Noiriel 1986: 266) and with the remarkable Northern coalfield strike that took place under German

Occupation in May–June 1941 (Lefebvre 2001). It had also marked its continuing presence with the mass strike and factory occupations of May–June 1968.

Class identities had become more durable. This occurred as five complementary elements knitted together. A second (and sometimes a third) urban generation was entering the same full-time occupation as their parents. The industries they worked in had much more in common with each other, quite commonly allowing skilled, clerical and managerial workers, as well as the unskilled labourers who had always done so, to move from one to another. The welfare state had expanded employment and job security in the state apparatus, while full employment, sectoral collective bargaining and the national minimum wage had reduced the inequalities in wages and living conditions of dissimilar groups of workers. The Socialist and Communist parties now openly appealed for votes on class lines, and by the 1960s, both large and small employers were well organised nationally to lobby for their economic interests.

The one area where change was possibly not so great, was in the area of the senior civil service. Despite or partly because of De Gaulle's 1947 reform when he had introduced an elite fast track route (the School of National Administration, *École nationale d'administration*) to enable some of his wartime supporters to be parachuted into senior positions in the French state, France had continued to be dominated by the same remote and arrogant self-perpetuating social elite that had governed France since Napoleon I. Even though the peasantry no longer provided a cushion of solid conservative votes, the state's top administrators still saw themselves as essentially independent of and even as *above* the democratic political process that had only finally extended the vote to women in 1944. This elitist view encouraged and sustained a view of the state as a 'co-ordinator' of last resort: when private capital, the trade unions or the Communists, appeared to be leading France in the 'wrong direction' it was up to them to co-ordinate the responses of private actors so that the 'public interest' would be achieved.

What then does a picture of French social class look like around 1970? I identify four occupational groups each possessing a more or less shared identity and broadly consistent relationships with the other classes. At the pinnacle of society remained a tiny hybrid class comprising major industrial and finance interests (half the biggest 200 French firms were still family-controlled), some senior managers and the very senior civil servants (including top judges and the generals who had staged the 1958 *coup d'état* that put General de Gaulle into power). This was a fairly stable class: during the late 1960s, 60 per cent of the managing directors of France's largest 100 public and private sector firms were the sons of business owners, merchants, brokers and bankers; between a quarter and a third were from other wealthy backgrounds. Nearly four out of ten of them were graduates of the same top Paris elite *grande école*, the *École polytechnic*. In 1978, two exceptionally powerful banking groups, Paribas, with 650,000 employees in hundreds of subsidiaries, and the

Banque de Suez in alliance with several huge industrial giants with over 100,000 employees each, co-ordinated most of French economic life (Marceau 1989). Closely linked finance–industrial capital had finally become a major power in its own right. But it had been obliged to share power with a state apparatus that had nationalised large rafts of industry and banking in 1945 and continued to play a key co-ordinating role both between France and the world economy and between this capitalist class and other classes. *Pantouflage*, the two-way movement of France's top civil servants into controlling positions in these private groups and back, was rife. The modernisers who had come to power after 1944 had taken France into the Common Market in 1957 and constructed huge state-supported 'social partnership' institutions to contain internal conflict, leaving France's capitalist class in a power-sharing arrangement with the state. Precise numbers are difficult to establish, but Piketty's (2001) excellent longitudinal study, suggesting the long-term stability of the distribution of French wealth and income, argues that there are about 3,000 super-rich households.

Distinct from this numerically small hybrid capitalist class, although largely working for it, was a large and growing, class of middle and junior managers, professional engineers and university-qualified teachers and civil servants. While often divided, their principal common interest and point of identity was in elevating their social and economic status above that of the small business and working classes.

The class of small businessmen and women was the historical legacy of the divisions between Paris (large business and finance) and Provence (small business) and of the importance of agriculture. It comprised of a broad grouping of smaller private owners of the means of creating wealth, the medium and small-sized employers, shop-keepers, medium and large farmers and landlords. This class was now relatively stable. Even by the mid-1970s, 68 per cent of all enterprise owners were themselves the sons of enterprise owners (Marceau 1989: 60). Its generally protectionist interests were often at odds with those of the big capital–state nexus. It was from this milieu in the 1950s that most support was given to the conservative shop-keeper and small farmer French Union and Brotherhood political party (*Union et Fraternité françaises*) founded by Pierre Poujade, and it was shop-keepers who contributed most to the 1984 European Parliament election breakthrough of French neo-fascism when an estimated 15 per cent of them voted for the National Front (Rollat 1985: 106). This class was highly conservative and was almost always at odds with the working classes.

Finally, the working class was much bigger than before, but still far from homogeneous: important divisions existed between the technicians, clerical white-collar workers and shop workers, and between all of these and the skilled, semi-skilled and unskilled industrial manual workers. Their common situation of being totally reliant upon their labour power, and hence at high risk within a capitalist market society, had forged mutual interests extending from employment rights and protection to social housing. After the political defeat of French unitarist–corporatist capitalism in 1944 this class was finally able to exercise some direct influence over the state. This overview of occupational class and the distribution of political power at a time when France's working population was about 22 million, is sketched in Figure 2.4.

There was considerable movement *within* each broad occupational class. This occurred particularly under full employment in the 1960s and 1970s, when many medium and large-sized firms practised upward internal skill enhancement (largely of 'French' rather than immigrant workers) through active training programmes, and when the children and wives of male manual workers began to move into technical white collar and service sector jobs (Noiriel 1986: 216). However, unlike one hundred years earlier, mobility *between* these four broad classes was low, particularly after 1918. This relative occupational rigidity lasted long enough both to confirm class identities and group cultures. Sets of class relationships were established that reflected both their historical origins and traditions and the contours of the new industrial society. These penetrated the social fabric, took on quasi-independent

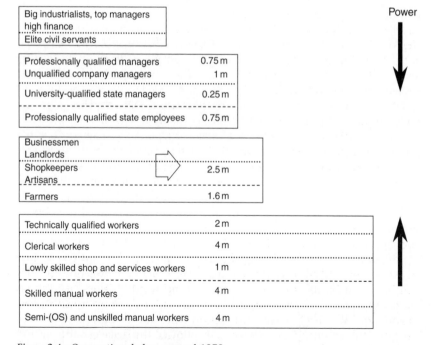

Figure 2.4　Occupational class around 1970

Sources: Marchand and Thélot 1991; Bordes and Gonzalez-Demichel 1998; Mendras and Cole 1988.

institutional and ideological forms, and helped shape political choices. Among the most important of these were the trade unions.

2.5 The origins and evolution of trade unions

Outlawed by the *Loi Chapelier* in 1791 in the name of *liberté*, it was nearly a century later before the 1884 Waldeck–Rousseau Law finally rendered workers' associations fully legal. This did not mean that workers stopped forming associations in the intervening years – they did so repeatedly, much to the authorities' chagrin. Indeed, in 1852, Napoleon III specifically passed a law legalising 'mutual' savings schemes that were to be controlled by local notables rather than by workers' own elected representatives (Dreyfus 1995: 18). When unions of hat makers, typesetters and tailors and the like were formed it tended only to be the more active – and the more angry – who would join, thereby risking fines or imprisonment. These early organisations rarely survived beyond the active life span of their founders. They rarely had a presence beyond the locality in which their founders lived, and they rarely asked for regular financial contributions from those joining. The unions that were formed did not therefore collect members' subscriptions to pay funeral or unemployment benefits. 'Mutual insurance', one of the Webbs' three fundamental purposes of trade unionism (the others being collective bargaining and 'legal enactment', achieving legal and political/legal progress) was not an option. Emile Pouget, the 'revolutionary syndicalist' editor of the CGT's weekly *La Voix du people* at its founding in 1900, rationalised this absence in terms of its neither 'overloading the struggle organisation nor (of) compromising its combative strength' (quoted in Reynaud 1975: 67). But it added to the unions' inherent instability. The fledgling local unions sometimes formed (what were frequently) short-lived national federations, normally where one stronger *syndicat* (local association) provided the vital corresponding secretary. But the further union activists went beyond their own localities, the more likely were the police to uncover or the employers to denounce their organising efforts.

The unions therefore came into legal existence with strong activist cultures already in place. Their focus was on the locality that they knew best and they grouped together all of those in the trade who hated the oppression of paternalism and small-scale capitalism. They wanted to raise wages and improve working conditions, but given their weakness in numbers within each individual workshop and the outright hostility of their employers, they were forced to organise outside the workplace. Meeting in cafes and halls and bringing together activists from many different workshops they could draft demands, organise demonstrations and even call strikes. Negotiation was never a real first option since the employers refused to recognise the unions. If enough workers followed the strike call they would wait until the employers, the mayor or the prefect responded, and then the strikers would decide whether or not to maintain the agitation.

Direct action, revolutionary syndicalism and reformism

The hostility the early union activists met with from the employers, as well as their small numbers (just 64,000 in 1880 according to Dreyfus 1995: 22), encouraged them to rationalise their minority status in relationship to their fellow workers. Their responsibility was to lead by example. If a minority took direct action on an important issue, then the majority might join in. 'Direct action' was thus democratic – it offered workers the possibility of participating in their own liberation – and it did not involve a dependency upon either the state or the employers. In the CGT's 1906 agitation for the eight-hour day, the confederation called neither for legislation nor negotiations: its aim was to have enough workers take strike action to convince everyone to simply impose the eight-hour day on the employers (Reynaud 1975: 66).

Most late nineteenth century and early twentieth century union members were male skilled workers, but local unions would generally recruit all workers employed within a given trade, not just those who had achieved a certain level of skill. A few would even allow women to join where they worked in the trade, and in 1900, the CGT formally acknowledged women's right to work and appealed for women to unionise. Women comprised 38 per cent of the industrial labour force in 1906, but just 89,000 out of a claimed total of 900,000 trade union members. Even in the overwhelmingly feminised clothing or tobacco trades, which had very high levels of unionisation, only a tiny number of women ever attended their union conferences (Guilbert 1966).

The industrial/vertical view of *trades* unionism dominated over the craft/horizontal view for several reasons. One was the historic memory of the corporatist pre-Revolutionary guilds that organised everyone from the labourer up to the master. Another was the new and growing influence of socialist thought and of a class struggle analysis of capitalism. Pragmatically, too, their very weakness on the ground meant that most local unions could ill afford to reject any potential member merely because they had not completed a lengthy apprenticeship. This was particularly obvious where several members of the same family, with different skill levels and positions, worked in the same trade and for the same employer. If a worker agreed with the union's objectives and was ready to participate in its decision-making processes and activities, then that was generally enough.

Many of the early legal union leaders were extremely suspicious of the strongly liberal and anti-socialist Third Republic. Most of them had witnessed at first hand the terrible repression exercised by the newborn Republic on the Paris Commune in 1871, when 30,000 workers were killed and thousands more transported or exiled from a city with a total population of under two million. Thus, most activists opposed the Waldeck–Rousseau 1884 law that obliged 'legal' unions to register with the local mayor and to declare their total membership. Legalisation, nonetheless, encouraged the survival of more stable federations of local unions and in 1895, a confederation of federations, the CGT was formed. The entry of unions into the universe of legally tolerated organisations also encouraged the creation of labour exchanges (*bourses du travail*) where workers could seek jobs, and local unions from different trades could meet together to provide mutual support, hold discussions and organise training. As occurred first in Paris in 1887, in those of France's larger cities and towns that had centre-left Republican majorities, a *bourse du travail* might even be provided with premises at the local taxpayers' expense if this was considered electorally expedient (Jefferys 1997). The 14 local *bourses* were much more active than the federal unions and they established their own Federation in 1892. In 1902, the statutes of the CGT were altered to give their growing numbers (74 in 1901 and 157 in 1908) seats on the CGT executive. This effectively merged the *national* federal trade unions with the *local* 'all trades' councils and transformed the moribund CGT into a living organisation for the first time (Groux and Mouriaux 1992: 66; Reynaud 1975: 64).

After the socialist Alexandre Millerand joined the Waldeck–Rousseau centre-left Republican government of 1899 to 1902 and then legislated the ten-hour day for women and children, a major ideological debate broke out about the nature and purposes of trade unionism. In one form or another the strategic differences that emerged then have continued to exist ever since, although they are often exaggerated and oversimplified. Reynaud (1975: 63) insists, for example, that one of the viewpoints, that of '*anarchosyndicalism* (after 1906 *revolutionary syndicalism*, the more historically accurate term) has left a deep impression on the French trade union movement'. What were (and are) the debates about?

Some see a sharp contrast between the movement's 'reformist' and 'revolutionary syndicalist' wings. On the 'reformist' side were three main groups of unionists: those in a few thousand small 'autonomous' local unions pursuing their immediate interests without clear aims for the wider labour market or society and who did not wish to combine with any others; then there were those in local and even national 'yellow' unions that were established by the employers to help maintain paternalist control; and the third group of reformists belonged to national federations, particularly in the public sector, but they did not affiliate to the CGT either because as civil servants they were not allowed to, or because, like the Catholic-influenced White-collar workers' union and the Miners and Railwaymen, they did not then see the need to become part of a larger confederation. In the main the 'reformists' tended to place their emphasis upon shorter and medium-term objectives that could be achieved through direct action against individual or groups of employers.

In contrast, the 'revolutionary syndicalist' trade unionists tended to place a greater emphasis upon the 'general strike' for longer term goals of social transformation and internationalism, and to stress the importance of generalising actions against the employing class as a whole. Many of them argued that neither party politics nor collective bargaining could be relied on to improve workers' conditions; workers could only rely on what was gained through direct action. Revolutionary syndicalists were sometimes politically close to a still sizeable anarchist movement, or tended to come from smaller firms and trades where the prospects of the employers ever agreeing to trade union recognition and collective bargaining were highly remote.

A different division was between 'party-political' and 'non-party political' trade unionism. At its heart this debate was between those who believed that trade unionists should either talk to and try and influence law-makers in their favour or build their own uncompromising workers' political parties, and those who believed that no trade unionist should have anything whatsoever to do with politicians and the state. This division seems clear enough but the reality was muddied. This is because many 'non-political' trade unionists still believed in the political process, just that it should take place through political parties and not through the trade unions, which they feared would fall victim to disunity if they became political debating chambers. Many of these helped give the French socialists under Jean Jaurès their highest parliamentary vote of 1.4 million in the 1914 national assembly elections (Lefranc 1977: 341). Figure 2.5 provides a sketch indicating the interlocking nature of the two debates in early twentieth century French trade unionism.

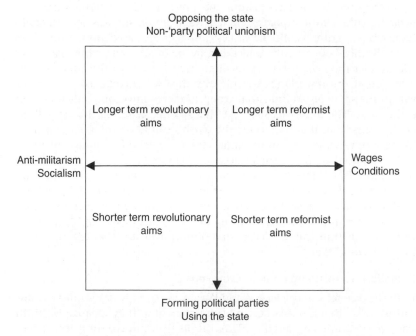

Figure 2.5 Typology of debates around union ends and means, around 1900

This wide range of possible strategic and tactical positions gave rise to a whole complex of alliances. While some activists kept to their corners, others varied their aims and the means they advocated according to the nature of the issue and its potential for mobilisation. In adopting its first full programme in the 1906 Amiens Charter, the CGT declared that local unions were both the base of resistance and the core of the future organisation of production and distribution, and that politics must be kept out of trade unionism. This was a defeat for the Guesdists and the supporters of Jaurès' Socialist Party (SFIO) that had just been founded in 1905, but it did not prevent the strongly reformist Miners' Federation from affiliating to the CGT in 1908. This was the Federation that had conducted France's first formal set of collective negotiations with the employers under the arbitration of the local prefect at Arras in 1891 (Kourchid and Trempé 1994). Although often wrongly presented as being the rejection of *all* politics by the CGT, it is thus better to understand the Amiens Charter as a tactical agreement by those from the four corners depicted in Figure 2.5 to coexist within the trade union movement and to do political battle outside of it (Moss 1994). Positions were not as fixed as is often made out, and cannot be deduced simply by examining the majority of votes cast at the CGT congresses, since each of the larger 'reformist' federations had just one vote, the same as the smaller federal unions.

Another important legacy from the pre-1914 CGT to the shape and debates within contemporary French trade unionism was its essentially industrial structure. While the earliest unions were based around quite narrow definitions of particular trades, beginning in 1902 and particularly from 1908 under the now pervasive revolutionary syndicalist discourse of common and identical working class interests, the CGT encouraged local unions within the same broad industrial group to merge into complementary federal unions. The industrial structure that resulted reflected this revolutionary discourse, but it also reflected the harsh realities of union organising in the face of vehemently hostile employers: it was rare for enough members to be recruited within a single occupational strata to make occupational trade unionism viable. More commonly the few who joined would come from several different occupational strata, and from several different companies. It made sense to organise them on an all-occupations-within-an-industry basis, and this early model was later taken up (with small variations) within the divided trade union movement that emerged from the First World War.

Catholic, reformist and Communist unions

With the outbreak of the First World War in 1914 many 'anti-militarist' and 'anti-state' trade unionists became supporters of a 'holy alliance' with the state to prosecute the war effort. This, they believed, was a short-term necessity. It would achieve victory over imperialistic Germany (whose trade unions and giant Socialist Party had broken with working class internation-alism by voting to support their government's war effort), and would enable French trade unionism to survive (Milner 1991).

The war and the 1917 Russian Revolution it triggered, however, actually led to the fragmentation of the CGT and to the crystallisation of new polit-ical and organisational structures that in one form or another have survived to the present day. These two world-shaking events tore apart the earlier debates on ends and means. People who had found themselves on the same sides in 1906 found themselves bitter enemies in the 1920s. The result was that in the years immediately following 1917 four distinct trade union centres appeared where previously there had just been one.

Two of the post-First World War centres were led by union leaders who had supported the war effort. They drew the lesson from wartime regulation and the 1919 laws introducing a legal 48-hour week and sectoral collective bargaining that the state provided a framework within which some greater equity and partnership with at least some employers could be realised. One group comprised the committed Catholics whom the Catholic Church asked to affiliate to the CFTC it set up in 1919 to counter the menace of Bolshevism. The Catholic international, to which the CFTC affiliated, called for collaboration between the classes and opposition to those who organised around class struggle:

> The goal of our trade union activity is to achieve the principle of pacific collaboration between capital and labour within the firm and to share equitably the profits it delivers.... Our Christian union ideal, based on brotherhood, our economic views demanding class collaboration and cooperation in production, will always prevent us from rallying around any doctrine based on class struggle.... We note that this class struggle exists in reality, born principally from the conflict between opposite appetites and from the abuses within a capitalism based on the law of strongest. (Quoted in Reynaud 1975: 86)

The CFTC believed that involving workers in discussions over the moderni-sation of production methods would benefit both workers and employers. But in the inter-war years its calls for consultation and the negotiation of collective agreements with the employers in the interests of both parties, fell on deaf ears. It was therefore pushed towards more clearly asserting trade union independence from the employers, and even to calling joint protest actions with the refashioned non-Communist post-First World War CGT. The CFTC's first president, Jules Zirnheld, defended this definition of trade unionism in these terms in 1925:

> The worker who unites with his fellow wants first and foremost to be able, thanks to this unity, to be able to claim and get what is owed to him.

> At the price of scandalising certain timid spirits, Christian workers believe that a trade union that does not have as its first aim demanding the just rights of the workers is not worthy of the name. (Quoted in Branciard 1990: 36)

The CFTC's Catholic ideology led it to campaign for the legal introduction of family allowances. Far from shying away from political activism three of its leading members were deputies of the Christian Democratic *Parti démocrate populaire* (PDP) in the early 1920s, and in the 1945 Constitutional Assembly, 38 of the 143 seats won by the PDP's successor, the *Mouvement républicain populaire* (MRP), were held by CFTC members (Branciard 1990: 40).

Another response to the radicalising outcomes of the First World War crystallised within the CGT. In 1921, the CGT executive expelled a minority (largely but not exclusively Communist) who were trying to set up Revolutionary Trade Union Committees in workplaces across the country. The CGT majority was a broad coalition embracing both pre-war reformists and wartime supporters of the war effort. The CGT majority (known as the *fédérés*) believed state intervention could improve workers' conditions, but still formally stuck to the 1906 Amiens Charter position rejecting any 'outside interference' from either the Socialists of the SFIO or from the Catholic Church – as occurred in the CFTC. With a claimed membership of 370,000 in 1922, rising to 740,000 in 1930, when over 300,000 public sector workers were affiliated, the CGT was formally recognised in 1924 by the government as the main representative of French trade unionists and given a seat at the International Labour Organisation (ILO). However, before 1936 the *fédérés*, too, had made few advances in collective bargaining and none in achieving workers' participation. After recovering from their initial fear of worker revolt in 1919–1921, the employers had reverted to type and proved less and less ready to give the time of day to any trade union, even ones as conciliatory as the CGT or CFTC (Reynaud 1975: 77–81).

The other camp of trade unionists had opposed the First World War 'holy alliance' and had welcomed the 1917 Soviet seizure of the state machine in Russia. Yet, this group also split in the early 1920s. Many of these trade unionists believed the French state should also be overthrown and captured by a French Bolshevik-type party. They saw the creation of favourable revolutionary political conditions as their most important duty as trade unionists. These activists generally joined the newly formed Communist Party. But others were more attracted to the workers' council ideal of the Russian Soviets than to Bolshevik Party influence and dictatorship. They believed the trade unions should continue to fight for its independence against any and all political parties. This group included both revolutionary syndicalists and many instinctive 'gut-militants' and tended to be anti-'party political'.

When both the Communists and the revolutionary syndicalists were expelled from the CGT in 1921 they responded by forming the *Confédération générale du travail unitaire* (CGTU). Initially the Communists were a minority of the CGTU *unitaires*, but within three years most of the revolutionary syndicalists had left (eventually forming a fourth tiny centre) while the Communists had recruited enough of the gut-militants to win the CGTU leadership. The CGTU had joined the 'Red' Trade Union International and remained affiliated when the 'Red' International accepted the political leadership of the Bolshevik-led Communist International. In France this meant that the CGTU became subject to the advice, instructions and discipline provided by the French Communist Party – the very antithesis of the 'revolutionary syndicalist' political independence that the CGT had stood for since 1895 (Dreyfus 1995: 126–37).

The CGTU's future up to 1936, when it merged back into the CGT, was to be treated by the Communist Party as a more or less direct transmission belt for its tactics and strategies to the wider working class. In the different situation after the Second World War, when the Communists became the majority of a much larger and more representative CGT, the PCF learned from the earlier experience to give the CGT more real independence, always, for example, ensuring that it had no more than half the members of its National Committee. Nonetheless, the leading role of the party ahead of the trade union in the broad working class movement was unchallenged by most PCF members who were also CGT activists (Reynaud 1975: 102–3). It was only at the PCF's 2001 congress that the current CGT general secretary stopped being automatically elected to its Central Committee (later National Council).

The contemporary mould of French trade unionism was thus largely set in the early 1920s. One essentially social Christian pole stood for cross-class partnership and social integration; it defended the Catholic, essentially passive, political concepts of *fraternité* and *solidarité* as representing ideals whose benefits trade unionists should bring to the attention of the employers, and believed that trade unionists should intervene politically to help bring these ideas about. A second pole represented market unionism, standing here for advancing workers' interests by negotiating collective agreements to reflect workers' strength in labour markets, but strongly insisting on the political independence of the collective bargaining process. It was not opposed to the state intervening to force employers to the collective bargaining table; but it did vigorously reject the idea that trade unionists should form political parties to win state power. A third pole embodied the class struggle perspective and rejected collective agreements as legitimating the conditions of subordination. Those who shared this view advocated the primacy of political action over the narrow trade union views they believed carried the danger of a narrow economism that would tend to trade short-term sectional gains against workers' long-term collective class interests.

The main centres' traditional positions are mapped onto Hyman's triangle in Figure 2.6. The CFDT union centre that was born out of the confessional CFTC in 1964 is shown, following a helpful suggestion by Richard

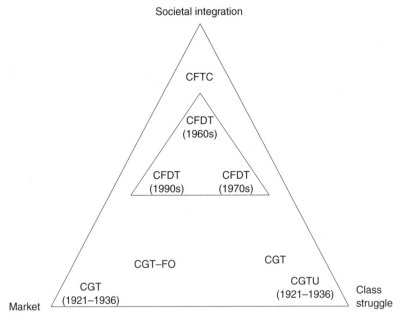

Figure 2.6   A map of the values of the principal trade union confederations

Hyman, as following a trajectory within its own inner triangle. The presence of competing organisations occupying each one of the three poles, made it difficult to create the dominant combinations of values Hyman (1996; 2001) argues occurs in Britain, Germany and Italy.

The CGT grouped the largest numbers of trade unionists until the late 1990s when the CFDT almost certainly caught it up, while FO was always much smaller (see Chapter 8). To interpret this ideological map and the changing membership of the distinctive three-pole configuration of French trade unionism from the 1920s to the 1970s, we must now consider the two new post-Second World War national trade union centres, CGT–FO and the CFDT.

CGT–FO

The origins of FO (CGT–FO) were in the inter-war reformist *fédérés*. Three years after the 1936 reunification of the CGT and CGTU that helped trigger that year's mass strikes and factory occupations, the majority leadership of former *fédérés* expelled the Communists again (for supporting the Hitler–Stalin Pact). A few months later the Vichy government then dissolved all the unions. The CGT was reunited in 1943 while still underground, but at the 1944 Liberation it was the Communists who emerged as having an overwhelming majority of support. In 1947, after PCF ministers had been thrown out of the post-war centre-left government and the Cold War replaced the 'battle for production', the American Federation of Labor (AFL) intervened. It agreed to funnel money through to the new minority of anti-Communist 'reformists', a contingent of 'anti-Stalinist' Trotskyists and a few remaining revolutionary syndicalists, should they split away to form a breakaway union confederation. The AFL, encouraged by the American CIA, consciously intended to weaken left trade unionism in France and believed firmly these ends justified any means.

The split occurred at the end of 1947. FO's founders took many public sector worker trade unionists with them. They were confident that under Communist leadership the CGT would rapidly lose members and decline as had the CGTU in the 1920s, leaving them to pick up the pieces. Yet the context was very different: the Communists were the largest political party and in 1947 the CGT's membership was in the millions. Despite the onset of the Cold War, the Soviet Union's prestige remained high among French workers, who saw Russia as having sacrificed hugely to help liberate the world from the Nazis. The new FO even failed to attract all the non-Communists within the CGT. Thus, outside the public sector, the traditional 'home' of reformist French trade unionism, FO was quite isolated. Its leaders were forced to accept aid from the French government, from the British and Belgian trade union movements, and, most compromising of all of their much-vaunted 'non-political' independence, key funding from the American AFL. This came with the 'political' price of committing FO to full support for North Atlantic Treaty Organisation (NATO) and European reconstruction.

FO's industrial strategy largely followed that of the inter-war CGT *fédérés*. It wanted the employers to negotiate and believed that negotiating was always preferable to striking. In response to price and wage controls between 1944 and 1950, FO demanded the restoration of 'free' collective bargaining – at the national and sectoral level but not at local level at which, particularly in the private sector, FO had very few members (Bergounioux 1982: 5–18). But its defining aggressive anti-Communism and 'moderate' public sector constituency combined a more politically conservative membership than the other major confederations with a top-down leadership that, in the 1980s and 1990s, increasingly wielded control with the help of a clique of anti-Communist Trotskyists.

FO's ideological stance, based on a market view of 'pure and simple' business trade unionism, is therefore often presented within a workerist, class struggle rhetoric. Despite its greater presence in the more feminised public sector, it has made little progress in opening up to women: its General Secretary (1989–2004), Marc Blondel, is renowned for his gratuitous sexist remarks, and in 2000 just one of its 17-strong delegation to France's tripartite National Economic and Social Council was a woman, compared to four and five respectively among the similar-sized CGT and CFTD delegations (Bulard 2000). This low prioritisation of women within FO was not new.

In 1989, only five of FO's then 95 federal union secretaries were women, compared to 13 out of 87 for the CFDT (in 1985) and 12 out of 88 for the CGT (in 1986) (Mouriaux 1995).

CFDT

The second new name shown on the map of French trade union values in Figure 2.6 is that of the CFDT. This centre emerged in 1964 taking with it nearly 90 per cent of the then CFTC membership. Responding to growing social tensions stimulated by De Gaulle's tough incomes policy in a period of labour shortages that eventually exploded in the strikes and occupations of May–June 1968, the overwhelming majority of CFTC members wanted a trade union centre that was both independent of the Catholic Church and more committed to the construction of a democratically structured economy and society. The 1964 report motivating the change in name and statutes adopted by the founding congress described the new union's common humanistic values:

> Putting man before the machine, a man without money, trade union struggles are dominated by the demands of people at work, in society and in the world. It is by remaining faithful to the purpose of man, to the dignity of the individual – free, responsible, united – that it has always opposed totalitarianism of both right and left. (Quoted in Cours-Salies 1988: 83)

The new confederation retained many of the CFTC's holistic values, but it also revisited the pre-1914 emphasis on trade union independence from outside influences – in its case from the Catholic Church. The old CFTC, left behind with a rump of members, was nonetheless still recognised in 1966 as a 'representative' trade union by the government for collective bargaining and running the *parity* welfare schemes (Branciard 1990: 186–94).

The change to a secularised union resulted from the convergence of several trends. The new post-Second World War generation of CFTC activists and members were both younger and more likely to be manual workers than the older, generally white-collar workers. Their experiences in the Resistance had given them a stronger sense of working class solidarity than the earlier generation. There was also a new politics in the air. The CFTC's impatience with the French employers' reluctance to permit any form of participation in the 1930s and 1940s had gradually led it to embrace a larger state role in the management of the economy and in arbitrating industrial relations. In the 1950s it attracted men like the young Jacques Delors, who ran its research centre between 1957 and 1961 and who was then appointed to work on the Fourth National Plan. The new aim of 'democratic planning' the CFTC had embraced in 1959 further encouraged the revival of ideas of workers' self-management and discussion of a 'third way' for advancing workers' interests that lay somewhere between Catholicism and Communism (Branciard 1990: 174–5; Cours-Salies 1988: 95–107; Reynaud 1975: 110–11). After 1968 it was this greater openness of the CFDT to ideas that encouraged the more dynamic Trotskyist groups to concentrate their members in that confederation rather than in FO.

The growing radicalism of the CFDT led it naturally towards a greater involvement in a perspective of struggle against the 'blocked' French society of the mid-1960s. Its values shifted towards a toleration of a societal form of *bottom-up* class struggle. While this was quite distinct from the *top-down*, structured and controlled, class struggle philosophy of the CGT, there nonetheless was a logic for the two confederations to come together and sign a joint action agreement in 1966. Mouriaux (1998) argues that May 1968 was one of the children of this new sense of wider working class unity. At its 1970 Congress, the CFDT embraced workers' control, planning and collective ownership of the means of production. In many ways the CFDT had become more radical than the heavily bureaucratic CGT, still tied closely to the political line of the Communist Party. However, with the PCF's 1977 decision to end its left unity agreement with the Socialist Party, the growing economic crisis and the end of trade union growth, the 1978 CFDT Congress announced the beginning of a shift back to its traditional values of *societal integration* and away from those of *class struggle*. Edmond Maire, CFDT general secretary from 1971 to 1988, successfully 're-centred' the CFDT on a more 'moderate' strategy of distancing itself from major struggles, such as the 1986 railway workers' and student strike waves, and of associating itself as closely as possible with the concept of social partnership with the employers. From 1993 to 2002 the CFDT was headed by a woman General Secretary, Nicole Notat, who continued the tack around its own inner triangle, taking the union still further towards the right and a position somewhere between the business union pole and social integration. With a claimed 42 per cent women membership it may now be the most feminised of the non-teaching trade union centres. Somewhere in the mid-1990s as we show in Chapter 8, while the numbers are still not very reliable, it probably equalled or overtook the CGT as France's largest trade union centre (Bulard 2000).

Managerial and teacher trade unionism

Two further trade union centres given 'representative' status by the government in 1948 are not mapped in Figure 2.6: the CGC and the *Fédération de l'éducation nationale* (FEN). We have omitted them because, unlike the four other centres, they do not claim to represent all French employees. If we were to put them on, however, the CGC would be located at the market pole, and the FEN somewhere on the axis between class struggle and social integration. How were these two institutions formed?

The CGC was reformed from an earlier 1936 manifestation in October 1944 with the encouragement of many employers. Its leadership aimed to try and create a distinctive trade union centre that would be much closer to the employers than the Communist-dominated CGT that had emerged after Liberation, although still retaining its independence (Bouffartigue 2001). Its first campaign protested the exclusion of managerial staff from the national social security system when it reversed that exclusion and negotiated the 1947 AGIRC managers' pensions and insurance agreement giving *cadres* an earnings-related supplement in addition to the national benefits. Its affiliated unions represented the groups of managers, professional engineers and technical workers *ingénieurs, cadres et techniciens* (ICT) who had begun unionising in certain industries during 1936, but whom neither the CGT nor the CFTC were initially very apt at assimilating (Reynaud 1975: 118–20). Since then it grew slightly up to the 1970s, and then went into decline. Its affiliated sectoral unions are largely made up of managers in large nationalised or formerly nationalised firms (like the electricity and gas and banking industries), but because of its representative status the CGC attends all national meetings between the unions and the employers, and can sometimes swing the odds in favour of the employers' position by joining with two of the other nationally 'representative' unions and signing an agreement – even when the three of them represent an overall minority of the workforce, as occurred in 2001 with the *plan d'aide au retour à l'emploi* (PARE) agreement (see Chapters 7 and 8).

The FEN became an independent autonomous Federation in 1948. It grouped the three largest unions representing teachers in the primary, secondary and higher education sectors and remained outside both the CGT and FO after a referendum in which the Primary School Teachers' union voted 82 per cent for independence. This severely weakened FO, which had been hoping the FEN's traditionally moderate members would join the other largely public sector workers it had succeeded in recruiting. But the teachers voted for the option that would retain their unity – something that was already challenged by the presence of a CFTC federation organising teachers in Catholic 'free' schools, and would later come under greater challenge from rival teacher unions set up by both the CGT and FO (Mouriaux 1996: 31–5). The FEN was given 'representative' status by the government to negotiate on teachers' pay and conditions and other educational issues, and the influence this gave it allowed its leadership to keep the lid on the internal tensions between primary and secondary school teachers and between left and right for nearly half a century before they exploded, as we shall see in Chapter 8.

2.6   Conclusion

This chapter has tried to explain some of the underlying reasons why state politics and social class are so important for French employment relations. Our argument is that a protracted process of class formation encouraged frequent mobilisations by both labour and capital, in their attempts to dominate the allocation of resources. Yet, France's populations grew slowly, remaining strongly rural and dependent upon immigration. This clearly influenced the slow rate of early industrialisation and helped to fragment social classes. It enabled a top administrative elite to run the state often at arm's length from the coexisting but distinct separate elites of big bankers and big industrialists whose interests they, nonetheless, attempted to second guess.

The worlds of commerce and work were highly heterogeneous up at least to the 1920s and 1930s, with agricultural and artisanal interests coexisting with rentiers, foreign bankers and industrial capitalists. This made the mobilisation of state power in the interests of a single section of society problematic. The urban left, did make bridges to the anti-clerical peasantry, but the generally conservatising strength of France's agricultural and rural-based industries kept working class political parties weak and made it difficult for trade unions to organise on clear occupational lines (Noiriel 1986: 266–7). Worker mobilisations took place against both the harshness of industrialisation and the experience of industrial discipline, but the divided working classes were neither large enough nor sufficiently politically coherent for their mobilisations to achieve permanent success. In each of the mobilisations of 1848, 1871 and 1936, the state wavered a little in front of the challenges, but eventually restored control to the dominant ruling elite.

As the population became more urban, more rooted and still more dependent on immigration, factory industrialisation progressed and the lines between France's four main social classes became more distinct. In particular the emergence of a working class steeped in the discourse of a unified class struggle renewed real fears on the part of the ruling elites. In the face of the growing risk to their interests of uncontrolled conflict the administrative elite responded by increasing the scope of state intervention. The ideologies of *laissez-faire* and *liberté* that had dominated France's ruling elites since the Revolution were compromised in the First World War, in 1919, in 1936 and again under the Vichy regime from 1940 to 1944. But it was the decisive political defeat of the right in 1944–1946 that led directly to the institutionalisation of many rights at work and to the reorientation of public policy towards a commitment to equality and solidarity for all. *Pluralism* and *fraternité–solidarité* tinged with elements of *égalité* became the policy of the early Fourth Republic, and while the Fifth Republic represented a swing towards *liberté* and a unitarist restatement of managerial prerogatives, De Gaulle's Catholic-conservative and *dirigiste* credo kept him working within pluralist and Keynesian frameworks.

In the next chapter we discuss how these social and political processes affected the labour process before the 1980s: not only the way managers managed and how work was structured but also how the state intervened.

3
Management, Work and the State before the 1980s

In 1980, a handful of extremely wealthy families still controlled more than half of France's top 200 firms. Far from being an anachronism, the way large French capitalists networked together in a combination of family ownership and interlocking directorships and their privileged access to the state were key to the success of French capitalism during the '30 glorious years'. Family networking was rooted in the most successful parts of French business culture. One study of 2,103 firms for which records exist in ten different French industrial centres over the whole period 1780–1935 found that 17 per cent defied the 'clogs to clogs in three generations' historical rule of thumb, and that there were extreme regional variations in firm longevity: in Eastern France (Alsace, Lorraine and Franche-Comté) over half the firms in 1935 were between three and six generations old, while in Normandy and Northern France the proportion was one quarter. The differences in survival rates appeared to lie in firm culture: those that survived longest appeared to stress practical techniques more, to be run by entrepreneurs with engineering and *grandes écoles* (*polytéchnique*) backgrounds, to have introduced social welfare schemes, to have a Protestant work ethic and to have remained under family control (Lévy-Leboyer 1997).

The enduring family-ownership culture of French firms had considerable implications for work, imposing distinctive forms of managerial control and values upon their employees. And at the same time this 'family-friendly' capital's toleration of the extent and scope of state intervention has had profound implications for welfare aspects of employment relations. The two-way association between welfare state and employment relations is an important although often neglected one (Carpenter and Jefferys 2000). This is partly because the modern state largely determines the conditions under which most people enter or leave (permanently or temporarily) the labour market. It provides their education, looks after their health, finds them work, often supports their housing and organises the structures that provide their pensions. Welfare considerations also act directly on working conditions through paying for periods of unemployment and training and in

70

shaping the provision and level of minimum wages, hours of work and health and safety measures. In the twentieth century the delivery of a growing range of welfare services and the creation of a substantial state-owned sector additionally transformed the state into a huge employer and obliged it to take an increasingly active part in the 'process of co-ordination' of France's industrial policy and employment relations (Birck 1998: 73). At the highest level many of France's elite administrators effectively became associate members of the family-network ruling elite.

This ruling elite was not the sole determinant of the evolution of employment relations. The labour process is also subject to its own dynamic. Managers, the state and workers all exercise some degree of choice in how they respond. Changes in production, technologies and industrial structure, in the age, gender and skill mixes of labour markets and in forms of employee resistance all help influence these choices. To try and understand the balance of influences, the chapter looks in turn at management, work and welfare against the background of the socio-political context described in Chapter 2. It argues that up to the Second World War the philosophy of nineteenth-century economic liberalism dominated management, work and welfare, and that it continued thereafter to exercise a strong influence among many employers. Their liberalism was usually limited in breadth by France's customs borders and in depth by an absolute hostility to any form of workers' independent activity. French liberalism was not very 'liberal', as can be seen in the repression of the 1871 Paris Commune. But the mass wave of factory occupations of 1936 and the political defeat of French authoritarian capitalism in 1944, shifted the dominant political ideology. The ideas that structured societal expectations and attitudes from then until the 1980s became those of *égalité* and *fraternité*.

3.1   The evolution of French management

When early French entrepreneurs expanded their companies beyond the numbers of employees they could personally tell what to do, they turned for managerial inspiration both to Catholic values and to the unitarist practices of the biggest organisations to hand, the state and the army. With the decisive defeat of Vichy's corporatist paternalism in 1944, the next major influence was American managerialism. Yet, in the same way that French family firms adapted the centralised state and military models without losing control, so they cherry-picked the managerial model, taking what they found valuable and discarding the rest. We look here in turn at the influence of the state, the military and of social Catholicism on the values of French employers and managers, and at the 'modernising' pressures on French managers after the Second World War. Finally we examine the paradox that France's intensely individualistic employers have also formed very tightly controlled collective organisations.

The French state exercised very considerable influence over the evolution of management thought and practice. It provided a bureaucratic model to emulate, with record-keeping and detailed rule-making at its core, and with competitive examinations as the principal path to promotion. It also provided a highly centralising model. All its core functions and personnel were in Paris, but senior national administrators had to be partly trained in *province*, and senior local administrators had to spend a lengthy spell in Paris before being returned to *province*, only rarely to their region from which they originated. This conscious attempt to forge a *national* caste of civil servants whose loyalties were to Paris rather than to their home towns was replicated by most large French firms in the nineteenth and twentieth centuries. This was not at all antithetical to family ownership. Typically, the son-in-law of the founder of Fromageries Bel who was president from 1941 to 1986 moved the company's HQ from Normandy to Paris during his own long reign (Fievet quoted in *Le Monde*, 4 April 2000).

Yet, the state shaped the evolution of French management still more directly. Both before and after 1789–1791 when all 'privileges' ended and economic liberalism was established, governments consistently and continuously intervened in business activities. As early as the 1660s, Louis XIV's Finance Minister, Jean-Baptiste Colbert invested in 400 manufacturing factories to reduce France's import dependence on high quality goods and military supplies and took the lucrative tobacco industry into state ownership (Castel 1995: 126). French businessmen today still denounce *Colbertisme* as being at the heart of all their problems. In 1794, revolutionary France created the *Conservatoire National des Arts et Métiers* and the *École Polytechnique* alongside the already existing *grandes écoles* (*École des Mines*, *École des Ponts-et-Chaussées* and *École du Génie Maritime*) to provide top rate civil and military engineers for public service (Birck 1998: 124). In the mid-nineteenth century the Second Empire legislated the limited liability company (1867) and as we have seen guaranteed the stocks that supported the risky building of a national railway network. In the 1890s, the Third Republic awarded the workers on these private railways official rights and civil servant 'status' in its capacity as the public protector of national safety (Noiriel 1986: 92). In all these and innumerable other ways, despite the dominant nineteenth century rhetoric of *laissez-faire* and the Napoleon III's signing of the Anglo-French commercial treaty of 1861, the senior civil servants became endowed with considerable and enduring powers of patronage.

As a result, long before implementing nationalisations and economic planning after the Second World War, before its 1930s' adoption of a 'global mission to secure economic recovery' (Birck 1998: 73), and even before its major co-ordinating role in the First World War, the French state's powers of patronage were a key point of reference for French employers and management. Adapting to state pressures while simultaneously learning how to turn them to their profit entered traditional French management ideology as a standard managerial value.

The military model

The myth of the highly efficient Napoleonic army, although tarnished by the defeat of 1870 and by the blood-letting of the First World War, survived both catastrophes. It was thus no surprise that with the emergence of mass production in the 1920s and 1930s, the term adopted to describe the growing ranks of professional engineers and of those delegated to command within the workplace was the military word, *cadre*. While originally meaning the frame of a picture or mirror, its military sense was of a superior rank commanding a 'square of men'. The choice of terms reflected a normative judgement about the differential contribution being made by those who were closely associated with the *direction* as against those who were merely workers. Managers were the new officer *corps* of industry, with total authority over their subordinates and whose obedience to their own hierarchical seniors (line managers are still called *hiérarches*) was absolute. The legal status of *cadre* was actually conferred on sales managers, administrators, engineers and technicians by the Work Charter of the war-time Vichy government (Bournois 1991: 26–8). Boltanski's (1987) historical study of the emergence of the French *cadre* argues persuasively that the status was created consciously as a mechanism for creating a distinctive, privileged managerial social group as a counter balance to the emergence of an organised working class. d'Iribarne (1989) suggests that while many French managers tend to exercise the authority their status gives them 'honourably', being bound by *ancien régime* values of duty, moderation and respect when requiring 'aristocratic obedience', others may act 'dishonourably' in demanding 'slavish obedience'. He offers in Figure 3.1 a sketch of the three discrete

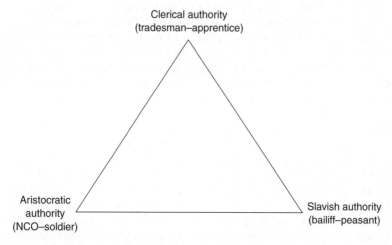

Figure 3.1   d'Iribarne's model of different contemporary forms of authority inherited from pre-industrial France

Source: d'Iribarne 1989: 114.

models of authority that he argues continue to influence French supervisory styles. While the 'aristrocratic authority', for which he gives a military analogy, and the 'clerical' authority are both seen as 'honourable', he argues that 'slavish' authority is 'dishonourable'.

The reduction of industrial co-ordination and the idea of 'handling men carefully' to the implementation of a military command structure provided a potentially fertile ground for the introduction and adaptation of Tayloristic 'scientific management'. Before the First World War, however, Taylorism was still largely viewed with suspicion. This was despite the efforts of a leading professor at the *Écoles des Mines* and of his *Revue de la Métallurgie* (Engineering Review) founded in 1904, and the introduction by Louis Renault of time-study into some of his French factories after a visit to the United States in 1911 (Kogut and Parkinson 1993: 185). In 1913, the prestigious *École des Hautes Études Commerciales* considered and then decided *not* to introduce 'American management methods' into its syllabus (Fridenson 1994: 82).

Scientific management was boosted by the experience of mass production during the First World War and afterwards. In the inter-war years the 'rationalisation movement' spearheaded by Henri Fayol became highly popular, even forming a joint organisation with the disciples of Taylor called the 'National Council of French Organisation'. Fayol was strongly opposed to nationalisation, writing in March 1921 of the 'industrial incapacity of the state' (Bouvier 1987: 176). His 'General Principles of Management' included 'the subordination of individual interests to the general interest', 'unity of command', 'centralisation' and '*esprit de corps*' (quoted in Hampden-Turner and Trompenaars 1993: 344). Fayol has been credited with articulating the need for and in fact presiding over the shift in large French companies from family-run to managerially run businesses with the appointment of salaried managing directors (Bouilloud 1998: 17). Robert Fievet, for example, applied Fayol's principles of hierarchical functionalism to Fromageries Bel after the Second World War, and created a new organisational structure with separate responsibilities for General Management, Technical Management, Commercial Management, Financial Management, Personnel Management and Research (*Le Monde*, 4 April 2000).

Fayolism also encouraged the widespread introduction into French manufacturing of a modified Taylorist time-and-motion method, the Bedaux piece-work system. The Bedaux Consultancy was, indeed, so successful that Paris-born Charles Bedaux returned to France from the United States and became a collaborator with the Vichy government after 1940. This should not surprise. The French management consulting firm *Commission d'études générales des organisations* (CEGOS) also continued to operate during the Occupation, helping companies innovate and reorganise in the face of exceptional circumstances. A CEGOS paper from 1943 is called 'Perfectioning Personnel Management Techniques' (Fridenson and Robert 1997: 215).

Nonetheless, the advance of 'modern' management methods was across a very narrow range of industries. Thus, in the 1910s and 1920s, while the Lorraine steel employers declared themselves avid readers of the *Revue de la Métallurgie* and expressed familiarity with Taylor's ideas, they did not implement them, largely for fear of alienating their skilled workers. Labour shortages were a stronger short-term influence on the French labour process than 'scientific management', leading to the employers' preference for extensive mechanisation. Fridenson (1994: 86–7) argues that 'this reveals a recurrent trait in French industry: to distrust management and to rely on technology'. Machines do what they are told and never answer back. Perhaps this too was one factor that encouraged a high rate of investment during the productivity 'miracle' after the Second World War?

Social Catholicism

The third core source of French managerial values was a blend of Catholic paternalism with utopian nineteenth century Saint-Simonian ideology. The Saint-Simonians favoured the unity of all productive and industrious elements (bourgeoisie, peasant and worker) against the useless aristocrats and rentiers (money lenders and landlords) in the interests of a functional administrative structure and a commitment to aggregate wealth and welfare (Maier 1970). Alongside this, but not necessarily in contradiction, French paternalism represented a powerful unitarist appeal to the *patron*'s inalienable *liberté* to do as he pleased within his family or *patrie*, provided he 'looked after his people'. In this vein the French foundry employers reminded association members in 1902 to look after their workers 'like a father does his family' (quoted in Castel 1995: 262). For many employers this was an ethical responsibility. The influential early sociologist Frédéric Le Play, whose views carried considerable weight with Napoleon III, considered it the moral duty of the wealthy to provide 'patronage' for the less fortunate (Frey 1995). The links with social Catholicism were very close. In 1889, a Catholic industrialist drafted this 'Catechism of the *Patron*':

> The authority of the employer should be as close as possible to parental authority ... (The employer) must aid with all his power larger families, thereby honouring the Law of God ... he must facilitate marriages between well-behaved young people, he must end illicite relationships, and, if unfortunately, children are the consequence, he must work to get them legitimated. (Cited in Savatier 1990: 52)

Although pro-active paternalism was regularly switched on and off according to the extent of labour shortage and the availability of substitute immigrant labour (Noiriel 1986), it remained the dominant managerial ideology. Frey (1995) adds the interesting argument that what was meant by 'paternalism' effectively evolved between the second half of the nineteenth and the first half of the twentieth centuries. He suggests that in response to the emerging socialist movement and the increase in average workplace size, the earlier 'industrial patronage' that was based largely on Christian morality and the metaphor of the family in employment relations tended to make way for a 'paternalism' motivated primarily by ideological anti-trade unionism and union-avoidance strategies.

The encompassing character of French paternalism has been superbly illustrated in an account of the foundry-village of Rosières, whose name today still signifies a brand of cooker. This was a tiny village with just 12 houses recorded in 1841, lost in the middle of France (20 kilometres from Bourges in the Cher Department and Centre Region). Pigenet (1997) traces how its old forge was bought in 1869 by Jules Roussel and transformed into a substantial business with 425 workers by 1877, the year he died. By then the village had 409 inhabitants, Roussel had acquired all 114 hectares of land in and around the village, built 59 houses for 'his' workers (typically semi-detached two rooms and garden) where key skilled moulders lived rent-free and other less critical workers paid low rents averaging annually just 3 per cent of the cost of construction. Before he died he changed the status of the company into a Société Anonyme (Limited company) called the *Société des Rosières* with ten shareholders and a *grande école* graduate and former marine officer, Léon Dupin, took over the reigns. Dupin remained President for the next 31 years, developing Roussel's early limited paternalism into a total control system in face of the growing challenge of trade unionism, as illustrated in Table 3.1.

By 1906, the village had nearly doubled to 739 inhabitants, of whom over half lived in the 102 tied-houses the company had built. Leaving to work elsewhere or being fired meant instant eviction. Dupin's rule was accepted and legitimated by most of the workforce, villagers and local people who worked for him. He was elected mayor in 1884 and stayed in office until 1908 when he retired, just two years after a major strike in 1906 had shaken his control system virtually to its roots.

France's reliance upon immigration may also have reinforced its engrained paternalism. Thus, Cross (1983: 16) argues: 'To a degree the new foreign labour system (of the interwar years) was a successful attempt to recreate, in a small but by no means marginal portion of the working class, the conditions which had once characterized the native citizen majority of the working class: a migratory workforce under the hegemony of the employers.' This intent is seen clearly in housing policy. Ever since the spread of factory industrialisation French employers housed many of their workers, subsidised their rents and made loans to local social housing associations in deliberate efforts to 'fix' otherwise highly mobile employees within their local labour markets. In 1930, in companies with more than 200 workers, one in five lived in employer-owned housing. The proportion varied according to the sector: in the mines it was 58 per cent, in engineering 28 per cent, and among railway workers 14 per cent (Groux and Lévy 1993: 36–7).

Table 3.1 Paternalism in practice: Léon Dupin's Rosières, 1877–1902

Year	Paternalist intervention
1877	Built Catholic church in village
1877	Built and funded Catholic boys' school
1878	Founded Mutual Aid society, presided by Dupin, deducting 2% from wages and receiving subsidy from the firm. This paid for workers' families accessing medical help and for days' off in the case of accidents at work
1891	Built and funded Catholic girls' school and nursery school
1892	Agreed to employee control of Mutual Aid society after a strike; subsequently Dupin's candidate won the election
1893	Fired the 20 leading trade unionists and socialists associated with the previous year's strike
1894	Established pension fund for 60-year-old manual and 65-year-old white-collar workers
1896	Supplied water to public fountains in village
1898	Built and funded a crèche
1900	Set-up shop to provide workers with wood, wine and coal
1902	Refused to provide land for building of a state public school in village

Source: Constructed from Pigenet 1997.

In some ways the Vichy period from 1940 to 1944 when France was divided into a German occupied zone and a smaller area administered by a government led by the octogenarian Marshal Pétain represented the pinnacle of success for Social Catholicism. His tryptique *Travail, Famille, Patrie* (Work, Family and Fatherland) replaced *Liberté, Égalité, Fraternité* in town halls and schools. One Vichy supporter contrasted the liberal capitalist and the paternalist capitalist in these terms:

> The liberal employer is a self-centred individual guided solely by their appetite. The paternalist employer is a leader responsible for a team to whom he is tacitly contracted to act as a good father of the family. The search for his own profit will be tempered by his desire to provide his collaborators with the means of living better ... to have a normal family life and to enjoy good health .... It should be noted that paternalism does not recognise any precise rights belonging to subordinates, only duties pertaining to the employer. (Cited in Frey 1995: 134)

But Vichy not only underlined France's enduring paternalistic management tradition. It also provided an unprecedented level of state intervention and pressure for modernisation. Stoffaës (1991: 448) argues that it 'marks the end of Malthusian economic liberalism and the birth of a technological and industrialising *dirigisme*'. In September 1941, the state authorised a 'Quality mark' for French plastics, and as late as 1 September 1944, 128 separate government organisations were in existence concerned with industrial production, involving as many as 20,000 people in enquiries and inspections (Rousso 1987).

The Liberation of France in 1944, however, represented a major blow to the authoritarian paternalistic perspective. An estimated ten thousand collaborators with the Germans were summarily executed, some of whom were employers who had denounced resistance fighters to the occupiers. Then De Gaulle's 1944–1946 coalition and the subsequent left governments built a new employment relations system based on the strengthening of the philosophy of employee rights. This was done, as we shall see, within a context where the family-owned firm and attitudes still survived, albeit alongside the much strengthened nationalised state sector.

New influences after 1945

Managerial practices and thought could not remain isolated from the new world economy established after the Second World War. Boltanski (1987: 97) argues that 'America has in one way or another dominated French social and intellectual life since 1945'. Part of the terms for accepting its $13 billion share of Marshall Aid in 1948 was that France opened its doors to American managerialism. The notion of 'management' as a distinct meritocratic 'profession' operating on universalistic principles was primarily an American construct. In 1952, the American Management Association defined the objectives of management as 'the preservation of a free society' through 'putting the real meaning of a free society to work within the organisation for which each individual executive is responsible' (quoted in Carew 1987). This implied there was 'one best way' of managing people shaped solely by the technical requirement to 'get the job done'. American managerial 'missionaries' saw themselves as a key mediating force that would obviate the need for class conflict, establishing a 'scientific' foundation for hierarchy through the realisation of the productive potential of 'industrial society' in the interests of all. And they preached on fertile ground to France's dynamic young Catholic managers. One of these explained:

> The Americans share our philosophical and moral views, because they believe that a worker who does not have a sense of freedom, who feels frustrated, and who is forced to work in unpleasant surroundings will not contribute all that he can to the company. (Quoted in Boltanski 1987: 127)

While America promoted its organisational methods as an ideological means for holding Communism at bay, it was also seen as a mechanism to secure the opening of European markets to US business. For both these reasons, the expansion of 'management education' became a significant element of Marshall Aid between 1948 and 1951 and of its successor Conditional Aid, between 1951 and 1960. Together they constituted a major conduit projecting American managerialism partly through US-influenced training, campaigns and consultancies and partly through direct funding of universities, where the new management practices could be permanently institutionalised and thereafter appear more 'home grown'.

The US Economic Cooperation Agency set up the *Association française pour l'accroissement de la productivité* (French Productivity Growth Association) to organise visits by French employers, *ingénieurs* and *cadres* to the United States. Between 1950 and 1953 4,000 individuals made the pilgrimage, including Robert Fievet of Fromageries Bel who discovered the presence of supermarkets, and as a result opened a business in Canada (*Le Monde*, 4 April 2000). In 1953, the European Productivity Association (EPA) was established as part of the Paris-based Organisation for European Economic Cooperation (OEEC), which remained dependent on US Conditional Aid until it became the OECD in 1961. The EPA and several other American-based or funded organisations then paid for several hundred French university lecturers to attend training courses in the United States. In 1962, the EPA and Paris's International Chamber of Commerce jointly founded *L'Institut européen d'administration des affaires* (INSEAD) at Fontainebleau, agreeing that its syllabi and staffing should be decided in conjunction with the Harvard Business School. INSEAD was funded in the 1960s by the Ford Foundation, as was the University of Paris-Dauphiné, which in 1968 launched the first French PhD programme in management (Gemelli 1994: 291).

Another route 'permitting the import and adaptation of the American model' was through management consultancies. Some were French. CEGOS was the largest French industrial training consulting firm until the arrival of subsidiaries of American parent firms like McKinsey, which opened its Paris office in 1964 and A. T. Kearney which arrived in 1967 (Cailluet 2000: 32). CEGOS ran training programmes based on combining automation and rationalisation with the 'human relations' approach developed in the United States by Elton Mayo in the 1930s. CEGOS grew from 40 employees in the 1950s to 600 by the mid-1960s, when its consultants also operated in Spain, Holland, Italy and Belgium. Its board of directors included directors of the main banks and the head of British Petroleum in France. *Société d'économie de mathématique* (SEMA), its principal rival, parent of the French polling company SOFRES and subsidiary of the giant financial holding company, Paribas, grew from 120 staff in 1960 to 2,000 in 1969. By then with Lille's Catholic University pioneering courses in 'human relations' in 1953, the message had already spread far and wide (Boltanski 1987: 118–26). Fayol, if not forgotten in practice, was put to the back of the class.

McKinsey's first French clients such as Péchiney and in particular Marcel Demonque, president of Ciments Lafarge, passed the word on to others. Cailluet (2000) argues that the close family and financial relationships between French firms favoured the diffusion of managerial fashions through the intermediation of 'popular' strategic and organisational consultants.

Thus, Etienne Dalemont, the head of the *Compagnie française des pétroles* (CFP – the future Total) in the early 1970s, recalls how CFP twisted and turned according to the latest American fashion. In the mid-1950s Standard Oil of California had helped it adopt 'job descriptions' and task analysis and to reorganise on hierarchical but operational lines. Then, in 1970 consultants reversed this organisational model by strengthening the role of the Board and decentralising control (Dalemont quoted in *Le Monde*, 4 April 2000). Essentially five or six McKinsey consultants spent around nine months in CFP before recommending – in the face of considerable senior management resistance – its standard recipe of separating line from strategic management, and of distinguishing clearly between strategic and executive functions. They also proposed the creation of a new strategic planning function, although this foundered in face of the oil price hike of 1973–1974. By the early 1970s, McKinsey had already implemented the same formula in a quarter of the top 100 British firms (Cailluet 2000).

Changing cultures

In the 1960s and 1970s, French managers still required 'educating' into the cultural assumptions of American managerialism. This was clear from comparative analysis of internal company surveys carried out by IBM in 40 countries where it had subsidiaries in 1968 and 1972. Geert Hofstede's analysis of this data suggested the presence of certain key cultural dimensions along which countries can be distinguished. One covers attitudes 'held by the majority of a country's middle class' towards 'human inequality'. These views, Hofstede argues, are 'usually formalized in hierarchical boss–subordinate relationships' which may be measured according to a 'Power Distance index' based on responses to questions about 'perceptions of the superior's style of decision-making and colleagues' fear to disagree with superiors, and with the type of decision-making which subordinates prefer in their boss' (Hofstede 1984: 65). On this index, while the United States had a moderate score of 40 (close to Hofstede's predicted score based on its latitude (!), population size and wealth) France had an exceptionally high score of 68, double its predicted score and suggesting a large distance between managers and managed. When broken down by occupation, IBM's highly educated French managers' power-distance score was four times higher than their equivalents in the United Kingdom, while the attitudes of manual workers in both countries were virtually identical (*ibid.* 1984: 78–9). France's exceptionally high 'authoritarian' score at the start of the 1970s was largely as a result of the attitudes of its managers.

France also scored very differently from the United States on a second index, 'Uncertainty Avoidance', with 73 compared to the United States's 36 when controlled for age. This index measured responses to questions about rule orientation, employment stability and stress. High scores are related, Hofstede suggests, to an intolerance of ambiguity, and hence embrace 'tendencies towards rigidity and dogmatism, intolerance of different opinions, traditionalism, superstition, racism, and ethnocentrism' (*ibid.* 1984: 112).

Drawing on a much wider range of cultural literature Hofstede then hypothesises the series of consequences flowing from the attitudes on these two issues. Some of these are listed in Table 3.2.

While the huge class differences between French IBM employees on several of these dimensions means it would be wrong to view Hofstede's work as telling the full story or as giving a full explanation of differences, as a description of French management attitudes in the 1960s and 1970s, this is quite close. Small wonder, then, that faced with intensifying international competition, French management educators had their work cut out to shift the dominant managerial cultural values away from the tradition that a formal mathematics training was the best way to prepare for leadership towards greater inter-hierarchical communication, less autocracy, less ritualism and more risk-taking and responsibility by middle-level management.

Table 3.2 Cultural consequences of high national 'power distance' and 'uncertainty avoidance' scores, according to Hofstede

Political systems	Ideologies	Organisations
High power-distance consequences		
Sudden changes in government (revolution and/or instability)	Ideologies of power polarisation	Greater centralisation with tall organisation pyramids
Labour unions tend to be ideologically based and involved in politics	Elitist theories about society	Large proportion of supervisory personnel
Autocratic or oligarchic governments	Religions that stress stratification	Large wage differentials
Where democratic government, right-wing parties dominant	Zero-sum theories of power in which all parties gain	Low qualification of lower strata
Tax system protects wealthy	Machiavelli, Mosca, Pareto, Michels	White-collar jobs valued more than blue collar
High uncertainty avoidance consequences		
Stronger nationalism	Theoretical contributions to knowledge	Managers more involved in details
Greater dependence of citizens on authorities	Theoricism in social sciences	Managers less willing to make individual and risky decisions
More elaborate legal system	Ideological thinking popular	More ritual behaviour
Stronger accent on expertise	Search for absolute truth	Lower labour turnover

Source: Hofstede 1984: 107, 142–3.

Although different aspects of the attempt to ideologically re-engineer management thought and practice were often resented and resisted, Carew (1987: 223) argues that its impact was 'cumulative' and 'pervasive'. Boltanski (1987: 104), too, suggests that it largely succeeded in France as the result of the support for modernisation orchestrated by the strong 'reformist avant-garde' network forged in the Resistance, and focused around Jean Monnet and Pierre Mendès France, that also extended to the planning commission, the commissioner for productivity, the Finance Ministry and to the *L'Express* magazine. It was its owner, Jean-Jacques Servan-Schreiber, who wrote in his best-seller, *The American Challenge*, that 'This war – and it is a war, is being fought not with dollars, or oil, or steel, or even with modern machines. It is being fought with creative imagination and organizational talent' (Servan-Schreiber 1969: xiii).

It is certainly true that between 1962 and 1975 the numbers of university-qualified management *cadres* and professional engineers in private industry rose from 440,000 to 775,000, while the numbers of qualified public sector managers rose from 157,000 to 212,000 (Bournois 1991: 30). It was this million-strong population, along with equal numbers of 'made-up' managers who lacked a higher education qualification, which then created the growing demand for more business education.

Increasing numbers of the brightest of French graduates wanting to enter management directly began to opt for post-graduate study at the *École des hautes etudes commerciales* (HEC), the equivalent of a *grande école* that had been founded by the Paris Chamber of Commerce in 1881. A study of 60 representative French texts published between 1959 and 1969 from the HEC library, including 11 translated from the original American, found the authors pre-occupied with motivating managers. The diet was essentially the application to France of the American human relations school (Mayo, Maslow, Herzberg, McClelland etc.) and the principal discourse (after praising the firm) concerned managers, subordinates and senior executives (Boltanski and Chiapello 1999: 100, 644, 653).

The consequences of failing to adapt could be serious. The Saint-Gobain company, for example, had been founded in Northern France in 1665 and by 1950 employed 35,000 workers making glass and chemical products. While publicly quoted and with 180,000 shareholders, none of whom held more than 2 per cent of the stock, family representatives still sat on the board as its turnover grew by 13 per cent a year between 1950 and 1970. Its objectives before the 1970s had been simply to maintain the firm's share of first European and then world production, which it did successfully with about 16 per cent in the mid-1960s. By 1969, it was a colossus in France, employing 100,000 people, but it was also flawed. Rising indebtedness had forced it to make new calls on shareholders, and the new shareholders expressed increasing dissatisfaction with the average annual 3.5 per cent net profit returned since 1950. The result was that in 1970 it was taken under the control of the Banque de Suez that bought 19 per cent of its stock and merged with another major chemical producer, Pont-à-Mousson (Daviet 1987).

Our argument is that it was only in the 1960s and 1970s that the process of the Americanisation of French 'professional' management education started to take deep root. In these decades – paradoxically the apogee of Gaullism – the government continued the process by financing hundreds of young French university lecturers to go to the United States to learn how to teach American management (Fridenson 1994: 83). In doing so the state trained the middle-class generation that has subsequently dominated university management teaching in France in the 1980s and 1990s, and whose ruling class peers are today's the 'captains of industry'.

Employers' associations

At first sight it might appear unlikely that France's *liberté-loving, unitarist* owners and the later generation of senior managers who were well-trained in the latest American methods should participate in what have become over more than hundred and fifty years quite tightly organised collective organisations. The impulses that led to the initial formation of French employers' associations have continued to motivate and mobilise employers right up to the present. First, there was a crude protectionism. This core motivation to influence state policy in the employers' sectional interests became more and more important after 1940 when the state adopted *dirigisme* and stepped into the role of principal co-ordinator for French capital. Second, there was the realisation that co-operation rather than competition could often bring mutual benefits, particularly in markets that were often far from 'free'. Third, there was the deep and enduring fear of workers' organisations that meant that when the employers were forced to recognise their actual existence, they tried to have as little to do with them personally as possible, in particular making it as difficult as possible for them to operate on the employer's own property.

The first industry-based employers' organisations were formed between 1835 and 1840 to organise against the lowering of import duties on manufactured goods and against the first legislative moves to restrict the hours worked by children. The second wave of employer organising occurred around the end of the nineteenth century in response to the appearance of French trade unions. The experience of continued labour shortages also encouraged French employers to associate to try and mutually control the inevitable pressures on wages. It was in 1901 that the largest current sectional association, grouping engineering and mining, the *Union des industries métallurgiques et minières* (UIMM), was founded by the oldest surviving association, that of the iron and foundry employers (the *Comité des Forges*). In 1919, the *Confédération générale de la production française* (CGPF), a national employers' organisation, was formed to lobby politically against the 48-hour week and the laws introducing sectoral collective bargaining procedures. This grouped 21 sectoral employers' associations each with a single vote. But in face of general employer apathy, it organised little and survived largely through state recognition. In 1936, the CGPF had just four staff, and effectively had to borrow people and facilities from the UIMM in order to provide even a minimum of day-to-day leadership to the employers. The pre-eminence of the iron and engineering employers was clear in that year's strikes and factory occupations, when it was the head of the *Comité des Forges* and not of the CGPF who contacted the prime minister Léon Blum to initiate negotiations to bring France's first successful general strike and wave of factory occupations to an end (Weber 1986: 56–8).

A third wave of employer organisation took place in the turbulent ten years from 1936. The employers immediately fired the representatives who had negotiated the 1936 Matignon Agreements and changed the CGPF's name (but not its acronym) to *Confédération générale du patronat français*, to assert more clearly their class interests (Mouriaux 2001). This hardening of their collective image reflected the fear-inducing events of 1936, the general strike, a first Socialist prime minister, the legal status given to staff representatives and mass unionisation. But this hardening process was encouraged under the German occupation and Vichy corporatism. When the existing employers' associations (and trade unions) were dissolved on 16 August 1940 by the Vichy government, sectoral Organisation Committees were rapidly put in their place. By Spring 1941, there were 91 of them and a total of 234 by 1944. Their object was to collectively organise war-time production and very quickly a liaison committee of the ten most important was established. The Organisation Committees were staffed either by people seconded from large companies or from the state civil service who distributed orders between the firms operating in each sector (Weber 1986: 56–8). Membership was compulsory and during this five-year period French employers got used to paying regular subscriptions to a sectoral organisation run by semi-state functionaries who told them what to do. Some historians have seen this enforced close liaison between the employers as a kind of 'golden age' in the evolution of employers' associations (Brizay 1975: 59–60).

The end of the Second World War saw the employers on the defensive, criticised for giving little patriotic support to De Gaulle and for having collaborated with the Germans. De Gaulle's disdain for the bulk of employers who were either strong Vichy supporters or reserved about the resistance was well known (Weber 1986: 67–9). Yet, he needed employer representatives to negotiate with on the future of the French economy as well as with the workers. Eventually three former senior civil servants who had made the *pantouflage* shuffle to industry or the Vichy Organisation Committees were found ready to lead a working group. They did the groundwork and on 21 December 1945 the CNPF's constitution was agreed. The *Conseil national du patronat français* would group all small and large firms, from both commerce and production as well as from the public and private sectors. Created as a 'council' rather than as a direct membership body, its members and finances came from the sectoral and regional employers' organisations that criss-crossed France. Rather than opt for either a 'trade' or a 'social' function, it decided to embrace both. At first it included among its members the potential competitor organisation representing small and medium-sized firms, the *Confédération générale de petites et moyennes enterprises* (CGPME formed in October 1944), but this liaison did not last long as France's larger firms increasingly found that they were the principal ones that could resource the CNPF with time and money. This tension between the interests of large and small firms within the CNPF has remained important throughout the organisation's history (Brizay 1975). Yet, the organisational tradition established under Vichy survived. A high proportion, around 70 per cent of all firms with more than 50 workers, continued to subscribe to at least one local or broad national single trade association of area multi-trade association that in turn affiliated to the CNPF.

This indirect affiliation mechanism allowed the CNPF's touch to be very light at first. There were and are huge differences between the organisational coherence and resources of the two big battalions, the engineering (UIMM) and building *Fédération nationale du bâtiment* (FNB) employers that themselves comprised both big and small firms, and tiny associations grouping a mixture of employers in a 'local union'. These differences had to be managed very carefully indeed, particularly when government interventions favoured the larger firm that had more resources both to dialogue with the state and to fill in the appropriate forms requesting subsidies.

The CNPF's first president was the head of a medium-sized Lyon engineering firm who had been deported to Dachau for protecting Resistance fighters. Georges Villiers could thus not be accused by anyone of collaboration. The choice was a clever one since it enabled the *polytechnique* graduates and representatives of France's largest firms to direct from behind closed doors an organisation whose titular head came from the small and medium-sized enterprise (SME) sector. On 12 June 1946 the CNPF was formally set up (Weber 1986: 72–7).

On the defensive from 1945 to 1947 the CNPF felt obliged to embark upon administering welfare programmes jointly with the unions in order to avoid them all turning out like the social security (*sécu*) scheme, where the contributors were initially given majority control (Pollet and Renard 1997). Individual employers had often initiated pension schemes, sickness benefit arrangements, health insurance and other forms of welfare as part of their traditional paternalism. Many charitable associations and mutual funds existed which were as opposed as the employers to seeing these taken over directly by the state. Yet, the political climate demanded that coverage be made as wide as possible. So in 1946, the CNPF very reluctantly endorsed the government's proposal to establish a national social security system that would cover those not previously covered, and gave them only one-quarter of its administrative council representatives. For the CNPF this was the very antithesis of the 'voluntary joint consultation' they would have preferred. It established open elections for the administrative councils and effectively reserved three quarters of the seats for the unions, while allowing the state to shape the comparative size of contributions paid by both employers and employees (Catrice-Lorey 1997).

In March 1947, under pressure from managers unhappy at being left outside any common national pension scheme, the CNPF signed an agreement with the CGT, the CFTC and the CGC (Reynaud 1975: 59). This established the *Association générale des institutions de retraite des cadres* (AGIRC) supplementary pension scheme that excluded the state and gave the employers equal representation with the already divided unions. It was a key moment in the formal birth of post-war *paritarisme* (joint management and consultation with the unions) since in 1967 this was the model of joint management that was used to replace the more democratic, elected contributor control over the social security (Friot 1997). The CNPF's preference in 1947 in terms of pensions – echoed again from 1998 – was for an individual insurance-based scheme that would build up a capital fund rather than the redistributive risk-sharing one proposed. But it finally acquiesced 'without resistance' in view of the balance of forces (Brizay 1975).

Nonetheless, the CNPF continued to call for the restoration of free trade and for reduced regulation. It publicly opposed the state's modernisation programmes, although those sectoral federations and large firms that benefited most under the First Plan and Marshall Aid welcomed them. The *patronat* (as it was known) also opposed the national minimum wage (*Salaire minimum interprofessionnel garanti* (SMIG)) and denounced its 1952 indexation 'by the bowler hats' – civil servants. It feared, in much the same terms as its predecessors in 1860, the removal of protectionism implicit in the formation of the European Coal and Steel Community and the Common Market (Weber 1986: 89–91). In 1958, it only signed an agreement with the unions on the unemployment insurance system, *Union nationale interprofessionnelle pour l'emploi dans l'industrie et le commerce* (UNEDIC), under the pressure of an ultimatum to do so from De Gaulle (*ibid.*: 127).

Against the background of the Fifth Republic's newly imposed political stability, with conservative governments continuously in presidential and parliamentary office until 1981, the divisions within the Patronat came to the fore. In passing a 'Liberal Charter' at its 1965 conference one section of the CNPF leadership raised the need for a shift away from Gaullist *dirigisme*, and its influence over the CNPF apparatus is accredited by René Mouriaux with some responsibility for the employers' particularly hard line in the run-up to the social explosion of 1968 (Mouriaux 2001). The 'Liberal Charter' stressed the 'natural economic laws' that held a strong appeal to the small and medium sized employers, but were viewed more sceptically by some of the larger 'national champions'. Nonetheless, the CNPF's new pressure for business *liberté* temporarily halted further national collective bargaining and in 1967 won the ending of formal elections and the trade union majority within locally-run Social Security *parity* schemes (Roger 2001).

While this anti-modernisation and anti-*dirigisme* majority was particularly entrenched in the individual federations and, naturally, in the CGPME, it was not unchallenged. Several internal employer 'think-tanks' or 'clubs' grouped different pluralist, *dirigiste* and modernising tendencies. There were Christian employers, young employers, an employers' research centre and more. By the early 1960s, their influence was beginning to grow, helped partly by the start of the turn to using professional managers. With the retirement of Georges Villiers the way was open for a new role for the CNPF. But it took growing social tension and the explosion of 1968, when the new president Paul Huvelin conceded to virtually all the union demands, to force the CNPF to clarify its new direction: the acceptance of pluralism and a readiness to pursue a nation level social dialogue with the unions.

The CNPF therefore changed its constitution in 1969 to give itself much more authority over its members. Its new leadership now wanted to negotiate binding agreements with the unions that would be directly applicable within its member firms. This was the last straw for the CGPME, which then completed the formal withdrawal it had begun in 1948 (Duchéneaut 1996: 88). From this time the CNPF became more openly the voice and representative of France's largest and generally more modern and managerial firms, all of whose headquarters were now located in Paris. Between December 1968 and March 1975, and against the background of a high level of industrial conflict, the CNPF signed nine major national-level agreements with the unions covering issues ranging from the reduction of working time, to the acceptance of trade union branches at the level of the firm and to rights to training (Sellier 1984). Most of these agreements were then enacted into law, confirming the clear link between the social partners and the state.

3.2 The transformation of work

If management core values only began to change significantly in the 1960s and 1970s, French workers' experiences of work altered fundamentally in the century that separated the Paris Commune from the mass unrest of 1968. The most striking change occurred in terms of job security. Right up to the Second World War, with the exception of jobs in the civil service, the army and on the railways, job security was extremely rare. For sure, many workers kept the same industrial jobs for as long as they wanted, and in certain occupations, generally where the employers experienced intense labour shortages, the sons of miners, dockers and printworkers even acquired 'rights' to enter the same firm as their fathers (Noiriel 1986). Certainly, too, the accelerating pace of factory industrialisation from the 1880s meant that

it was only relatively rarely that business slumps created so much unemployment that it threatened the steady expansion of the worker side of
the peasant–worker economy. Significant unemployment did occur in
1904–1906, 1918–1921 and 1932–1935, but France's low birth rate and
periodic blood-shedding meant it was not an enduring endemic issue.

Work provided little or no sense of security or of dignity to the overwhelming majority of French workers whose peasant parents and grandparents had usually experienced one or the other or both. Exposure to the
vagaries of the weather was not the same as holding a job totally exposed to
free market forces and the vagaries of the business cycle, with wages, hours of
work, length of unpaid holidays and working conditions determined almost
exclusively by management dictate, being trapped in employer-owned or
subsidised housing, and experiencing paternalistic authoritarian management. Discontent even spread to male clerical workers. 'What a cantankerous
group our clerical employees have become,' complained the Director of the
Parisian Gas Company in 1893 on the eve of the appearance of a broad
white-collar protest movement (quoted in Berlanstein 1991). The emerging
worker–peasant economy no more integrated them into an increasingly
wealthy society than had the different insecurities of the peasant–worker
economy before it. As French workers began to savour the possibilities of
exercising voice provided to them by their concentration in larger numbers
and by the communication made possible by the spread of daily newspapers
and the railways, it was little wonder that the choices open to them often
appeared starkly between total passivity and total revolution.

Post-Second World War transformations

By the 1970s the world of work had totally changed and so had the available
choices. French workers had experienced 25 years of full employment.
Admittedly unemployment doubled between 1960 and 1974 to 2.8 per cent,
850,000 on ILO definitions, but during those same years the size of the
active population over the age of 15 had grown from 19.9 million to
22.3 million (OECD 1996: 45; Bordes and Gonzalez-Demichel 1998: 27, 128).
Unemployment was seen largely as seasonal or temporary and as a choice or
source of mild annoyance rather than of insecurity and fear. Nearly continuous and rapid economic growth had engendered a deep sense of job security.
Once in a job it commonly became a job for life – not merely in the nationalised and government sector or in the huge bureaucratic banks, but also quite
widely in the substantial manufacturing sector. Working hours had finally
started to come down again towards the historic low achieved briefly immediately after the factory occupations of 1936. This level was regained in the
1970s after the legislation of four weeks' annual holidays. Figure 3.2 shows
how annual working hours for industrial workers employed full time in
larger factories or building firms nearly halved between the inception of the
factory-economy and its peak in the mid-1970s in a process validated and
institutionalised by the state.

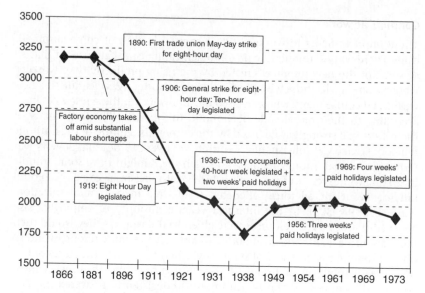

Figure 3.2   Annual working hours in industry and construction, 1866–1974
Sources: Marchand and Thélot 1991; Jefferys 2000.

Workers' real wages also increased significantly. Pushed by labour shortages and the provision of rights to sectoral collective bargaining – whose outcomes could be extended by the state to all firms within the sector – the purchasing power of the average net annual wage rose on average by 4.3 per cent a year between 1950 and 1978 (Friez 1999).

Along with improvements in nutrition, living conditions and urban sanitation, this liberation of workers' lives from the common experience in the 1860s of working 12 or more hours a day from the age of eight, totally transformed the quality of their lives. First it gave them more of it. At birth French men born in 1900 had a life expectation of 45.9 years; by 1935 this had risen to 55.4 years; and by 1975 to 69 years. The equivalent figures for women show an increase in life expectancy from 49.5 years in 1900 to 61.1, and then to 76.9 years in 1975 (Daguet 1996: 16). Of course these figures conceal significant continuing disparities of social class. Skilled male manual workers in work and aged between 30 and 64 at the start of 1975 were 90 per cent more likely to die in the following five years than were managers or highly qualified professionals; while unskilled manual workers were 160 per cent more likely to do so (Mesrine 1999: 230). But the huge increase in years lived was not a chance: it was a reality. And with it, particularly following the establishment of rights to four weeks' paid annual leave in the 1960s and 1970s, came a second huge benefit: the opportunity to exercise a real degree of choice about personal preferences in consumption and leisure.

Conflicts at work

These improvements in workers' living standards did not come automatically. There was no inherent logic in French capitalism that ensured that all or some of the new resources created by the rising productivity of workers' labour would go to those who physically lived shorter lives creating this new wealth. Of course many who exercised most power over these resources lived according to their moral code of 'honour' (d'Iribarne 1989); and many of them were still strongly influenced by the corporatist culture of the Catholic religion. French Catholicism never entirely got over the idea that poverty was virtuous and that 'money lenders' and 'rich men' might have some trouble in getting to heaven. In France, after 1789, Catholicism 'became the central rallying point for all forces alienated from (free market) modernization' (Crouch 1993: 301). In the inter-war years a minority of employers also believed that if greater resources were given to the workers they would then purchase more goods and create more wealth, receive more resources and so on. But despite this plethora of sympathy, when those with the least control over the distribution of resources asked for more from those with most control, the employers' short-term interests consistently answered no. The result was that decent working conditions, shorter working hours, paid and longer holidays, improvements in wages, fair treatment at work, a say in company investment decisions, good quality and independent (of the employer) housing, clean water supplies, reasonable provision of transport and other social amenities in workers' areas and so on, were almost all areas of social conflict. This occurred increasingly from the 1880s as parts of the still minority worker part of the peasant–worker labour market started to unionise and organise politically. Figure 3.3 shows the nearly steady growth in the numbers of strikes in market sector industries reported annually in France from the 1870s to the 1970s.

Strike data in France has to be interpreted cautiously, since public sector strikes were not counted at all until 1982, and subsequently are still not officially published for the public health sector and central and local government. Nonetheless, the pattern of an underlying increasing combativity from the 1880s to the 1970s is clearly established, with major strike waves occurring around 1906, 1919, 1936 (when the number of strikes recorded reached a record 16,907), 1947, 1950–1951, 1955–1957 and 1968 (when no data was collected).

These conflicts provided a critical test for the semi-independent self-perpetuating state administrators. This elite had negotiated the end of the Napoleonic Empire and the transition to the Third Republic quite successfully. But its members were acutely concerned lest 'disorder' provide the occasion for a new Napoleon or an old King in alliance with the Catholic Church to stage yet another *coup d'état* that would destroy the secular Republican state and their privileges with it. The Republican civil service elite did not risk leaving education in the hands of a hostile Church. It was

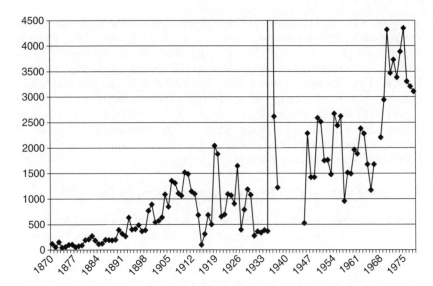

Figure 3.3   Numbers of French market sector strikes, 1870–1979 (except 1939–45, 1968)
Sources: For strikes 1870–1938, Shorter and Tilly 1974: 361–2; for strikes 1945–1979, Simon 1981.

in their interests, as well as in the interest of unifying France, that the anti-Communard Republican Jules Ferry introduced free secular Republican primary education in 1881 and 1882. This imposed a national, secular curriculum aimed at teaching civic duty, at keeping the workers in their place in society and at combating socialist ideas (Winock 1995: 96–7). By 1900, 86 per cent of French children were enrolled (compared to 74 per cent in England and Wales at the same time) (Ambler 1991: 8). Not only was France early in starting to invest in 'human capital', but national education was also politically astute in a Third Republic dominated by representatives elected with peasant votes. For it meant expanding public employment and placing school teachers (as well as postmen – the by-product of rising literacy) in every village, creating new (and Republican) jobs in rural areas (Cross 1983: 8).

When labour–capital conflict occurred, the Republican state had three different ways of responding. It could stand back and do nothing, it could use the police and army to support the status quo, or it could intervene to try and mediate the conflict in the public (i.e. its own) interests. What usually happened is that the state did all three at different moments, and sometimes even at the same time. Partly its reaction depended upon the scale of the struggle, partly on the issue involved, and partly on the parliamentary arithmetic that became much more sensitive in the twentieth century with the emergence of first a Socialist and then from 1920 and particularly from 1945 until 1976, a Communist-voting working class electorate. The important point, however, is that if a conflict went on long enough and the issue was serious enough and still not resolved, then the state *might* get involved, when it would attempt to impose a settlement that would bring the conflict to an end. Thus, increasingly from the 1880s to the Second World War the state itself took on the role of social peace 'co-ordinator' in the *last* resort. The defeat of the racist, conservative Catholic elements linked to the Vichy regime helped create a new political economic dynamic: the construction of a large part of the French welfare system and the emergence of the state as France's major direct employer in the for-profit sector. These changes transformed the state into an actor of the *first* resort.

3.3   State intervention from the *ancien régime* to the 1970s

French state concern with employment-related issues has its origins in the elite's three principal motives behind early charity and welfare: their self-interest in curing the diseased poor so that they no longer carried infection and could return to work; their fear of the uncontrollable character of the poor; and for some, their genuine sense of Christian *fraternité*. From the sixth century the monasteries provided a monopoly of care for the local sick and poor, and later this was extended to pilgrims and other travellers, including the dispossessed 'wandering poor', who were housed in *hospices*. From about the twelfth century a growing merchant class began to leave donations for the founding of hospitals, whose poor and sick residents would pray for their souls. In 1544, the Church founded the first recorded public assistance agency, the *Grand bureau des pauvres de Paris*, and by 1789 it was running 1,800 public charities. The guilds, too, were often an important source of collective aid to old, sick or travelling guildsmen (Carpenter and Jefferys 2000: 105; Ambler 1991: 3; Castel 1995: 232). Yet, although these early forms of social policy often sought to aid the mobility of labour, they were totally overwhelmed in periods of rural famine when large numbers of the poor made their way to the towns and by the Black Death. Following it France (like England) saw a flurry of welfare legislation to cope with the combination of a social catastrophe and a sudden improvement in the bargaining power of common people, marking a shift towards the secularisation of the control of the poor. The Royal Ordinances of the second half of the fourteenth century laid down that workers must stay where they were in rural areas, to keep up or improve agricultural output, or in the towns to keep up the industrial production of the incorporated trades, and that those who were expelled or escaped from their place of origins should be treated as outcasts and not given work (Castel 1995: 87–9).

The demonology of the migrating landless labourers and wandering poor, the beggars or vagabonds as they were disparagingly known, lasted until late in the nineteenth century. It really only ended with the inter-war reshaping of France's peasant–*worker* economy into a *worker*–peasant one. In the sixteenth century vagabonds could be executed. From the fourteenth to the eighteenth centuries they could be sentenced to hard labour (for five, ten years or life). Cardinal Richelieu declared in 1625:

> We wish that all the towns in our kingdom control and regulate their poor, not only of their own town, but also of the neighbouring areas, so that they are locked up and fed and the able-bodied employed on public works. (Quoted in *ibid.*: 137–8)

More common in the eighteenth century was confinement to workhouses: between 1768 and 1772 nearly 112,000 were captured and set to work. The *ancien régime* even paid a per-head bonus (*ibid.*: 98). Under the growing intellectual influence of Physiocrats like Turgot and Malesherbes this represented an 'enlightened despotism' compared to hard labour or deportation. The state then increasingly adopted social policies of an 'improving' kind that would stimulate commerce, population growth, taxes and the numbers of conscripts. Not only did the Crown directly promote emerging forms of economic discipline, either producing for the market – the workhouses were among the first factories – or seeking to 'train' new forms of behaviour appropriate to market discipline, but it also centralised control of human and cattle epidemics, promoted the establishment of the Royal Society of Medicine, and in 1730 introduced regulation of midwives in order to reduce infant mortality (Carpenter and Jefferys 2000: 105).

Welfare after the French Revolution

Under the 'free' labour market established in the French Revolution there was a sharpening of the earlier distinction between the 'good' poor, unable to work for genuine reasons, and the 'bad', the 'able-bodied' poor. In 1791, one speaker told the Revolutionary Assembly that the 'able-bodied' could normally be expected to find work for themselves and, 'known as professional beggars or vagabonds, refusing any work, they disturb the public order and are a blight on society and demand to be judged severely' (quoted in Castel 1995: 189). Thus, while Article 21 of the new 1793 Constitution declared that 'Society owes subsistence to its unfortunate citizens, either in finding them work, or in providing the means of existence to those who are incapable of working', the mover of a law on begging passed four months later justified instead 'imposing the necessity of work (on the able-bodied non-working poor)' (quoted in *ibid.*: 190, 196). The Napoleonic Penal Code defined vagabonds as 'all those without a profession, or a trade, or a fixed home, or means of subsistence, (for more than six months) who cannot be vouched for or certified to be of sound moral quality by a gentleman' (quoted in *ibid.*: 91–2).

Through most of the nineteenth century French social policy remained dominated by this fear of the poor, and perhaps for good reason: there were four major revolutions in 1789, 1830–32, 1848 and 1871, several major riots and revolutionary plots, and an estimated 200,000 beggars and 1.6 million destitute (about 6 per cent of the population) in 1834. Castel (223) argues that 'what can properly be called an anti-worker racism was spread right through the nineteenth century bourgeoisie'. Punishment rather than responses based on *fraternité* or *égalité* ruled the day. Thus, by 1871, the only welfare agencies present in France were the Church charities that had been restored after 1815, an additional 1,500 hospices and hospitals for the destitute sick (generally run by town councils and four-fifths of which also dated from before 1789), and the precariously-funded (by a 10 per cent tax on public entertainment and by donations) local public charity offices that were initiated by Napoleon I and only existed in less than 40 per cent of French communes (*ibid.*: 233).

The establishment of the Third Republic (1871–1940) on the eve of France's military defeat by Germany, however, greatly concentrated the minds of the state's administrators. Mere repressive control of the poor increasingly appeared ill-suited to the new interests both of French industrialists in a productive supply of labour and of French generals in a fit supply of conscripts. Under the influence of the state paternalist Le Play and social Catholicism a consensus slowly developed among the state administrators about the need for the government to do 'something' about poverty – short, naturally, of tackling its causes (*ibid.*: 242–5). France therefore pioneered free medical care (in 1893, but only for the able-bodied poor who could return to work once cured), child welfare clinics, supplies of free milk, and family policy generally (Quine 1996). The elaboration of welfare protection was an extremely slow process. It took 18 years between the first parliamentary proposal for a law on accidents at work and its passage in 1898. Industrialists and liberals fought long and hard to resist the incursion of the state into the 'private' contract, although many paternalist employers provided benefits to 'their' workers individually. It took 20 years before the 1910 passage of a law giving pension rights to seven million workers and peasant–workers, and even by 1921 only 1.7 million were actually covered since the courts refused to make contributions mandatory. We can see the state beginning to intervene, but with French trade union density still below 2 per cent and the French socialists receiving only 1.7 million votes in 1914, there was little compulsion on the state elite to act rapidly.

In 1884, however, the Third Republic finally legalised the trade unions originally banned under the *Loi Chapelier* of 1791. It was the first of a series of measures that by the end of the nineteenth century slowly helped define the concept of social *rights*. These measures were both a challenge to *laissez-faire* capitalism and a form of safety net for it. Their message was that the employers must fund *insurance* to cover the risks faced by their workers. In 1892, for example, one of the demands of the Rosières strikers was for proper accident insurance rather than grace-and-favour entitlements to paid days off under the paternalistic employer-dominated Mutual Aid scheme (Pigenet 1997: 19).

Both Castel (1995) and Friot (1998) powerfully make the case that in linking the *right* to a pension, sick pay and unemployment benefit to the job and the specific employer, workers collectively forge links across the workforce and between themselves and future generations of workers. They see these links as constituting far greater constraints on the employer than does the 'universal' provision of general taxation-based 'assistance' that has been the hall-mark of Anglo-Scandinavian welfare regimes. Thus, the French socialist leader, Jean Jaurès, defended the 1895 miners' pension scheme in these terms: 'This has nothing to do with a charity organisation; it's about the recognition of a right confirmed by equal sacrifices' (quoted in Castel 1995: 289). It was from this period, and from workers' real experiences of each measure as representing an actual struggle against the employers, that the notion of *droits acquis* or *acquis socials* (acquired welfare and employment rights) starts to take hold.

State-imposed dual representation

In 1919 and 1936, in response to huge worker mobilisations, the state created and then strengthened legal frameworks for national collective bargaining in France's different industrial 'branches', and in both periods tried to force life into them by making the negotiators responsible for the way in which shorter working hours would be introduced. These measures required employers' associations to offer a formal recognition of the unions at sectoral level. Under the 1919 legislation there was no mechanism to extend the agreements' reach to all who worked in the sector, whether or not members of their respective employers' association or trade union. When this facility was included in the 1936 law it effectively put into the hands of the Ministry of Labour a procedural power to coerce employers to implement collective bargaining outcomes – a power that was renewed in the Collective Bargaining Law of 1950 and is still in operation today. This largely explains the paradox that France has the European Union's highest collective bargaining *coverage*, while also having the European Union's lowest level of trade union density (Traxler 1994).

While negotiations in a handful of sectors had taken place sporadically since the early 1890s, the 1919 and 1936 laws were at the heart of establishing formal trade union recognition – in so far as labour market issues outside the workplace were concerned. Within the workplace the situation was very different. In the same 1936 law workers in establishments with 50 or more workers were given the right to elect Personnel Delegates. But while the unions tried to ensure that the law specified that they should be trade unionists, this was rejected on the grounds that given the small size of the trade union movement that would exclude too many from the benefits of representation. Thus, a dual representation system was born, with both elements of it imposed on the employers against their will by the state. *Outside* the workplace trade unions were recognised, while *within* the workplace – at least when elections were actually held – the often but not necessarily overlapping category of Personnel Delegates (and from 1945 Works Council delegates) were supposed to be recognised. It was only in 1969 that the trade unions acquired the right to nominate a *trade union* delegate within the workplace, thus partially uniting the two systems.

Some of the more important measures taken by the Third Republic in the areas of welfare and employment rights between 1874 and 1936 are shown in Table 3.3.

Table 3.3 The extension of welfare and employment rights, 1874–1936

	Welfare rights	Employment rights
1874		Creation of Labour Inspectorate to monitor 1841 law limiting child labour
1884		Legalisation of trade unions
1890		Right to individual legal action against an employer for improper dismissal
1892		Abolition of night-work for women Paid Labour Inspectorate with special status established
1898	Industrial accident insurance (compulsory for employers from 1905)	
1900		Ten-hour day for women and children
1906		One rest day per week Ten-hour day for men
1908		Ministry of Labour created Women eligible to vote and stand for Industrial Tribunals (first established 1806)
1910	Workers and Peasants Pensions (limited application)	
1913		Unpaid 8 weeks' maternity leave
1916		Tripartite representation on boards of nationalised industries
1917		Local conciliation and arbitration committees
1919		Eight-hour day (48-hour week) Sectoral collective bargaining
1928	National Social Security for low paid workers with insurance covering: health, maternity, disability, death and old age	
1930		
1932	Family allowances paid by employer	
1936		40-hour week Two weeks' paid holiday Personnel delegates at work State extension of collective agreements

The flowering of French welfare and employment rights thus occurred under a wide variety of influences. These ranged from the Catholic employers who first introduced family allowances and the paternalists who often sought to both geographically 'fix' and morally and politically control their employees, to modernising employers who wanted to take employment regulation out of competition; from the Catholic Church which wanted to encourage large families and discourage women working after marriage to the state administrative elite who wanted to reinforce Republicanism and reduce social conflict; and from the shopkeepers, wealthier peasants and landlords who wanted to avoid higher taxation to certain skilled occupations who wished to gain increased protection for their particular professions. Finally, but by no means least, there were the interests of the savers and administrators of the nineteenth century mutual insurance funds that had been encouraged under Napoleon III as a substitute for trade unions.

The lack of domination of any one of these elements or even of a stable coalition between different ones had two significant effects. First, it took a very long time before France introduced the full twentieth century panoply of welfare coverage; and second, when it did, it occurred in a multiplicity of forms, as sketched in the simplified diagram in Figure 3.4.

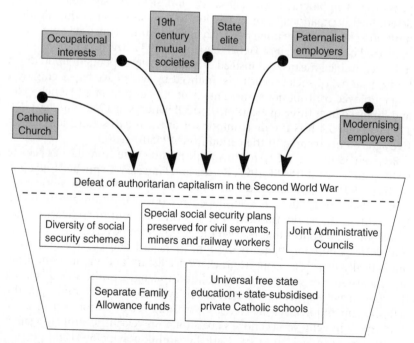

Figure 3.4 Influences and outcomes in the formation of the French welfare state

After the Liberation the pension schemes already in existence were threatened with being nationalised or brought under state regulation. The employers strongly opposed the foundation of the post-war social security system by the decree of 4 October 1945 because it replaced their paternalist control with a system managed by those who paid their contributions – or at least by their trade unions – and threatened to include management staff (Pollet and Renard 1997). At the same time, building upon the 1931 encyclical *Quadragesimo Anno*, the Catholic Church was anxious to restore the role of intermediary bodies between the state and the market (apRoberts *et al.* 1997: 28). Rather than allow the creation of one new national occupational scheme for all workers in which they risked being a minority on a central management board, the employers decided to reach 'voluntary' agreements with the unions setting up national associations whose pension schemes would provide additional cover for special groups of workers. Under these agreements, beginning with the *cadres'* AGIRC in 1947, they negotiated shared control – with parity of representation in the management function between the contributors and the employers. By 1984, the result was that there were as many as 117 different state retirement pension schemes covering virtually the whole population (Ambler 1991: 21). The strength of egalitarianism within French politics, however, meant that while access to pensions, unemployment compensation and sickness pay were generally determined occupationally, or in relation to a certain level of qualification, most other benefits were universal, with means testing being used only rarely. It affected only 6 per cent of French benefits in 1983. The occupational basis of French welfare means that instead of being largely dependent upon direct taxation, most of social security is financed by workplace-based employer and employee contributions: these made up 43 per cent of all French taxes and financed over three-quarters of all social benefits in 1982 (Ambler 1991: 12–13). Table 3.4 lists the most important of the *acquis sociaux* and collective agreements secured in the period from 1945 to 1980.

Between 1949 and 1981 French social transfers rose from 12 per cent of GDP to 26 per cent (INSEE 1997; Bordes and Gonzalez-Demichel 1998: 96). Ambler (1991: vii) commented that 'much of the world failed to notice that in the 1960s and 1970s France developed into one of the more generous welfare states in the world, translating an old commitment to "solidarity" into a body of social polices that rescued the elderly from poverty, drew virtually the entire population beneath the tent of health and old-age insurance, dramatically expanded opportunities for secondary and higher education, and increased aid to the handicapped and to single mothers'. Comparing the French with other European welfare systems, another study put the achievement differently: 'in France everything seems to happen as if we were trying to achieve Beveridge's goals (of a universalistic struggle against Want) using Bismarckian methods' (Palier and Bonoli 1996: 31).

Table 3.4 Welfare and employment rights, 1945–1980

	Welfare rights	Employment rights
1945	Compulsory education to 14 Free education available to 18	Personnel Delegates restored Works Council Delegates introduced (in workplaces with at least 50 workers)
1946	Social Partner managed Social Security Insurance Funds set up for all occupational groups Minimum Pension (AVTS)	Special employment status established for all national and local government employees 40-hour week restored 20 hours ceiling on overtime Two weeks' paid holiday restored Suppression of concept of 'women's wages'
1947	Social Housing Act Managers and Professionals Pension fund (AGIRC)	Health and Safety Committees
1948	Rent Act	
1950		Collective bargaining and trade union representation National Minimum Wage (SMIG) National Job Classifications
1953	1 per cent company tax to go on workers' social housing	
1956	National Solidarity Fund (FNS) for the low income uninsured	Three weeks' paid annual holiday
1958	Unemployment insurance agreement (UNEDIC)	
1959	School leaving extended to 16	
1961	Supplementary non-managerial pension agreement (ARRCO)	
1963		Public sector workers obliged to give five days' notice of strike action
1966		Recognition of five nationally 'representative' union confederations
1967	Redundancy payments scheme National Employment Agency (*ANPE*)	Minimum working age raised from 14 to 16
1968		Legalisation of workplace union organisation Union workplace delegates introduced
1969		Four weeks' paid annual holiday Job security agreement
1970		National Minimum Wage SMIC (partly indexed to wages) replaces SMIG Maternity leave agreement
1971		Industrial training agreement Monthly Pay law Continuing Skill Training law with 0.5% apprenticeship tax
1972		Equal Pay law

Table 3.4 continued

	Welfare rights	Employment rights
1973		Bankruptcy wages guaranteed
		Dismissals only for real and serious fault
1974	Start of school year allowance to parents	Agreement on additional unemployment benefit
1975	Realistic guaranteed minimum old age pension (MV)	Labour inspector authorisation necessary for redundancies
	Disability benefit (AAH)	Agreement on minimum working conditions
1976	Single parent benefit (API)	
1977	Housing benefits (APL, ALF)	Law requiring large firms to include social audit in their annual reports
1980	Minimum family income (for 3-child families)	

From an employment relations perspective the source and dynamic of French welfare is highly significant. This is because in a political context where *acquis sociaux* are guaranteed by the state, the maintenance of what is still a *collective imposition* by past, present and future workers on their employers (individually and nationally) had two significant effects: it made it more difficult for the employers or the state to withdraw them (if they wanted to), and it reinforced a *logic of collectivism*. This logic both continues to play a role in shaping class awareness (as we shall see in Chapter 4), and in legitimating industrial conflict (as we shall see in Chapter 8) and it creates a dynamic element favouring the extension rather than the restriction of rights.

The employment rights listed in Table 3.4 also created a vast extension of 'hard' law covering both substantive and procedural work regulations, some of which created still more 'soft' law in its wake since with the extension and statute status of collective agreements provided by the state, 'more than 300 national sectoral collective agreements mean effectively more than 300 occupational laws' (Lyon-Caen 1990: 68).

Finally, in this growth of state intervention in employment relations (including the nationalisations of 1945–1946) France not only experienced centralised wage controls from 1944 to 1950, but in each of the three following decades, the state intervened directly to control wage rises: in the 1950s with the Pinay plan of 1953 and the Pinay–Rueff plan of 1959, in the 1960s with the Stabilisation plan of 1963, and in the 1970s with the Barre plan of 1976 (Jefferys and Contrepois 2001). The government also created a central planning agency whose long-term plans are credited with having helped directly shift resources to those sectors most significant for industrial recovery and then rapid sustained growth. The First Plan covered the years 1947 to 1951(Bouvier 1987), while the subsequent two were four-year plans and those in the 1960s five-year. An idea of the scale of this intervention is provided by the strategic steel industry, which, between 1948 and 1965, was loaned some two billion francs (in 1970 money – the equivalent of 38 francs per head of the population) by the government's investment agency (*Fonds de développement économique et social*). In the early post-war period, 1949 to 1954, public funds made up as much as 40 per cent of the industry's annual resources (Mioche 1987).

3.4   Conclusion

The French state intervened extensively in management and employment relations before the 1980s. In management and economics it moved from implementing economic liberalism after 1789 to 'co-ordination' and 'planning' in the 1950s and to encouraging professional American managerialism in the 1960s and 1970s. Its directing elites worked ultimately to ensure the best possible political conditions in which capitalism could operate. But this long-term aim required taking into account the labour shortages and volatility of labour in the nineteenth century, and the growing radicalisation and solidarity of the industrial labour force in the twentieth century. Where work is concerned the state established labour codes that drew the limits of *procedural* workplace subordination by giving workers a series of minimal individual freedoms to join a union, to take strike action and in firms with more than ten workers to elect representatives. It also framed the context of collective bargaining and compelled some degree of participation by employers by introducing the possibility of legally extending agreements reached by a minority of employers and unions to all, whether or not the others had participated in the negotiations. Shaping the limits of *substantive* subordination it legislated the length of the working week and the numbers of paid holidays, and introduced a national minimum wage. In the area of welfare, first after the employers experienced deep political instability in 1944–1945 and then after their experience of industrial instability in 1968, the state extended workers a considerable degree of 'decommodification' based on statutory job-based rights.

These interrelated changes may be viewed using the analytical frameworks we developed in the Introduction. Far from understanding them as merely reflected past customs and practice and a specifically French 'cultural history', we see the changes in the economy, in management, in the state and in employment relations as representing the outcomes of a century of struggle around priorities and choices. The French Revolution and its Bonapartist sequel structured a society around the *unitarist* bedfellows of Catholic paternalism and economic liberalism. *Pluralism* largely remained unattractive to French employers. The minority of workers who became political identified with *class struggle*, mounting several insurrections and strikes that all failed, ultimately, to overthrow capitalism. But they did succeed in embedding a *struggle* ideology within the first permanent independent workers' unions. These workers' organisations were quite divided: a few 'yellow' unions were formed under the employers' aegis, but since the employers' generally rejected the idea of collective bargaining, *market trade unionism* had little influence before 1914. Meanwhile, those who preached *social integration* unionism fared little better until the State decided it needed their support in the First World War.

Much changed, after the outcome of the Second World War weakened the grip of many old discredited bankers and industrialists, giving sway to the minority of capitalist modernisers. *Pluralism* subsequently became the key employment and welfare strategy driven by the State. It could not force the employers' to adopt pluralism at firm level and to bargain with the unions locally. Where they could, most employers remained *unitarist*. But the State could and did require that the employers recognise and bargain with the unions at national (and more rarely regional) level. Within the unions ideological differences matured into a clear triangle opposing distinct organisations representing *class struggle*, *market*, and *social integration* unionism. By 1980, the political ideal of *liberté* still motivated most employers and managers, but the values of working class *égalité* and of *fraternité* and *solidarité* had a much greater presence at work and in political life. But as we shall see in the rest of the book, the following 20 years saw these more collective values and the aspirations they encouraged experience a considerable reversal. The world moved on, but not without considerable and continuing struggle.

4
Values, Class and Politics since 1981

What are the key developments that have shaped the political context of contemporary French employment relations? For most non-French observers the most difficult elements to grasp are why in an essentially conservative society the left was in power for virtually the whole of the 1980s and 1990s, why the right appears to be less attracted by neo-liberalism than by neo-corporatism, and why is it that France's minority unions continue to exercise such dramatic mobilisation capacity?

To explain these issues it is important to understand that French society has experienced both change and continuity since the 1970s. There was a real weakening and fragmentation of workers' voice in the face of dramatic reductions in job security and deindustrialisation that created high levels of unemployment, and were accompanied by the renewal of a much more combative capitalism trying to extract profits under conditions of lower inflation than during the 'thirty glorious years'. This renewed exposure to a much more competitive labour market encouraged some workers to try to protect themselves by investing massively in education for their children; others responded by adopting racist attitudes to the perceived threat of competing immigrant labour. Yet although there was a shift from manual to white-collar work, the different weights of the French social classes remained relatively stable. The potential for mobilising workers thus remained, although it simultaneously became much more difficult to do.

Individual *liberté* and capitalist neo-liberalism staged a comeback, but largely under the tutelage of left governments that used the discourse of *pluralism* and *market unionism* to smooth the way. *Égalité* as the struggle for equality and redistribution remained present, but its values became less identifiable with what was a shrinking manual working class constituency. Thus, by the elections of 2002, Lionel Jospin, the left coalition prime minister of 1997–2002, listening to the advising sirens from New Labour in the United Kingdom, even believed it was in his political interests to run for president independent of the 'socialist' label. How were manual workers' political links to French Communism and Socialism broken?

103

Two key contextual socio-economic factors were decisive: high unemployment and low inflation. They both impacted considerably on the relative mobilising capacities of French labour and capital. Fear of unemployment inhibited workers from taking strike action that might as an outcome lead to the loss of their jobs; while low inflation meant that the pressure to renegotiate the terms of subordination appeared much less frequently than when inflation had been high. At the same time high unemployment gave capital a stick with which to threaten the workers, and an opportunity to restructure away from less profitable sectors; while low inflation intensified pressures on French capital to maximise non-price competition through improving quality, sales and marketing and productivity. The decisive cross-over of the trends in unemployment and inflation since 1950 is shown in Figure 4.1 to have occurred at about the time that the first Socialist–Communist coalition government of the Fifth Republic came to power in 1981.

France's OECD standardised unemployment rate stood at 7.4 per cent in 1981 before rising to a peak of 12.6 per cent in June 1997, just after Jospin took office (OECD 1992: 284; 1998a: 190). It then fell to 9 per cent in January 2001 with one million people fewer unemployed, before the decline bottomed out and the numbers actively seeking work started to rise again.

French unemployment rose in the 1980s and 1990s essentially because the growth in the active population since 1975 exceeded the rate at which *new* permanent jobs were created. It did not, therefore, strike the workforce

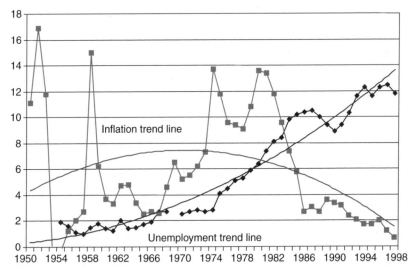

Figure 4.1   Inflation and unemployment, 1950–1998
Source: INSEE 2001a.

equally. It was these 'new' workers, those younger men and women entering (or re-entering after having children) the labour market, and all women, who were the hardest hit.

Lower rates of unemployment among older workers did not alter the fact that the work experience changed significantly for a high proportion. Thus, the permanent job for life that had been available to nearly all working men and many women in the 1960s and 1970s, became restricted by the mid-1990s to just half the working population – to most public sector workers and one in four in the private sector (OECD 1997). In 1970, one estimate is that 76 per cent of the active population had a 'stable job', but by 1994 this had fallen to 54 per cent (Deschamps and André cited in Duchéneaut 1995: 112). In 1998, some 22 per cent of French workers had worked for the same employer for 20 years or more, and 45 per cent for ten or more. The least job security was experienced by young workers, hotel and restaurant workers, shop workers and business sector workers – in the main those who worked in the most rapidly growing parts of the economy (Auer and Cazes 2000).

Against this background it is not very surprising that people's images of the world changed. For many the 'we' with whom they identified socially and collectively became a much less obvious point of reference. This chapter focuses first on changes in people's values and then on the resilience of class divisions. Finally, it reviews the changing political fortunes that reflected these ideological and structural pressures. The argument here is that despite important structural changes and growing insecurity the political system failed to adapt. Political inertia in the face of the globalisation of American managerialism left the State as much in the centre of things – and as such a target of mobilisation – as ever. France did move in a neo-liberal direction, but it did so under the close observation of a State chaperone.

4.1   Changing lives and values

One of the structural explanations for the strength of the political right across much of France is that urbanisation – and its associated exposure to collectivist socialist needs and experiences – took much longer to achieve than in France's industrialised neighbours. While factually true, the argument's logic is challenged, of course, by the tradition of anti-clericalism and left politics that survived from the 1850s to the 1980s among the 'red peasants' of Southern France. It is also challenged by the near completion of French urbanisation by the end of the twentieth century. Between 1990 and 1999, as more people went to live in towns with their employment possibilities and amenities, the proportion living in communes having more than 2,000 people at their centre rose from 73 per cent in 1975 to 80 per cent in 1999, while communes with fewer than 200 inhabitants continued to lose population (Amossé 2001). But this higher degree of urbanisation does not appear to have created a consciously more collective approach to life, in

Table 4.1   Support for left-wing political values, 1999 (1 = complete disagreement and 10 = complete agreement)

	Average
The state should take more responsibility for providing people's needs	4.04
There should be more nationalisation of firms and industries	4.05
The unemployed should have the right to refuse a job that does not suit them	4.54
Competition is dangerous. It encourages what is worst in people	4.74
The state should regulate firms more effectively	4.90
Incomes should be more equal	5.14

Source: Bréchon (2000).

at least as far as any indentifiable readiness to agree with or express left opinions is concerned. In a major longitudinal representative survey of social and political attitudes in France, the values of the old left are clearly in retreat. Fewer French in 1999 than 18 years earlier were consistently critical of capitalism and in favour of state intervention. Table 4.1 presents the average of views on six key issues using a 10-point scale.

A majority of survey respondents tended to disagree with all left-wing views, although aspirations for more effective state regulation and particularly greater income equality came closest to dividing opinions down the middle.

Is socialist-collectivism on the retreat because despite urbanisation, the reality of contemporary life is becoming more individual? Since 1980 travel-to-work distances have increased considerably, allowing employers to seek labour from a much wider area than before, while house building, motorway and associated civil engineering works kept the construction industry busy. Cars are more common. Their numbers rose from 379 to 437 per 1,000 of the population between 1985 and 1996, by when only one in five households did not have one (Andersen *et al.* 1999: 156; Bordes and Gonzalez-Demichel 1998: 43). As a result more people could live further from their place of employment, and the character of urbanisation changed. It became less city-centre focused: by 1999 about 20 per cent of the population lived in the peri-urban borders between town and country, mainly in new housing estates (Besset 1999).

Are values changing because family life is becoming less collective than before? Between 1984 and 1999 two million additional individual houses and one million apartments were added to the housing stock. Fewer families lived with their parents or parents-in-law. Home ownership, increased – from 46.7 per cent in 1978 to 54.7 per cent in 1999 – although largely at the expense of private rather than social house renting, which rose from 13.3 to 16 per cent (Amossé 2001: 250). Not only did women have smaller families, thereby freeing themselves more readily for labour market entry, but they were more likely in the 1990s than before not to marry, or to be divorced;

women increasingly lived on their own, with or without children. By 1994, 13.4 per cent of all couples were unmarried. Between 1980 and 1996 the marriage rate fell from 6.2 to 4.8 per 1,000 inhabitants and the proportion of divorces per marriage rose from 24 to 43 per cent (Bordes and Gonzalez-Demichel 1998: 27; Andersen *et al.* 1999: 76). The proportion of single-parent families rose from 6.7 per cent in 1990 to 7.3 per cent of all households in 1998 (Amossé 2001: 110). As family life was restructured it was accompanied by a decline in another collective form of coping: the proportion of French who did not belong to any religion rose from 26 per cent in 1981 to 42 per cent in 1999 (Lambert 2000: 137).

Finally, do the origins of a less socialist-collective view of the world lie in the continued rise in living standards? A key measure of this, while partly reflecting technological innovation, is the spectacular improvement in infant mortality, where deaths under one year per 1,000 live births halved from ten in 1980 to 4.8 per 1,000 in 1999 (Amossé 2001: 75).

Each one of these demographic evolutions plays a part in shaping people's experiences and views of the world they live in more or less critically, and more or less unamiguously. But the complexity of changing values goes beyond a simple left–right continuum. Thus, since 1981, the French have become both more tolerant and slightly more authoritarian. The Bréchon study (2000b) found greater acceptance of individual freedoms, such as the right to divorce or to have an abortion or the toleration of homosexuality, alongside stronger respect for authority and the law, including a greater readiness to condemn business bribes and social security fraud.

Paradoxically, too, while they respect the law more, French people as a whole also appear more ready to participate in collective protest than two decades earlier. In 1981, 50 per cent of the population declared that they had never participated in any kind of protest activity, from signing a petition to participating in a boycott, a demonstration, a wildcat strike or a workplace occupation. But by 1999 only 28 per cent had never done so, and 40 per cent of the generation born between 1973 and 1981 had already participated in at least two protests (Bréchon 2000b). The French were also quite ready to support protest by others. In a survey conducted by *Sofres* on the eve of the Genoa G8 summit in July 2001, 63 per cent approved of the anti-globalisation demonstrations (*Le Monde*, 19 July 2001). And this support for protest was not just for 'away matches'. A series of *CSA* surveys on the 26 national strikes that occurred between 1995 and the end of 2000, found that 41 per cent supported the strikers and 28 per cent were sympathetic. On average only 17 per cent were hostile or opposed to the strike movements (Courtois and Jaffré 2001).

Values have changed as people experienced slower economic growth, higher levels of unemployment, the shrinkage of traditional industry, the collapse of Communism, a growing internationalisation of national capitalisms and the growing ideological strength of neo-liberalism. Yet, all values did not move in a single direction towards *liberté*, an acceptance of managerial *unitarism* and *market trade unionism*. The State and significant sections of both the employers and the unions still stress the advantages of *pluralism*, *social integration* and *solidarité–fraternité*. And despite the presence of individually experienced uncertainty the collective *class struggle* response remained legitimate, often but not always consistently linked with *égalité*. Here we will turn to look at what continues to underpin a collective potential and occasional reality, the survival of social class divisions.

4.2   Class divisions around 2000

How has occupational class changed since 1970? Our answer is ambivalent: in some respects considerably but in others very little. The outcome, a stronger ruling class voice, a weaker sense of manual working class voice, but a broader awareness of collective interest among many white-collar workers, explains the continuing unpredictability of French employment relations.

The most evident occupational shift between roughly 1970 and the turn of the twenty-first millennium is the decline in the numbers and proportion of manual workers and the increase in white-collar workers, particularly managerial staff. With the dramatic fall in the numbers of unskilled or semiskilled manual workers, manual workers as a whole have become a minority within an extended working class. Even while many two-income families now declare themselves 'middle class', France is at least as class divided as it was 30 years earlier. This may be seen in Figure 4.2.

The 200 families

Far from becoming less powerful during the 1980s and 1990s, a tiny fraction of the ruling elite consolidated its wealth and power. By the end of 1997, the richest 5 per cent of French households possessed 40 per cent of the total of individually owned property, and the richest 1 per cent alone owned 20 per cent (Chambaz *et al.* 1999: 279). The average annual *income* declared by the 3,200 very richest (top 0.01 per cent of) households in 1998 (*after* the legally approved non-declaration of a considerable proportion of their financial investments) was over seven million francs (of which over four million derived from stocks and shares), while the next 28,000 households averaged a mere two million francs a year. The bulk of the wealth of 3,200 highest earning households derives from *unearned* income: only one-fifth of income came from wages or pensions (Piketty 2001). Their salaries, often gained from heading up France's biggest businesses, had risen too. A study of the salaries paid to the 473 directors of the top quoted 40 firms in 2000 showed they averaged 2.3 million euros, and in 17 of these the highest salary paid averaged 498 times higher than the national minimum wage (*Le Monde*, 6 February 2002).

Piketty's (2001) exhaustive study of income tax returns has confirmed that a numerically very small group of super rich people still exists today – he

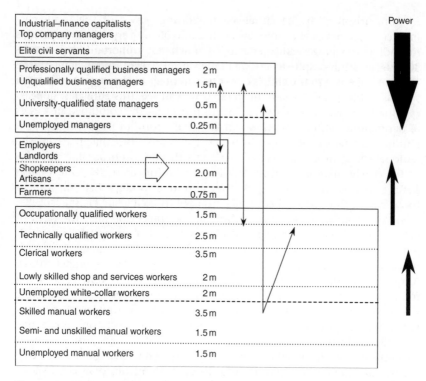

Figure 4.2   Occupational class around 2000
Sources: INSEE 2001b; INSEE 2001c.

calls it '200 families' to stress the similarity with the polemical construct, the '100 families' that controlled the France of one hundred years ago. Michel Pinçon and Monique Pinçon-Charlot (2000) go further. They argue that Marx, Weber and Bourdieu rightly described this group as a 'bourgeoisie'. They too find that the seriously wealthy are few in numbers. The 'solidarity' wealth tax, for example, detected the presence in 1999 of 800 households whose accumulated wealth exceeded 100 million francs (excluding works of art and only partially including their principal residence). They show that these people belong to the same exclusive clubs, that they send their children to the same exclusive private schools and that they defend their wealth by interbreeding. Far from becoming less exclusive with the weakening sense of identity among the wider working class, this bourgeoisie has become still more active in pursuing its identity and interests:

> No other social group presents to the same degree the unity, consciousness of itself and mobilisation. (Pinçon and Pinçon-Charlot 2000: 7)

By comparison with the enhanced mobilising power of the industrial–financial sections of this bourgeoisie, the role of the very top civil servants (including the judges and generals) is much less important than it was 30 years ago. But despite a very small meritocratic recruitment element (the route to full entry to the elite is either by parentage or through examination success to the *grandes écoles*), in so far as we can see, this elite class appears essentially stable. Hancké (2001: 73) confirms that the combined processes of nationalisation, privatisation and financial reform in the 1980s led 'to a national capitalism of a few, in which the same elites that had run the national economy before, reappeared – only this time as heads and directors of the newly privatised firms'. Studies of recruitment to the elite *grandes écoles* from 1950 to 1990 suggest they continue to perpetuate the rule of those whom Bourdieu called 'the state nobility' (cited in Plaisance 1998: 103). Most *grandes écoles* students are like Bertrand Collomb, the head of Lafarge who became president of the *Association française des entreprises privées* (AFEP) in December 2001: a *Polytechnique X-Mines* graduate as were his father and grandfather before him (*Le Monde*, 15 December 2001). Among the 61,000 students (out of a national total of 1.3 million) studying full-time to secure entrance to the elite *grandes écoles* in the academic year 1996–1997, just 6.9 per cent were the children of manual workers (compared to 27.1 per cent manual workers among France's economically active over-15s) and 8.9 per cent were the children of white-collar workers without a technical or professional qualification (compared to 29.3 per cent among the working population) (Bordes and Gonzalez-Demichel 1998: 57, 73).

The managerial class

Below the bourgeoisie there is now an even larger managerial class that is distinguished from the rulers partly by their income levels but largely by the fact that its members derive most of their income from work. Thus, below the wealthiest 5 per cent, the next 5 per cent of high earners derives 90 per cent of their revenues from earned income (through salaries or pensions) (Piketty 2001). The managerial class is not only more numerous than it was two decades earlier, its members are also both more qualified and less certain of their futures. Under an expanding economy in 1970 almost all managers had been convinced that their individual road to promotion and the good life was secure. But these convictions were shaken in the 1980s and 1990s by the emergence of managerial unemployment, by the increasing trend to measure managerial performance that subjected them to neo-Taylorist controls, and by the need to join an upward spiral of accumulating qualifications (Baron 2001). Thus, while the numbers of people carrying out 'management' tasks increased enormously in the 1980s and 1990s, the status of many of these 'new' managers has fallen far below that of a superior technical or 'officer' class. Hundreds of thousands of potential new recruits were 'trained' for management within higher education, yet they entered the managerial labour market in a period of rising managerial unemployment: in the ten years to 1997 *cadres* unemployment rose from 2.9 to 5.1 per cent (André-Roux and Minez 1999: 141). Even recent pressures on the *cadres'* advantageous national pension scheme may be interpreted as helping draw them towards a more collective culture and away from the ruling elite world of private income and inheritances, the world of the traditional petit-bourgeoisie (Friot 1998).

The values of this managerial class are far from being homogeneous. Unsurprisingly, one 1997 survey found that nearly three-quarters of *cadres supérieurs* identified with 'economic liberalism' (Baron 2001: 306) – but this still left a quarter who did not. Rozès (2001) argues that most managers supported market neo-liberalism in the 1980s, when they saw this as bringing both progress and their own social mobility. However, in the 1990s, their beliefs were shaken by the increasing hold of international finance, and by the weakening of their sense of control over their own destiny. Thus, while they continue to support modernisation and cultural liberalism, many also want some form of economic regulation to give them a minimum of confidence about the future. The conclusion of recent French studies of managers appears to be effectively 'watch this space' (Bouffartigue 2001).

The working class

There are fewer manual workers in 1999 than in 1982, more qualified white-collar and technical workers, and more low-skilled service sector workers, as shown in Table 4.2.

Table 4.2   Working class occupations, 1982–1999

	Employment (in thousands)		Change 1990–1999	
	1982	1990	1999	%
Intermediate occupations				
Public sector, health and teaching	1,688	1,916	2,272	+19
Private sector admin and sales	898	1,279	1,621	+27
Technicians	653	723	880	+22
Foremen and supervisors	546	546	545	0
Clerical workers				
Public sector clerical	2,038	2,310	2,679	+13
Private sector administrative staff	2,060	1,921	1,749	−9
Wholesale and retail white-collar staff	622	732	865	+18
Personal service workers	781	937	1,362	+45
Manual workers				
Skilled workers	3,686	3,725	3,497	−6
Unskilled workers	3,089	2,586	2,163	−16

Source: Amossé 2001.

Do these evolutions prove there is a general tendency towards upskilling? The data in Table 4.2 describes the workers, not the jobs they are actually doing. If the work people do is analysed, then the trend picture is more complex. Far from unskilled work disappearing, an INSEE study found its presence had increased from a low point of 4.4 million in 1994 to 5.1 million five years later (Chardon 2001). The reality is that many 'skilled' French workers work at 'unskilled' jobs.

It is well known that the skill level of work is associated with different sorts of risks to health and from accidents. Class – and whether your job is unskilled or skilled – still makes a large difference to life chances. A longitudinal government study from 1982 to 1996 of 190,000 married men and women who were born in France (thus excluding many of France's lowest paid immigrant workers) reveals enduring differences in mortality rates between social classes, along with evidence that they increased in the first half of the 1990s, probably as a result of rising unemployment. The evidence is charted in Figure 4.3.

Male employers and managers between the ages of 30 and 75 died roughly 40 per cent *less* frequently than the average man, while unskilled male manual workers died 30 per cent *more* frequently. Among women shopkeepers mortality was 6 per cent *less* than average, while among women skilled manual workers it was 8 per cent more than for all women. The same study showed that over the period 1982 to 1996 the risks of dying between the ages

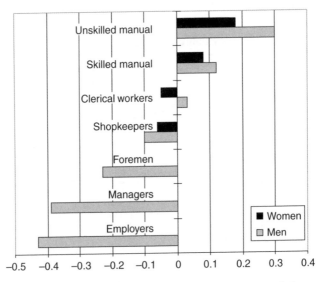

Figure 4.3 Standardised mortality ratios between socio-occupational classes and men and women, 1982–1996

Source: Mesrine 1999: 229–33.

of 35 and 65 were 10.5 and 13.5 per cent higher, respectively, for clerical and manual workers than for employers. Further, the greater risk faced by the unemployed than the employed in 1990 of dying over the next five years had risen from 270 per cent in 1982 to 310 per cent (Mesrine 1999: 230).

Social mobility and social fragmentation

How much social mobility is there between French social classes? One study (Goux and Maurin 1996) found that in 1993 only 35 per cent of sons occupied the same socio-occupational category as their father, compared to 43 per cent in 1977. Yet, after the emergence of new jobs in management, professional and white-collar occupations and the decline of jobs in agriculture are taken into account, family social origin still has a major effect. Fifty-six per cent of male manual workers were the sons of male manual workers, while three-quarters of the sons of managers were either managers themselves or above-average income earners; 42 per cent of the sons of employers became managers, the other half entered the professions. This study (based again on a French-born sample, which therefore is likely to provide a higher estimate of social mobility than if it had included immigrants and their sons) found no change between 1977 and 1993 in the relative chances of a worker's son and a manager's son of making it to the top. Its authors conclude that 'society is becoming more mobile, but not towards greater equality in the chances of social improvement' (*ibid.*: 315).

Most of those dependent upon salaried employment to live are now white collar, and their ranks extend far beyond clerical workers and the technically qualified to the university-qualified professionals who teach or who work in the health service or in commercial services. The social mobility discussed above has most often occurred within this broader employee class, with half the sons and daughters of manual workers taking up often university-qualified white-collar jobs in other segments of the same broad grouping or even rising to the lower ranks of the managerial class. Education became the route to mobility.

By 1999, one in four of the whole population was either a student or still at school (Frickey and Primon 2001: 163). Between 1980 and 1997 the proportion of eighteen- and nineteen-year-olds staying on at school rose from 34 to 68 per cent, and those gaining a *baccalauréat* or its equivalent increased from 26 to 61 per cent (Plaisance 1998). In 1973, of every 100 young people who left the education system nine had a basic university qualification or higher; by 1997 the figure was 21. Many more of these also acquired post-graduate qualifications. Between 1984 and 1997 the numbers of students who left university after five years of study (*Bac +5*) doubled to just under 50,000 a year, to which must be added the 23,000 a year who graduated from engineering schools after equally long studies (Frickey and Primon 2001: 164, 177). Fall in activity rates for young men and women between 16 and 24 were thus dramatic. Young people now sought qualifications in the *lycées* (high schools or sixth forms) or in higher education. A child's expectation of education had been 16.7 years in 1982 but by 1998 it had risen to 18.9 years (*Le Monde*, 30 March 2001). In higher education enrolments doubled from 1,175,000 in 1980/1981 to 2,108,000 by 1994/1995 (André-Roux and Minez 1999: 113).

For the children of manual or clerical workers, getting the *bac* or to a university usually means 'promotion' to a higher occupational classification than their parents. But given that State universities are only in third rank behind the *grandes écoles* and *écoles de commerce* in guaranteeing access to the managerial class senior managers, their social mobility rarely goes much further than the same broader working class.

When asked in the French social survey of 1999 to indicate to which social category they felt they belonged, 9 per cent chose 'the privileged' or 'well-off', 29 per cent chose 'upper middle class', 36 per cent chose 'lower middle class' and 24 per cent chose 'working class' (*la classe populaire*) or 'the poor' (Bréchon 2000b: 272). But it is one thing to passively 'belong' to a social class encompassing between 'lower middle' and 'working' classes some 60 per cent of the whole population, another to be able to identify with it and still another to be able to consciously articulate its interests.

What about the attitudes of different occupational groups to the trade unions? In the employee survey of over 10,000 workers in workplaces with more than 20 workers carried out in 1999 in association with the *Réponse* workplace employment relations study, manual workers (63 per cent) showed themselves the most convinced of the irreplaceable role of the unions in employee representation. But technical workers were at virtually the same level (61 per cent) while a bare majority (54 per cent) of clerical workers, foremen and front-line managers, and professional engineers and middle-level managers were also either totally or largely in agreement with that view. It was only when the degree of identification of the different occupational groups with the unions was measured by testing employees' responses to another statement that a clear hierarchy of attitudes opened up. When asked whether they believed the unions put their own agendas and interests before those of the firm's employees, just a third (34 per cent) of manual workers agreed, compared to 42 per cent of clerical workers and 48 per cent of technical workers. Over half the foremen and front-line managers (54 per cent) and professional engineers and middle-level managers (56 per cent) shared this cynical sense of distance from the unions (Zouary 2002). While technical workers were as supportive of a union presence as manual workers, the degree with which they (and the slightly less supportive clerical workers) identified with the unions was much less. The effects of high levels of unemployment and considerable structural change on both white collar and manual components of this broader French working class has meant that its identity and voice mechanisms have been fragmented and partially disarmed.

This fragmentation can be traced in two major ways. Its manual component has been acutely divided by racism. In the 1995 presidential election a *Sofres* exit poll found that 30 per cent of manual workers voted for Le Pen, compared to 21 per cent for Jospin, 19 per cent for Chirac and just 8 per cent for the PCF candidate, Robert Hue (Courtois and Jaffré 2001). In the first round of the 2002 elections an *Ipsos* exit poll found the same 30 per cent of manual workers voting NF, but the proportions of the unemployed had risen from 25 per cent in 1995 to 38 per cent (*Le Monde*, 28 April 2002). Manual workers and the unemployed together were clearly more ready to protest against their experience of the capitalist and/or political system by voting for a racist presidential candidate than by voting either Communist or for the Far Left.

While manual workers and the unskilled working class have far from disappeared, the second sea change in voting preferences has seen the Communists who used to receive the largest share of the vote among these most disadvantaged workers, shoved aside. The PCF share of the vote fell nearly continuously from 22 per cent in the 1973 national assembly elections to less than 5 per cent in those of 2002. Of the few who still reported voting Communist in 26 *CSA* surveys undertaken in 2000–2001, 24 per cent were retired, 23 per cent (compared to 18 per cent in the population as a whole) were clerical workers, 21 per cent (compared to 14 per cent) were manual workers and just 8 per cent were professional white-collar workers (compared to 12 per cent) (Courtois 2001).

One collection of essays produced in the early 1990s bore the title: *Working Men and Women: a fragmented and silent world*. Its editor, Azémar (1992), summarises the issues. Manual and unskilled workers continue to exist in large numbers, but they no longer appear to share a common political or cultural voice. Verret (1992) points to the 'deworkerisation' of the heartlands of French industry and the renewed exposure to commodification as abstracted labour faced by those still in work.

Does this mean it is no longer helpful to talk at all about the working class? Should we instead focus on individualism? Terrail (1990) addressed these questions in a longitudinal study of factory workers' lives in northern France. He argued that the end of constant shortages and deprivation for most workers and the improved control workers now have over their own lives have not killed off working class culture, but rather have 'modernised' it and in many ways rendered it more 'political' in a very broad sense of the term. It is more difficult to voice, and can be more difficult to mobilise, but for Terrail a greater degree of 'worker individuation' may have as much potential to be transformed into a project advancing workers' rights in the face of ruling class interests, as those projects that were based upon the now-disappeared 'massed ranks' of undifferentiated manual workers.

4.3   Political change since 1981

The growth of a wider less homogeneous working class with a more fragmented agenda, in a period in which values have become less politically left-wing, but more socially radical and more ready to protest, has been largely reflected in recent political history. The three key political developments since 1981 that provide the context for the detailed consideration of contemporary employment relations in the rest of this book were the emergence of the National Front as a major political force, the continued divisions among the democratic right-wing parties, and the eclipse of the Communist Party by the Socialists, whose own ambivalence between a modernising and a social democratic agenda may have led to parliamentary election defeats after each five-year period in which Socialist Party prime ministers held office, in 1986, 1993 and 2002.

The emergence of the National Front

Blaming immigrants was a popular response to the breakdown in the 'golden years' pattern of rising expectations. This was not new: it had previously occurred in the 1930s. France had already closed its frontiers to permanent immigrants in 1974 and had initiated an aided-repatriation programme in 1977. Subsequently, under right-wing governments in 1986 and in 1993, it first eased the expulsion of 'undesirable' immigrants, and then denied automatic citizenship rights to children born in France or to any 16–21-year-olds who had received prison sentences of six months or more, even if they had lived their whole lives in France (Schor 1996: 280–2). The country also became less hospitable to refugees: only 147,000 entered France in 1997, compared to 187,000 entering Sweden and 119,000 entering the Netherlands, countries with populations one-sixth and one-quarter France's (Andersen *et al.* 1999: 69). As immigrants sought other means of entry the rate of political asylum rejections sky-rocketed: up from 15 per cent in 1980 to 84 per cent in 1990 (Schor 1996: 277). This trend continued in the 1990s. In the single year 2000, the numbers held for an average of 5.1 days each in 13 of France's 23 immigrant detention centres was 17,883, a rise of 25.4 per cent over 1999, with nearly half (44 per cent) subsequently being deported (*Le Monde*, 27 July 2001).

The official freeze on new permanent economic immigration did not survive the 'push' effect of deepening Southern Mediterranean economic crisis, the Balkans crisis, the fall of Communism and the Algerian civil war, but it did help change post-war French politics. Publicly halting immigration was tantamount to pointing the finger of responsibility for rising unemployment and poor housing conditions at the existing immigrant population. Earlier waves of immigrants had been assimilated over one or two generations and normally experienced social mobility out of the worst jobs, but this route became increasingly barred to most of the children and grandchildren of the majority North African immigrants of the 1950s and 1960s. Between 1975 and 1990, as many as 40 per cent of the jobs occupied by non-French citizens disappeared, creating the equivalent of half a million redundancies. By 1996, 24 per cent of all temporary workers were foreigners, and three-quarters of these came from Algeria, Morocco or Tunisia (*Conseil de l'emploi* 1999).

Youth unemployment, particularly for those young French who were of African or North African origins, became endemic. Whereas in 1975 just 9.1 per cent of all under 25 were unemployed, in January 1990 this figure had reached 19.1 per cent and by March 1998, 25.4 per cent (Marchand 1999: 106). By 1990, not only were there more than four million 'foreigners' living in France, having been born elsewhere than the 'hexagon', in addition there were some ten million children or grandchildren of 'foreigners' (Schor 1996: 231). These identifiably 'non-white' families are largely concentrated in Paris and France's other major cities, and in the more industrial North and East and along the Mediterranean coast from Marseille to Nice. Within increasingly depressed *quartiers* or high-rise estate *cités* the descendants of North Africans in particular became a dispossessed or excluded population. They were both victimised by and contributed to the spread of an increasingly racist political discourse aimed at the votes of other low-skilled French workers who felt at risk in the increasingly insecure labour market.

The FN was founded in 1972 by Jean-Marie Le Pen from the fragments of the fascist sects and reactionary populist movements based largely on small shopkeepers that had existed since the 1930s. Le Pen's political career had begun when, as a serving army officer who had participated in torturing prisoners in the Algerian War, he was elected the youngest of 53 far right deputies to the National Assembly at the 1956 high point (11.5 per cent) of Poujade's French Union and Brotherhood small shopkeeper/peasant alliance. In 1974, when he first stood for president he received just 0.74 per cent of the vote and at the next election in 1981 he could not even achieve the necessary 500 signatures of elected national or local government figures to stand. Yet, in the European elections of June 1984, as French unemployment started to rise and the Mitterrand government performed a U-turn away from Keynesianism, fighting on an explicitly anti-immigrant platform the FN won ten Euro MPs with 10.95 per cent of the vote (2.2 million electors), and nearly double that in the Alpes-Maritime department (Rollat 1985: 13, 64, 82, 104).

Subsequently Le Pen made still further progress in taking racism into French daily political life: in the first rounds of the 1988 and 1995 presidential elections his vote rose from 14.4 to 15.1 per cent won; and in the June 1995 municipal elections the FN took control for the first time of significant parts of local government, in particular of Toulon, Orange and Marignac, which it began to run on the basis of 'putting the (white) French first'. In 1996, the FN launched FN-linked trade unions among prison officers and in the Paris RATP local transport, although the Industrial Appeal Court ruled them illegible to stand in representative workplace elections, deeming them essentially political rather than trade union organisations.

In 1999, however, against a slowly improving economic context, and personality and political divisions about trying to forge an alliance with the conservative right, the FN split. In that year's European elections Le Pen's FN received just 5.9 per cent of the total poll compared to 3.5 per cent for Bruno Mégret's dissident *Mouvement national républicain* (MNR). This setback proved to be only temporary. Le Pen's score in opinion polls began to climb immediately after the attack on the World Trade Centre in New York of 11 September 2001. This created a huge anti-Muslim backlash in France, reinforced by the Socialist government's 'anti-terrorist' measures that included the requirement to show identity cards when sending parcels through the post office, and continuously broadcasting appeals for 'vigilance' in railway and underground stations. In the 2002 presidential election campaign both Chirac and French television played very much into Le Pen's hands by focusing on the issue of street crime and physical insecurity as a means of undermining the Socialist prime ministerial candidate Jospin. The result was that while abstentions rose to 30 per cent, Le Pen's share of the vote increased sufficiently to put him in second place behind Chirac in the first round of the 2002 presidential elections, as shown in Table 4.3.

Le Pen's vote cannot be dismissed as an aberration. From 1984 to 1998, in opinion poll after opinion poll, between 16 per cent and 32 per cent of

Table 4.3   First and second round presidential election share of votes in Metropolitan France, 1981–2002

Election round	1981		1988		1995		2002	
	1st	2nd	1st	2nd	1st	2nd	1st	2nd
Right								
Chirac RPR	18.0		19.8	46	20.7	52.7	19.4	81.96
UDF	28.3	47.8	16.5		18.5*		6.9	
DL							2.1	
Le Pen (NF)			14.6		15.1		17.2	18.04
Mégret (MNR)							2.4	
De Villiers (MPF)					4.8			
Chasse Pêche							4.3	
Centre								
Chevènement							5.4	
Left								
PS	25.9	52.2	34.1	54	23.3	47.3	15.9	
PRG							2.1	
PCF	15.5		6.9		8.7		3.4	
Verts	3.9		3.8		3.3		5.3	
Lutte Ouvrière	2.3		2.0		5.4		5.8	
LCR							4.3	
Votes to Left of PS	*21.7*		*12.7*		*17.4*		*20.9*	

* Balladur was actually an RPR member, though supported by the UDF.

Sources: Frémy and Frémy 2000: 754; *Le Monde*, 23 April, 7 May 2002.

French over-18, interviewed in their homes by *Sofres*, declared themselves more or less in agreement with Le Pen's ideas (Courtois 1999). This is not to say that the French are growing more tolerant of racism. Many of those who voted Le Pen told the media their intention was to protest against a system that appeared to be letting them down. Some other evidence points to growing distaste for the NF. A growing proportion of people declared that they would not wish to have someone from the extreme right as a neighbour, up from 14 per cent in 1980 to 44 per cent in 1999 (Bréchon 2000). The scale of the million-strong 1 May 2002 demonstrations against Le Pen, and the failure of Le Pen in the 2002 presidential second round to go beyond the combined share of the first round vote received by the FN and the MNR, is further evidence to put on the other side of the scales.

Yet, on top of poor housing, the absence of jobs and the lack of social mobility, the knowledge that half of French people disliked racist political parties intensely and are proud of the 1998 multi-racial French World Cup football champions does little, however, to help those with less education get jobs. Continuing systemic racism continues to deny children of North African immigrants both integration and dignity in the labour market, and in poor urban areas throughout the 1980s and 1990s this generation regularly exploded in anger at frequent examples of excessive police brutality used against them. And in terms of work, more than 40 years after large numbers of North African workers first joined French unions, there are still almost no trade union leaders from ethnic minority backgrounds. In this context the credibility extended to a racist party through its taking on the mantle of the opposition to Chirac should not be underestimated – particularly in terms of its potential demobilising consequences on attempts to revitalise employee solidarity.

The Gaullist inheritance

The emergence of the NF from the mid-1980s exacerbated the tensions within France's traditional right. The democratic but authority-focused alliance successfully created by De Gaulle between the Catholic-inclined small employer–landlord–farmer class and the big industrialists fell apart in face of the difficulties involved in adapting to global neo-liberalism while simultaneously retaining a populist nationalist mass vote: the small proper-tied classes generally wished to retain their protectionist privileges, yet large-scale capital wished to open up France to international capitalism. For the Gaullist politicians the trick was how to try to retain the nationalist conser-vative vote established by De Gaulle while simultaneously directing France towards neo-liberalism. It was a trick they failed to master. The difficulties the right had in mobilising conservative republicanism around a single political party or project was that between 1981 and 2002 France either had a Socialist president or a Socialist prime minister or both for all except the years 1995 to 1997. And this despite a political situation where the combined vote of the right and the extreme right in the first round of each of the five National Assembly elections that occurred between 1986 and 2002 exceeded that of the combined left.

The right was beset by political divisions. In each of the presidential elections between 1981 and 2002 Chirac was challenged by a UDF candidate who represented a pro-European, liberal and modernising centre-right, and in the last three elections also by Le Pen. In 1988, Le Pen called upon his supporters *not* to vote for Chirac in the second round (in 1995 he gave no advice). Possibly as a result, despite the right having a majority in the first round of the 1988 election, Chirac lost, while he won in 1995. But that victory came at a price. To beat both his RPR colleague, Edouard Balladur, then supported by the UDF, and Jospin, the PS candidate, Chirac had shifted his political discourse away from his 1988 neo-liberalism to traditional one-nation *dirigiste* Gaullism. Thus, in the run-up to the 1995 election he called for workers to have higher pay rises and for an end to the 'social fracture' of increasing poverty. Chirac's shift reflected the difficulties the right had in making neo-liberalism electorally popular.

Elected president in 1995, Chirac totally ostracised all those RPR and UDF colleagues who had supported Balladur and gave the premiership and seats in government only to his closest personal supporters. Alain Juppé, the RPR Mayor of Bordeaux and a remote, aloof *énarque*, became prime minister, and in the autumn of that year it became his responsibility to announce to the French public that Chirac had changed tack. 'No more Mr Soft Guy', the government announced a freeze on public sector wages for the following year. It then decided it would increase parliamentary control over the levels of social security established thus far by joint employer–trade union parity organisations, and most combatively announced that state employees would in future have to work five years longer to qualify for their full pension. The result was the biggest strike and demonstration movement France had seen since 1968, with mass support reaching far outside the ranks of state employees. Juppé, and for a time Chirac, became highly unpopular (Jefferys 1996a).

In 1997, Chirac dissolved the National Assembly a year early, calculating that the right would do better then, than a year later. He had not expected French voters to refuse to give the right an unimpeded five-year control of both the presidency and the national assembly. But once again – and to most commentators' surprise – they opted for the compromise of *cohabitation*. When the divided right-wing parties lost, Jospin became Chirac's first *cohabitation* prime minister, and the political right turned in on itself in a search for a scapegoat. In the 1999 European elections, although the turnout was only just half the electorate, and the NF had split, the right's divisions became still more pronounced. The RPR and UDF found themselves beaten not only by the Socialist Party, but also by a new temporary Euro-sceptic nationalist alliance of the former RPR 'Home Secretary' most identified with a strong anti-immigrant stance, the Gaullist Charles Pasqua, and the neo-liberal Catholic Philippe de Villiers (of the Movement for France – MPF).

In the build-up to the presidential elections of 2002 there were as many as eight right-wing candidates campaigning more or less actively to secure nominations to stand against the incumbent Chirac (RPR): Madelin (DL), Bayrou (UDF), Boutin (ex-UDF), Saint-Josse (Chasse-Pêche), Le Pen (FN) and Mégret (MN). Pasqua (RPF) and de Villiers (MPF) were also in there at first, but never made it to the starting post. Little wonder, then, as we shall see in Chapter 7, that to better mobilise their own neo-liberal political clout against both the interventionist, *dirigiste* right and the regulatory left, France's large employers in 1998 transformed the CNPF into a new political campaigning organisation, the *Mouvement des entreprises de France* (Medef). In many ways, with Chirac's overwhelming 5 May 2002 re-election in a massive electoral display of republican values, and the subsequent June 2002 rout of the socialists, and as one of the Medef leaders became Chirac's Finance Minister, it was the large employers who became the biggest winners of the 2002 elections. Not only had the regulatory socialists been obliged to vote for Chirac as president against the racist Le Pen, and had then been roundly defeated in the National Assembly elections, but for the first time in nearly 40 years, the same right-wing party was solidly in power in both branches of the State executive, and its successful presidential candidate had neither been forced to take on a left social policy nor to openly embrace protectionist trade policies in order to win. Profiting from the moment to try and create one single right republican political party, Chirac dissolved his RPR and formed the *Union pour la majorité présidentielle* (UMP), which then decisively won the June national assembly elections.

Socialist rise and fall

The unexpected resolution of the right's political divisions in 2002 was largely the result of Lionel Jospin's poor electoral performance in the first round of the presidential election. As shown in Table 4.3 in 2002 he slipped 7.4 percentage points below his first round score of 1995. This marked a new low point in the modern Socialist Party's (PS) 30-year roller-coaster existence in which the PS had first eclipsed the Communist Party as the principal left opposition party in France, then had seen its candidate François Mitterrand elected president in both 1981 and 1988, but which had also suffered electoral defeats after each of its two earlier five-year periods of government – in 1986 and in 1993. The 2002 defeat exposed once more the internal difficulties the PS has as a governing party in reconciling its 'capitalist modernising' and 'social democratic reformist' wings with the expectations it raises among a broad swathe of the electorate that it can offer greater protection from a European and world context that is being increasingly pressurised to accept American regulation of international trade and finance.

The overshadowing of the PCF by the Socialists took a long time. In 1971 at the founding conference of the PS, François Mitterrand, who had joined just a few days earlier and became its First Secretary, famously declared that

> Anyone who does not accept the rupture...with the established order,...with capitalist society, cannot, I say, cannot be a member of the Socialist Party. (Quoted in *Le Monde*, 10 May 2001)

Emphasising his social democratic face, Mitterrand went on to create a Common Programme with the PCF and the *Mouvement des Radicaux de Gauche* (MRG) that lasted until 1977. His unity strategy was successful. For the first time since 1936, in the National Assembly elections of 1973 the Socialist 21 per cent of the vote nearly equalled that of the Communists; in 1976 the PS became the single biggest left-wing party. From then, despite the emergence of both a Green and a Far Left vote, the hegemony of the PS appeared assured. Mitterrand outmanoeuvred the long-standing PCF leader Georges Marchais by constantly appealing for socialist unity between 1977 and 1981, making Marchais appear sectarian and responsible for dividing the left. Then Mitterrand offered the PCF a place in government, a tactic Jospin used again in 1997. The result was that the PCF became identified with the Socialist government's policies and found it more difficult to mobilise independently of it and against it. It pulled out of the government in 1984 after Mitterrand's 'u-turn' towards monetarism, but it became increasingly dependent upon the PS's electoral largesse. Subsequently, the fall of the Berlin Wall in 1989 and the end of the Soviet Union and its satellite regimes, the changes to its traditional manual working class constituency and growing political competition from both the racist FN and the Trotskyites, saw both the PCF's vote and its membership decline.

At the end of 1999, although the PCF was still France's largest membership party, it claimed only 203,600 members. By June 2001, Robert Hue's own estimate was around 150,000 (*Le Monde*, 19 June 2001). Its vote in cantonal (local government) elections fell from 13.3 per cent in 1988 to 9.8 per cent in both 1998 and 2001, and even more critically, in the 2001 municipal (town council) elections it lost 23 of the 74 Communist mayors who had been elected in 1995 in towns with more than 15,000 inhabitants. This compared to a PS loss of just seven from a total of 177 Socialist mayors (*Le Monde* 17, 20 March 2001). The PCF has been reduced, through its own inadequacies as well as through Mitterrand and Jospin's absorption strategies, to a small core within the wider Socialist front. In the legislative elections of June 2002, when many left voters who had used the first round of the presidential elections to protest against the Jospin government's failings returned to casting a 'useful vote', the PCF vote fell below 5 per cent. This percentage is critical for any French political party, because it is the level that triggers state funding. The collapse is shown in Table 4.4, although as a result of its

Table 4.4 National Assembly first round election results, 1981–2002,* in per cent

	1981	1986	1988	1993	1997	2002
Right						
RPR/UMP	20.9	11.2	19.2	13.0	15.7	33.3
UDF	19.2	8.3	18.5	12.2	14.2	4.9
RPR-UDF		21.4		25.9		
MPF						0.8
DL						0.4
Other right	2.7	3.9	2.9	2.9	6.6	4.0
Chasse-Pêche						1.7
Extreme right						
FN	0.4	9.7	9.7	8.1	14.9	11.3
MNR						1.1
Right total	*43.2*	*54.5*	*50.3*	*62.1*	*51.4*	*57.5*
Centre						
Chevènement						1.2
Environmentalists						1.2
Left						
PS	37.8	31.0	34.8	11.4	23.5	24.1
PRG						1.5
PCF	16.1	9.8	11.3	6.0	9.9	4.8
Greens	1.1	1.2	0.4	7.0	6.4	4.5
Far left**	1.3	1.5	0.4	1.1	2.5	2.5
Other left	0.6	1.5	2.8	1.8	2.8	1.1
Left total	*56.9*	*45.0*	*49.7*	*27.3*	*45.1*	*38.5*

* 1981–1997 legislative election results are based on Metropolitan France alone; for 2002 the results include the *Départements d'outre mer* (DOM).
** Combined LO and LCR.

Sources: Frémy and Frémy 2000: 763–4; French Home Office website for 2002.

electoral pact with the PS and the Greens, the PCF was still able to secure 21 deputies compared to the 138 for the PS, seven for the PRG and three for the Greens in the 2002 National Assembly.

Why is it that the socialists performed so badly after each of their three periods when they held the prime minister's position and nominated the government? Part of the reason is the tension between their internal 'modernising' and 'social democratic' tendencies. They neither fully satisfied either. They alienated the employers by introducing new regulations to improve workers' rights, and they alienated many workers after 1983 by embracing a monetarist neo-liberal economic orthodoxy.

Mitterrand's 10 May 1981 election was a profound shock to the French ruling elite. The panic on the Paris *bourse* (stock market) was so great that sales were suspended for the next two days. His first prime minister from 1981 to 1984, Pierre Mauroy, implemented a classic Keynesian relaunch policy. Demand was stimulated through raising the national minimum wage by

10 per cent, housing benefits by 50 per cent and family allowances by 25 per cent (Fléchaire 2002). Public expenditure went up by 21.5 and 16.5 per cent in 1981 and 1982, respectively, helping create 240,000 jobs in the public sector alone (Cochet 1997: 94). In addition the Socialist–Communist coalition government intervened massively in industry. In 1981 and 1982, it embarked on a huge nationalisation programme: five major diversified groups (including Saint-Gobain, Rhône-Poulenc, Compagnie générale des Eaux, Thomson), two steel companies (Usinor, Sacilor), two arms firms (Dassault, Matra), 36 commercial banks (including CCF and CIC) and France's two financial giants (Suez and Paribas). Complementing the nationalisations of 1936 and 1945, the state controlled virtually the whole of the energy, transport and communication sectors, basic industry, leading manufacturing industries and banking and finance. The state regrouped its acquisitions into a series of national champions and embarked on massive investments in research, rising by 25 per cent each year from 1981 to 1984. Even in the shrinking private sector it supported sectors facing particular difficulties like machine tools, textiles, shipbuilding and paper (Stoffaës 1991: 463–4).

However, faced with a 27 per cent devaluation against the Deutchmark between 1981 and 1983, an investment strike by France's capitalist class, political isolation in Europe and inflation climbing up to 15 per cent, in June 1982, Mitterrand followed the advice of his 'minimalist' 1981–1984 economy and finance minister, Jacques Delors, and put the brakes on. A year later he embraced monetary liberalism (Northcutt 1992: 102, 113). Henceforth, the control of the economy would be through deflationary policies aimed at maintaining a strong currency linked to the Deutchmark, combined with financial liberalisation to fully open up France to external capital. The international financial markets rather than the French state would now be largely responsible for directing investment, and the Anglo-Saxon style 'market economy', where firms raised much of their finance through surrendering family ownership to the stock markets and the wealthy kept a higher proportion of their assets in shares, would be given free reign.

The election of a right-wing National Assembly in 1986 confirmed France's turn away from Mitterrand's left Keynesianism of 1981 and 1982. Chirac's ambitious privatisation programme included 65 public sector companies and almost all the banks nationalised in 1982. Following the example of Mrs Thatcher in the United Kingdom he aimed particularly to increase the numbers of French shareholders. It began with Saint Gobain (1.6 million small shareholders), Paribas (3.9 million), Suez (1.6 million), Société Générale (2.3 million), CCF (1.7 million), one of France's public TV channels, TF1 (0.4 million), the petroleum giant Elf Aquitaine (3.5 million) and three large insurance companies (GAN, UAP and AGF – subsequently taken over by Groupama, AXA and the German company Allianz respectively) (INSEE 2001b: 143). The sales gave renewed life to the French stock market, increasing its capitalisation by 30 per cent and quadrupling the number of share holders, although the price of restoring their profitability to private sector levels has been estimated as a total loss of 80,000 jobs (Stoffaës 1991: 466–7; Euzéby 1998: 59).

The surprise re-election of Mitterrand in 1988 and the subsequent return of a majority left government moderated the onward rush towards neo-liberalism. Yet, the fall of the Berlin Wall in 1989 and the subsequent collapse of Russian Communism, conferring victory in the Cold War to the United States, endorsed further withdrawals of the state from direct economic management. It also reassured potential investors that stock markets were nearly as good as banks for safeguarding their savings.

Successive Socialist prime and finance ministers then continued to support the strong franc, tying it first to one deflationary icon, the Deutchmark, and then to another, European Monetary Union. To do so meant squeezing the French economy hard and allowing unemployment to rise, shifting economic power decisively back towards the ruling class. Based on Milton Friedman's 'economic freedom' ratings, which judge performance under 17 different attributes of liberalism (covering money and inflation, government operations and regulations, taxation and restraints on international exchange), France moved up from a well below average 3.6 out of ten in 1985 to the OECD country average of 6.1 by 1995 (Henderson 1998: 38–40).

This orientation did not change significantly with the surprise election of a 'plural left' government in May 1997. Under Jospin the privatisation programme decided by the right in 1993 and dubbed 'openings to capital' continued. By 1999, the state had sold 40 per cent of France Télécom (6.7 million shareholders) and Aerospatiale Matra (2.7 million), 50 per cent of Air France (2.5 million), 56 per cent of Renault (1.1 million), 60 per cent of Thomson CSF, 90 per cent of Crédit Lyonnais (3.5 million) and 100 per cent of the BNP (2.8 million shareholders) (INSEE 2001b: 143). All in all its privatisation receipts had amassed 380 billion francs as against the 47 billion costs of the 1981–1982 nationalisations and the 217 billion invested in the nationalised industries subsequently (Orange and Rocco 1999). By the beginning of 2002 only the huge firms who provided electricity (EDF) and gas (GDF) and postal services (La Poste) and virtually all public transport remained 100 per cent in public hands. In 1985, one in ten of French employees who were not employed directly by the government worked in the nationalised industries; by the year 2000, this proportion had fallen to one in 20 (*Le Monde*, 9 April 2002). After this huge privatisation programme had brought in 31 million euros between 1997 and 2002, more than the right had achieved in 1986–1988 and 1993–1997 combined, Jospin may have been honest but he further alienated many social democrats by describing his 2002 presidential platform as not being a specifically 'socialist' one.

There are issues of probity and style as well behind the negative electoral evaluation of the PS in government. The Socialists were implicated in several

corruption scandals during the Mitterrand era, taking illegal political donations from France's major firms nearly as readily as did the right. Under
Jospin the Socialists failed to effectively bridge the gap between the French
political–industrial elite and ordinary workers. Jospin, himself, was an
énarque graduate (as was Giscard d'Estaing and Chirac), and so too was
Martine Aubry, his minister of labour and the daughter of Jacques Delors.
The traditional *pantouflage* (soft passage) of top civil servants moving to take
up jobs in private industry continued unabated. In 1998 alone, according to
a government report, the cases of 813 former civil servants, half of whom
were in the top Category A grade and nearly a third of whom came from the
Ministry of Finance and the Economy, were investigated to check whether
their new jobs were linked to their earlier government functions (*Le Monde*,
20 July 1999).

This is not to argue that French Socialists have entirely abandoned redistributive social democracy. The continuing presence of the PCF, even if
reduced to a small core compared to its former strength, has meant that in
power the Socialists have been forced to consider criticisms from their left
as well as from the right. In 2001, for example, it ended up approving a measure limiting large employers' rights to declare redundancies that it would
never have contemplated without the Communist presence. Without the
left in government it is nearly certain that France would have been closer to
the United Kingdom's 7.3 or Switzerland's 7.4 ratings on Milton Friedman's
index, and there would also have remained far fewer of the continuities with
the attitudes and values of *égalité* and *fraternité*. Measures taken by the
1997–2002 Jospin government, such as the extension of free health care to
some six million French who previously had to pay, the 35-hour week that
may have helped create an additional half a million jobs (Husson 2002b:
27), and the placing of additional consultative obstacles in front of companies wanting to relocate their business, would have been unthinkable under
a government of the right. In the following chapter we consider the evolution of state interventions affecting employment and welfare rights that
flowed from the left dominance of the French political process.

4.4   Conclusion

We have painted a picture of considerable ideological, social and political
evolution in the 1980s and 1990s. France has become more urban, less
socialist and less religious. Yet, at the start of the twenty-first century it is
also more tolerant – both of people's sexuality and ways of living, but also
of people's right to protest. It is less industrial and has a larger managerial
class, yet at the same time a tiny bourgeoisie and a large working class remain
strongly present. Social mobility is very limited. Within this wider working
class, however, there are new divisions along both racial and educational
lines. It is still very far indeed from coalescing around any clear ideological

view of the world let alone endorsing a common political project of its own, although high levels of participation in strikes and other forms of protest suggest that such a project is not unthinkable.

All political parties have shifted to the right with the biggest developments being the strengthening of the racist right, the possible emergence of unity among the rest of the right parties, and the eclipse of the PCF. Until 2002, although there has been a major weakening of workers' voice in French society, the political right were unable to take full advantage of this. The largely hegemonic Gaullist Party of the 1960s splintered and like Humpty Dumpty, no one was able to put it back together again. Attempts by Philippe de Villiers and Alain Madelin to create distinctive neo-liberal right parties have so far failed in face of three principal factors: the difficulty of reconciling French nationalism and racism with liberalism and globalisation; the remaining vested interest of a huge state apparatus in centralised control; and the deep attachment of different segments of the French population to protective business regulation, extensive employment rights and to one of Europe's most generous welfare states. It remains to be seen whether the new UMP right political party can now take the whole right forward in the same direction. Even with the encouragement of the Medef it is no foregone conclusion that it will hold together as the next election tests approach.

France has followed a 20-year trajectory towards *liberté* and neo-liberalism. Nonetheless, in a country where, as we have already seen, the state largely structures employment relations, the electoral 'accident' of successive Socialist governments had profound effects. Their shift towards neo-liberalism was far from unambiguous. Hence, not only did they advocate employer *pluralism* and union *social integration* but they rejected *unitarism*, and retained a commitment to *égalité*. They also remained strongly *dirigiste*, and against the backcloth of a triumphalist American view of the inevitability of globalisation, sought to retain the capacity for the state to influence employment relations. In the following chapter we consider what this meant for business, employment and welfare.

5
State Intervention since 1981

This chapter argues that despite the increasing importance of American managerialism and of non-French share ownership, the state remains at the heart of the organisation of relations between capital and French labour. It is not that the state is neutral. Rather its directing groups see their interventions as modernising France so that it can perform better within global markets. Yet, how these interventions occur is still shaped by the mobilising powers of a range of actors, from the employers and trade unions, to political parties and distinctive interest groups such as the military, the Church, the state elite itself and the whole body of state employees and even the hunting and fishing lobby. In turn the pressures these actors exercise reflect the continuing tensions on them of the interrelated but distinct ideological poles representing *liberté, fraternité* and *égalité* – of the market, of society and of class.

Hancké (2001) has argued powerfully that the strong economic performance of France in the 1980s and 1990s that confounds the neo-liberal critics of any state intervention cannot be wholly explained by the performance of the French state. While he concedes that 'state policies … mattered in industrial and economic readjustment', he suggests that neither the state, the market, or cultural traditions should be seen as the key driver. He prefers to locate the driver of change in 'a bottom-up perspective that builds on the capacities of firms to restructure their environment' (*ibid.*: 40–1). Later on, in Chapters 6 and 7, we will qualify his conclusion by suggesting that its truth lies more in the resilience and adaptability of the French bourgeoisie than in any particular sociology of the large firm, in which we show that behavioural continuities from before 1980 are still commonplace. Here, however, we insist that whether Hancké's 'large firms' or our view of a small, collective ruling class (Hancké's (2001: 46) 'small group of top managers, government officials and bankers') are seen as the key drivers of change, it would be unwise to underestimate the 'stickiness' of the French state to power.

We first sketch the state's direct influence, as an employer and purchaser of services. Next we glance at its role in regulating the wider business environment before turning to its regulation of the employee–employer interface. Finally, we consider its welfare roles in mitigating the dislocating and potentially conflictual effects of the capitalist labour market.

5.1   The weight of the state

In 2000, the French government and its associated social security organisations took 45.2 per cent of the country's gross domestic product in taxes and social security deductions. This compares with 1998 figures of 37.2 per cent for the United Kingdom (after 17 years of Thatcherism) and with 52 per cent for still social-democratic Sweden. As in virtually every country in the world these figures for the end of the 1990s were higher than in 1980, when in France they were 40.6 per cent, in the United Kingdom 35.3 per cent and in Sweden 47.1 per cent (INSEE 2001c: 125).

Nearly two-thirds of this total tax take (28.5 per cent of French GDP in 2000) is transferred through a myriad of state-associated social security organisations to old age pensioners, the sick and the unemployed, as we shall trace below (in Section 5.3). Some of the rest is redistributed to private firms to aid research or re-equipment programmes; a great deal is spent on France's military ambitions; and some is redistributed to the tax payers via subsidies to public transport and housing and other public works. But the bulk of the money raised in taxation is spent on providing government services. This means placing orders for goods and it means employing people. The state's strength as a customer allows officials to exercise considerable sway over the structure of French industry: its most senior officials still drop heavy hints to their former class mates from the elite post-graduate universities, ENA, the Polytechnique or HEC, who head up France's private sector, about which products they would like firms to manufacture, at what price and with which companies they would prefer French firms to collaborate or merge.

There are three specific areas in which the state is taking a growing role as an employer: health, on which the French spent 9.5 per cent of GDP in 2000; education, which took a 7.1 per cent share; and central and local government (INSEE 2001a). The growth since 1981 and the distribution of state employment is shown in Table 5.1.

Despite a decline in the numbers of full-time military personnel (conscripts and reservists are excluded from these totals) and against the trend elsewhere in Europe (Carpenter and Jefferys 2000: 106), the closing decades of the twentieth century saw a steady although slowing rise in the state sector employment under both left and right governments.

But in addition to those *directly* employed by the state sector the 1,540 nationalised companies in 1999 employed a further 1.1 million workers at the end of that year. They still made up 5.3 per cent of all French employees, even if down considerably from the 9 per cent of 1991. Of these firms,

Table 5.1   State sector employment* (thousands), 1981–1999

	1981	1984	1987	1990	1993	1996	1999
Civil service	1,926	2,004	2,024	2,077	2,151	2,281	2,286
Local government	1,114	1,216	1,234	1,326	1,407	1,463	1,505
Public health	726	781	797	802	826	844	857
Defence	454	452	442	413	393	387	370
All state employees	4,220	4,453	4,497	4,618	4,777	4,975	5,018

* Excluding those employed in Catholic and other private schools who are largely paid for by the state as well as those employed on special 'youth job contracts'.

Sources: INSEE 2001a,c.

95 employed over 200,000 staff, while the big four, *La Poste*, *SNCF* (French national railways), *France-Télécom* and *EDF* (French Electricity) and their subsidiaries employed some 750,000 between them (INSEE 2001b: 143). In the main their employees still have permanent civil service status with very similar rules on conditions such as promotion procedures and pensions (in the case of France Télécom new employees hired since the partial privatisation of 1998 now have a different status). A little further removed are many workers in the health, voluntary and education systems whose jobs largely depend upon state subsidies. For example, in 2000 a total of 1,650,000 people worked in health of whom only half were directly employed by the state with most of the rest being effectively subsidised by the state; the same is true of the 145,000 private (largely Catholic) school teachers (Montalembert 2001: 171; Triclin 2001: 29).

Three factors help explain the French state's continuing huge influence: the massive budget it wields; its role in appointing the chief executives of all the nationalised companies in which it holds all or a majority of shares; and the six million people it effectively employs along with the up to two million more whose wages it pays at once removed. Depending on who is counted this means it employs between one in five and one in four of the whole French active working population of 26.1 million people in March 2001, and nearly one-third of all those in salaried employment. This sheer weight of numbers creates a powerful force making it politically difficult to role back the state.

5.2   Regulating the business environment

France has been at home with *laissez-faire* liberalism since the Declaration of the Rights of Man and of Citizens of 1789. Yet the weaknesses and divisions among its ruling elites and their constant (and not irrational) fear of revolt from below since then have had a major impact. They legitimated continued state intervention not only as the country's defender (the classic role of the state) but also as the integrator and key arbitrator over business and labour markets. Rousseau's Enlightenment view of a 'social contract', where the rule of law (including, as the 1804 Napoleonic Civil Code puts it, 'legally issued decrees') is what distinguishes barbarism from civilised society, still holds sway (Briant 2001).

The state remains omnipresent in the business environment. Some regulations date back to pre-revolutionary times. In 2002, for example, the official January and July sales periods are still regulated by law: these are the only periods in which shops can legally sell goods at a loss, and then only if the goods have been on display and available for sale at a higher price for the previous month. Other regulations are much more recent: for example, the one requiring all non-French manufactured cars (including those manufactured elsewhere in the EU) to be certified as being 'up to French standards' before they can be registered. While the first example shows the state still seeking to ensure a 'level playing field' between French stores in such a way as to help ensure the integration and survival of small and medium-sized businesses, the second shows the state in its more classic role of protecting French-manufactured products against imports.

These examples would have to be multiplied thousands of times to fully capture the continuing importance of state regulation for French business. Of course, many regulations have fallen out of common use, for others the means to ensure compliance are lacking, while for many more it is well known that a word with the local village or town mayor or key ministry official will secure an exemption. Yet their presence and acceptance over generations creates an expectation that business activities that impinge on the collective should somehow be socially regulated. Thus, although the right protested against the 1981 nationalisation and some on the left challenged the 1986 and 1993 privatisation laws, the state's right to act was not questioned.

In this context, the state's pursuance of business regulation on a European-wide scale poses very few ideological problems to the French ruling elite. Certainly neither Jean Monnet, widely recognised as the European Union's 'founding father', nor Jacques Delors, largely responsible for the push towards the Single Market and Single Currency, saw any major difficulty with setting *laissez-faire* economic practice within a much wider European regulatory framework. Thus, as a part of Mitterrand's turn away from Keynesianism, financial reforms in 1983 and 1984 liberalised French capital markets and banking, creating a single market covering both long and short-term capital and pulling the state out of its mediating role in short and medium-term capital markets (Cochet 1997: 98). The preferential interest rates that were the hallmark of French state tutelage were reduced almost overnight as a share of all loans from 44 per cent in 1985 to 17 per cent by 1988. Then, under the 1986 Single European Act – agreed after an understanding reached by Mitterrand with the British Prime Minister Margaret Thatcher – France abandoned all exchange controls from 1 January 1990

(Jeanneney 1991). In 1989, the giant Crédit Agricole bank was first taken out of state control and established as a mutual society. Finally, in 1996 a liberalisation measure was enacted transposing the 1993 EU directive giving a common European status to share trading and investment services.

The French state thus committed its people under the Maastricht (1992) and Amsterdam (1997) Treaties to a 'strong franc', lower rates of public expenditure and sustained deflation through the 1990s without any major challenges, even though these policies entailed very high levels of unemployment. Neither the legitimacy of such macro regulation nor their goal of achieving a single European currency in 1999 and the 2002 launch of the Euro were questioned by any significant section of business interests. This was not the case, by contrast, with the evolution of employment regulation, which is often seen as a challenge to managerial prerogatives.

5.3   Regulating employment relations

The state still has a major influence over rule-making on both substantive and procedural issues in French workplaces. Here we first sketch out one piece of the evidence. Table 5.2 summarises the contents of the contemporary Labour Code listing the hundreds of issues on which laws and directives with the force of law have been issued.

The range of areas of intervention is huge and we are not arguing that actual workplace behaviour automatically follows the letter of the law. But we are suggesting that the detail of this national rule-base represents a continuing restraint upon both large and small employers that they would love to see largely torn up. In part at least because they recognise that its presence constitutes a key element in the continuing survival of independent workplace trade unionism. To illustrate this argument we will give three examples of the way the law and changes to it continues to influence employment relations, looking in turn at employee representation, the Auroux laws and working time.

Employee representation

A key area of state intervention in terms of institutionalising workplace level employment relations has been the Labour Code's enactment of measures guaranteeing the election, rights and status of employee representatives. It includes 111 text pages on Works Councils (*Comités d'entreprises* – CE) alone and 43 about personnel representatives (shop stewards or office reps). The law establishes that personnel reps (DP) – who may not be related to the owner – should be elected in all firms with 11 or more workers, while Works Councils (and Health and Safety Committees) are supposed to be established in all firms with 50 or more workers. Depending on the numbers of employees and their composition the election is divided into 'colleges': some have just one representing everyone; others have two, representing manual and

Table 5.2 Contents of the French Labour Code, 1998

Books	Section titles	Chapters	Text pages
Work agreements	Apprenticeship contracts	6	58
	Work contracts	10	197
	Collective agreements	7	40
	Salaries	9	45
	Fines		1
Work rules	Working conditions	3	58
	Rest and holidays	7	58
	Health and safety	9	224
	Work doctors		37
	Work social services		2
	Fines		1
Placements and jobs	Placement	3	22
	Jobs	7	120
	High commission on professional equality	2	3
	Overseas labour and the protection of national labour	2	22
	Workers without jobs	3	31
	Fines		1
Workers organisations, the representation, participation and involvement of workers	Trade Unions	4	43
	Personnel reps	6	43
	Works Councils	10	111
	Involvement and participation	4	21
	Economic, social and trade union training	2	2
	Workers expression rights	2	4
	Workers' funds		1
	Fines		1
Work disputes	Individual disputes – Industrial Tribunals	11	141
	Collective disputes	6	34
	Fines		1
Monitoring application of law and work rules	Monitoring services	2	13
	Employers' obligations		6
	Fines		1
Special measures for certain workers	Mining industrial	2	8
	Process industries	2	13
	Building and public works	2	10
	Transport and telecommunications	4	27
	Travellers and sales reps		27
	Journalists, artists and models	3	50
	Concierges and residential workers	3	20

Table 5.2 continued

Books	Section titles	Chapters	Text pages
	Measures for certain workers and firms	4	10
	Fines		1
Special measures for overseas departments	Work agreements	4	4
	Work rules	2	12
	Placements and jobs	4	23
	Work disputes	1	1
	Monitoring work legislation and rules	2	1
	Special measures for certain workers	1	1
	Fines		1
Continuing professional training within permanent education	Institutions of professional training	2	16
	Professional training agreements and contracts	2	10
	Individual and collective rights of workers on training	3	22
	State aid	2	3
	Employers' participation in the development of continuing professional training	4	24
	Financial aid and social insurance of training placement students	2	22
	Measures concerning state and local authority employees		5
	Work-placed based professional training	2	16
	Monitoring continuing professional training – various steps – fines	3	8
Uncodified Laws, Decrees, Orders	General measures	10	3
	Penal measures	10	4
	Monthly pay	1	3
	General social contribution	1	1
	Holidays and work absences	5	1
	Health and safety	11	10
	Health	2	1
	Jobs	4	1
	Length of working time	5	1
	Personnel representation	8	2
	Locally elected representatives	2	2
	Security occupations	2	1
	Employee financial participation	2	1
	Continuing professional training	6	7
	Workers productive co-operatives	3	1
	Intellectual property rights	2	2
	Firms in difficulties	9	1
	Work medal of honour	1	1

Source: Desjardins *et al.* 1998.

clerical workers, and other workplaces have three separate 'colleges', where managers and professionals are also represented separately. In order to 'simplify' procedures for small and medium-sized firms, most of which ignore the law unless some trade union employees call them to order or a conflict erupts, the Balladur cohabitation government passed a new employment law in December 1993. The *Loi Quinquennale* allowed firms with between 50 and 200 workers to let their *délégués de personnel* (DPs) double as Works Council delegates, effectively increasing the real threshold for works councils to 200 employees, while simultaneously extending the period of office of personnel reps to two years with their elections to coincide with those for the works council (Ministère 1994).

The four legally required representation channels available for dialogue between employers and employees in firms with at least 50 workers are shown in Figure 5.1.

Personnel reps (first set up in 1936) are present in 80 per cent of 50+ workplaces, works council reps (created in 1945) in 88 per cent, trade union reps (created 1969) in 67 per cent and health and safety reps (created 1982) in 81 per cent (Ruelland 2001a,b).

Together these four channels create a potentially very dense network for employee–employer dialogue. A key issue is the degree of freedom the

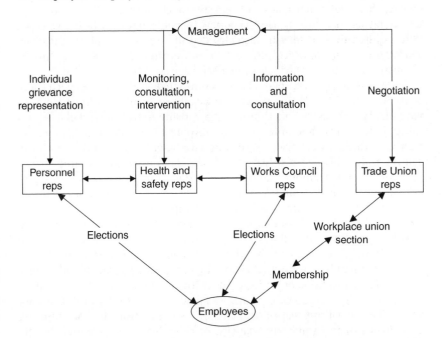

Figure 5.1 Legally-available employee representation channels available in private and semi-public firms with more than 50 staff

representatives have in which to operate. Companies are legally obliged to give the four kinds of personnel reps time off for representative business. The Health and Safety representatives, who are nominated by a joint meeting of works council and personnel delegates, are given time on a sliding scale according to the size of the workplace. This rises from two hours a month in workplaces with less than 100 workers up to 20 hours a month in workplaces with 1,500 employees or more. A less complex allocation operates for the directly elected personnel reps. Each is entitled to 10 hours a month in workplaces with less than 50 workers, and to 15 hours a month in larger ones. Where, in workplaces with 50–199 workers the works council function is combined with the personnel reps, the combined rep get a total of 20 hours a month – something that occurred in 23 per cent of 50–199 workplaces in 1999 (Zouary 2000). Any time spent in meetings with the employer would be paid in addition to these hours.

All elected Works Council reps have a legal entitlement to 20 hours a month, while in workplaces with more than 500 employees, each union present can additionally nominate a rep to sit ex-officio on the works council. These union delegates also receive a 20 hours a month allocation. The reps are free to use these hours to move around inside or outside the workplace, provided they are acting in the interests of their CE. In reality, of course, this means that many of them use much of their time up on 'trade union' rather than strictly 'works council' business, but the line between the two is quite fine. The reps are also afforded some protection from dismissal during their terms of office and for six months afterwards: they can only be dismissed with the authorisation of a Ministry of Labour Inspector.

Trade Union reps (DS) may also be nominated in workplaces with more than 50 staff. There is one for each officially recognised union branch in workplaces with less than a thousand staff, rising to five in workplaces with more than 10,000. The union reps are responsible for the local union section and conduct workplace based collective bargaining with the employer. They too can move freely within or outside the workplace and receive between 10 and 20 hours a month paid trade union duty time according to the size of the firm. Time taken in meetings called by the employer are in addition to this allocation, while if the meeting is called by the union rep it is deducted from his or her allocation. Where firms have more than 2,000 staff in at least two sites, then the unions can additionally each nominate a Senior Trade Union rep covering the whole company (Ministère 1994).

The argument here is not that all employee representatives take advantage of their full allocations of hours. Many, probably most, do not – for a multitude of complex reasons. In some workplaces there is little or nothing for them to do; in others fear of dismissal or lesser sanctions by the employer or manager may inhibit the exercise of their legal entitlements. In still others pressure from colleagues who would have to pick up the representative's workload is a sufficient restraint (Contrepois 2002). But in other companies, particularly the larger ones, the entitlements are often taken in full. Among 71 extremely experienced delegates to the CFDT Banque union's 1999 congress, virtually all of whom held at least two representative positions, half spent between 15 and 35 hours a week on union business in the employers' time, a fifth spent 35 hours or more, in other words were effectively full-time working for the union and/or the Works Council, but 30 per cent spent less than 15 hours a week (Jefferys 1999).

While companies are legally entitled to ignore the opinions of their works councils (decided by majority vote), these have the right to consult external experts – and do so in a quarter of workplace CEs, and in 39 per cent of company-level CEs (IRES-DARES 1998: 199). They also have the legal right to be formally consulted over a substantial range of issues, five of which are regularly considered by more than half of France's workplace CEs, as shown in Table 5.3.

In firms with less than 150 workers CE meetings should occur at least once every two months, and at least monthly in firms with over 150 staff. The employer or his representative chairs the works council meetings and has an individual vote. The CE has to be given an office and the necessary equipment with which its secretary and members can work, and it is entitled to two grants from their employer that are entirely at their disposal: a subsidy equal to 0.2 per cent of the gross company wage bill, plus a variable contribution to support social and cultural activities. One out of six CEs has a large enough income to employ full- or part-time staff in its own name (IRES-DARES 1998: 197).

The law is not fully respected, particularly by smaller employers. In 1999, more than half of all 10+ workplaces employing nearly one in five workers had no employee reps. Only 23 per cent of all these workplaces had Health and Safety reps and only 27 per cent works council reps. But the proportion of 50+ workplaces with no reps at all falls to 7 per cent and these employ just 2.3 per cent of the workforce. Thus between 73 and 81 per cent (according to which survey you use) of these larger workplaces had Health and Safety reps and 88 per cent had CEs (Ruelland 2001). In a national survey of CE in 1995–1996 (one-third of which were company works councils and two-thirds workplace-based) researchers found that 11 per cent of CEs had taken their employer to court within the previous five years for non-respect of their rights or disagreements on a critical issue (IRES-DARES 1998: 195, 200). As many as 61 per cent of works councils had also approached the Labour Inspectorate for information or an intervention. Some of those requests for intervention concerned the dismissal of 'protected' workplace reps. In the four years 1991–1994 the Labour Inspectors were asked to approve 2,700 rep dismissals per year for 'disciplinary' reasons and 12,500 for economic motives. But over the next four years, as the economic recession bottomed out and the requested 'economic' dismissals fell to 10,700, the annual average number of 'disciplinary' dismissal requests rose to 3,250

Table 5.3   Works Council legal rights to and regularity of consultation, 1996

Theme	Object	Works councils discuss (%)	
		Regularly	Never
Company results, annual report, legal, economic and financial changes	Any issue arising of interest to the workers Consultation on management strategy, especially take-overs, mergers etc. and before any announcement of closure	83	5
Jobs and personnel management	Consultation on changes in numbers, lay-offs, redundancies	68	8
Training and development	Consultation on strategy and plan and on objectives and induction	64	8
Social and cultural activities	Organises social expenditure put at its disposal by the firm (tourist outings, Xmas parties, subsidised canteen etc.)	61	15
Working conditions and health and safety	Consultation on workplace rules, impact of any changes on working conditions, work measurement, health and safety trends	55	16
Working time	Consultation on modifications to collectively agreed working patterns, compensation rest periods, overtime, part-time hours, holiday arrangements	44	15
Wages and remuneration		38	30
Welfare	Housing help, various company insurances,	36	21
Participation	Involvement and the functioning of 'right of expression' within the workplace	33	39
Profit sharing	Consultation on results and scheme	29	44
Technological change	Consultation on change	26	34
Qualifications, promotions	Skill composition of workforce	22	37
Union rights and employee representation	Any proposal to dismiss worker representatives	13	55
Firm organisation	Consultation on important changes to production		
Research	Company research strategy		
Equality	Discuss report on equality and measures proposed		

Sources: Ministère 1994; IRES-DARES 1998: 198.

(INSEE 1994, 1998, 2001). Underneath this trend was another: between 1995 and 1999 the proportion of trade unionists among the representatives in the firing line rose from 31 to 38 per cent (Merlier 2001).

While general levels of employer non-implementation and hostility to employee reps are high, their legal status nonetheless provides a kind of residual bedrock to which workplace union activists attach themselves. As Contrepois' (2002) detailed study shows, despite the constraints imposed by 'institutionalisation', it can help them retain their capacity to act in workers' interests independently of the employer. Employee reps have a legal right of access to company information and a process of 'meaningful consultation' that means that at the very least the company can be challenged in the courts if it does not meet and inform the representatives prior to any significant decision. This is particularly the case in redundancy situations where the very last employment law passed by the 2002 Jospin government gave even clearer signals to the employers that they had to consult their employees. Based on regular elections among the whole workforce the employee representatives thus acquire a public legitimacy that often spills over into workers' acknowledgement of trade union legitimacy – even if they do not actually belong to a union.

Modernisation of labour regulation

Labour regulation has been a key area of state policy debate since 1981. Different governments have had different short-term objectives reflecting struggles around the allocation of resources. But they have largely shared a common approach: to try and improve French competitivity further by getting French employers and workers to cooperate more closely together. The Auroux Laws and decrees of 1982 may in part be viewed as a catching-up exercise with an earlier European Keynesian response to the 1973 oil price hike and slowing down of the world economy. Although the minimum wage and social welfare expenditure rose dramatically under France's right-wing governments of the 1970s, their business links made it more difficult for them to experiment with the more radical forms of worker participation that were launched or discussed in countries as distinct as Sweden, West Germany and the United Kingdom, where governments were actively canvassing ways of reducing worker combativity and encouraging wage restraint in the face of sky-rocketing inflation (Carpenter and Jefferys 2000). So when Mitterrand came to power on a Keynesian platform it appeared both natural and politically expedient that space be given to attempting to institutionalise a whole range of ways of inserting worker participation and collective bargaining into French management processes. The outcome, the laws and decrees implemented by the Catholic Socialist employment minister, Jean Auroux, provided individual 'free speech' rights for employees, strengthened representation rights and set the target of the progressive reduction of working time to 35 hours. They also imposed workplace-level negotiation obligations on the employers. There was to be both 'a change in rulemaking…and a change in the rules on the organisation of time' (Thoemmes and de Terrsac 1997: 55). The setting of substantive targets which must subsequently be implemented by negotiation has been a recurrent feature of French state employment interventions since 1919 (Jefferys 2000).

The main features of the Auroux Laws are summarised and contextualised with the modernising measures of the following 20 years in the top part of Table 5.4.

Table 5.4   Employment laws, 1981–2001

Year	Measure	Effect
1982	Auroux Laws	Suppression of language qualification for workplace representative elections Right of expression in the workplace Employers must establish clear disciplinary procedures Health and Safety Committees Group Works Councils Requirement to conduct annual negotiations 39-hour week Fifth week of paid holidays Retirement at 60
1986	Redundancy Law	Suppression of requirement that redundancies be approved in advance by Labour Inspectors
1992	Recruitment Law	Discriminatory recruitment practices outlawed
1993	Retraining Law	Employers obliged to provide a retraining plan for their ex-employees
	Five-year Employment Law	Incentives provided for firms to use part-time and temporary workers Threshold for formal Works Committees raised to 200 workers with personnel delegates doing the job in firms with 50–199 staff
1996	Robien Law	Incentives provided for voluntary introduction of shorter working hours
	European Works Councils	Transposition of EU directive establishing Works Councils in multinational European companies
1998	Aubry Law 1	Incentives given to employers for negotiating job-creating 35-hour week agreements Non-trade unionists to be allowed to be mandated by a recognised union to sign 35-hour agreements with their employer
2000	Aubry Law 2	35-hour week for all working in 20+ firms from 1 February
2001	Guigou Law	Companies to face a delay of at least 21 days after declaring redundancies to allow negotiations Workers can subsequently demand mediation Minimum redundancy payment doubled to 20 per cent of a month's wage per year employed

For our purposes what is important to retain from the Auroux laws is that if their intention was to strengthen the trade unions, they clearly failed. While there was a steady advance subsequently in the number of workplace meetings between employers and worker representatives, trade union membership declined significantly down to what may be viewed as a hard core of around 8–10 per cent of employees, largely those working in very big private firms or for the state. Legislation appears capable of preserving real gains won by workers in action, but only very rarely can it achieve new advances when workers are either not mobilised or are being actively de-mobilised, as when following Mitterrand's U-turn of 1983 the government abandoned the target of the 35-hour week.

In terms of its modernising objectives, the Auroux balance sheet is much more positive. Many employers were nudged into taking a series of measures that their fellow European employers had been doing without any difficulty for years, such as meeting four times a year with employee reps in Health and Safety Committees (half of all 50+ workplaces were meeting at least this regularly by 1998, when three-quarters of all the 50+ workplaces actually had such CHSCTs) (Coutrot 2001a). Group works councils were widely established across multi-divisional organisations; 25 days' paid holiday a year became a national minimum; retirement at 60 became the norm.

Perhaps the Auroux Laws' greatest achievement, however, was in pushing thousands of employers into annual workplace negotiations with the unions. Decentralised local bargaining had long been identified as the big absentee in French employment relations, leaving little room for establishing common ground and improved personal relations between employers and employee reps. When the unions were stronger the employers had always resisted bargaining within the workplace, fearing that through the acceptance of *pluralism* their managerial prerogatives would be irreversibly weakened. But in the face of rising unemployment and nearly free-fall union decline in the 1980s, the prospect of turning local collective bargaining into another means of responsibilising employee reps into the firms' problems was jumped at by many. By 1987 there were roughly 6,000 firm-level agreements a year and ten years later there were twice as many (DARES 2000). The numbers were increasing particularly because of a new state incentive for employers to negotiate over shorter working hours.

Working time

In the context of the renewal of broad working class solidarity in the strikes of November–December 1995, a centrist UDF deputy, Gilles de Robien, successfully introduced a law trying to tackle the issue of high unemployment through a voluntary work-sharing scheme. The Robien law allowed firms that negotiated shorter-working hours and as a result hired more staff to be rewarded with reductions in their employers' social security deductions. Working time had never entirely left the political agenda, but it was now back with a vengeance (Jefferys 2000). Thus when the French socialists wrote up their manifesto for the surprise legislative elections called a year early in 1997 – particularly as they did not think they would win them – it was natural for them to hark back to the pro-worker 'radicalism' of 1981 by repeating the promise of a 35-hour week.

Five months after forming his new coalition government Jospin announced that despite failing to reach agreement with the employers, he would honour the Socialist election pledge to reduce the working week from 39 to 35 hours. A new law would, he claimed, reduce unemployment while increasing leisure time. At a time when four million were unemployed and the average working week was 41 hours, and getting longer for the growing numbers of managers and professional workers, and when statistical advice suggested that it cost the state less to create a job than to pay unemployment benefits, the 35 hours had a commonsense logic (Notat 1998: 49). Yet the Aubry Laws of 1998 and 2000 also reflected another logic: that of a continuing process of state modernisation of industrial relations in which working time was held out as bait. Those employers who implemented it would be obliged to raise productivity with greater flexibility and new forms of work organisation and wage moderation, and to do so would have to negotiate more seriously with workplace-level employee representatives than ever before. Working time legislation was once again being used to reshape a French post-war industrial relations settlement where pluralist reformers believed that too great a legitimacy had been afforded to the *national* French trade union confederations and their sectoral federations, and too little to the workplace level.

The impact of the Aubry laws on the labour market was considerable. They undoubtedly helped to create hundreds of thousands of new jobs, possibly up to 500,000 between March 1997 and March 2001 (Husson 2002b). It is impossible to say exactly which jobs they created, but of the overall total of 1.3 million new jobs 87 per cent were full-time and 79 per cent were permanent (Husson 2002a).

Evidence in support of their impact on industrial relations may be drawn from the huge immediate increase in the volume of collective bargaining at firm level, up from 11,800 agreements reached in 1997 to 31,000 in 1999 and 30,434 in 2000 (DARES 2000: 40; Triclin 2001: 35). And working hours for many workers did come down. The changes in average agreed working hours for full time workers in firms with ten or more workers over the whole period since 1980 are shown in Figure 5.2.

By the end of 2000, average working hours for full-time workers in all 10+ firms had fallen to 36.6 hours, a more than two-hour fall from the average second quarter hours from 1993 to 1998 (*35 Heures La Dépêche*, 10 April 2001). Those employees most favourable to the shorter working week appear to be those eligible to take the cuts as extra whole days. Thus the principal immediate beneficiaries are the growing numbers of white-collar workers

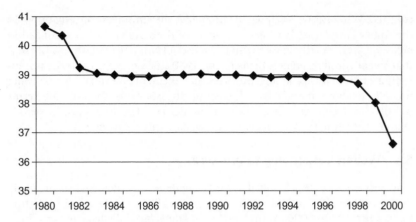

Figure 5.2 Average agreed working hours for full-time workers in firms with ten or more employees, fourth quarters, 1980–2000

Source: INSEE 2001a.

and managers whose overtime hours were rarely counted and who have acquired the right to take an extra ten days' holiday a year. According to French hoteliers they are now taking more mini-breaks then ever before. More than half the managers who had worked shorter hours for at least one year took at least one mini-break away as a result, compared to just 13 per cent of manual and clerical workers. Yet for the manual workers most subject to reductions in overtime hours, to pay moderation and to the flexibilisation of their traditional working hours, the 35-hour week has been experienced more ambiguously. In a DARES survey of those who have spent a year or more under 35-hour week agreements, only 49 per cent of unskilled workers reported an improvement in the quality of their working lives (*Le Monde*, 15 May 2001).

Little wonder, then, that the Aubry Laws became differentially popular. In November 2000, a national opinion poll reported that the overall approval reached 61 per cent (compared to 30 per cent who disapproved), with managers (64 per cent), the unemployed (72 per cent) and technical and professional white-collar workers (74 per cent) being the most supportive. Overall, 71 per cent of those questioned believed it improved the quality of life, a proportion that rose to 87 per cent among employees already working 35 hours (quoted in *35 Heures La Dépêche*, February 2001). Nonetheless, by the 2002 election only one-third of all employees had been actually affected by the law, and the uncertainty surrounding the timing and the real impact of its implementation in smaller and medium-sized firms, may have turned a potential electoral asset into a liability for Jospin.

This brief review of recent employment regulation should not be read as making the case that the state was the only industrial relations actor that counted. While, as we shall see in Chapter 7, the employers bitterly opposed the Aubry Laws, it is also clear that most of the state's other modernisation measures were exactly in line with the prescriptions of the new wave of HRM that swept through French firms in the 1980s. Before we turn to the refashioning of French capital and business management, we must also consider the other labour market role played by the state: its shaping the terms of entry and departure from the labour market. The final section of this chapter therefore turns to recent state welfare interventions.

5.4   Welfare responding to pressures

Transfers under France's social security (*protection sociale*) rose from nearly 26 per cent of GDP in 1981 to 30 per cent in 1993 before declining slightly to 28.5 per cent in 2000. At the same time France's public debt rose ten times between 1980 (when it equalled 15 per cent of GDP) and 1998 when it reached 48 per cent of GDP. Meanwhile the share of social security transfers in average gross family income (estimated at 16 per cent in 1950) rose from 34 to 36 per cent between 1990 and 2000 (Montalembert 2001: 174; Bordes and Gonzalez-Demichel 1998: 81, 116). Why has French state expenditure risen so far and so fast in the era of globalisation, neo-liberalism and the 'rolling back of the state'?

We argue that the French state has continued to borrow and spend in order to sustain a substantial degree of protection from exposure to the 'free' labour market for French workers. It has done so largely because of the political context described in Chapter 4 where high levels of welfare expenditure and cross-generational subsidies have been legitimated by the ideological resilience of values embracing *égalité*, society and pluralism. But it has done so also for two institutional reasons. First there is the very size of the state apparatus, which makes it difficult to create both the will to dismantle it and a big enough political coalition to do so. Then there is the state elite's continued lack of confidence in French or multinational capital's ability to modernise France on its own without stirring up massive social conflict.

Of course there has been change in a neo-liberal or 'targeted' direction. Means testing is more prevalent in 2002 than it was in the 1970s, and cuts in provisions are now being introduced across the board: the 1983 government circular instructing French hospitals to serve inpatients tap instead of mineral water has been followed by many more significant restrictions (Wilsford 1991: 106). Yet one result of the continued strength of the equality and solidarity poles within French politics means that this means testing has generally not been imposed on France's insurance-based systems. Instead it has used on the new schemes designed to reduce poverty among the growing numbers 'excluded' from occupational schemes. Generous existing insured workers' rights (*acquis social*) have been largely defended successfully, as by the mass strike of 1995, while a safety net of new (and less generous but generally above poverty-level) rights has extended a substantial degree of 'decommodification' protection to the growing numbers of highly exposed citizens. Overall, protection increased in the 1990s and, accompanied by annual rises in the national minimum wage, appear to have resulted in France avoiding the sharp rises in inequality and poverty that marked the British and American experiences since the mid-1980s (OECD 1996a).

Welfare and the labour market

The relationship between state interventions and employment can be illustrated as a series of concentric rings around the individual job, as graphed in Figure 5.3.

Closest to the individual worker and their working conditions are *substantive* rules on such things as the minimum wage, basic job classifications and laws laying down such things as the 'legal' length of the working week (or year) and of the duration and breaks between shifts. Outside that 'ring' are the *procedural* rules that regulate the form and institutions of employment relations, including requirements for works councils and for annual collective bargaining. Both of these two 'rings' are monitored by the French

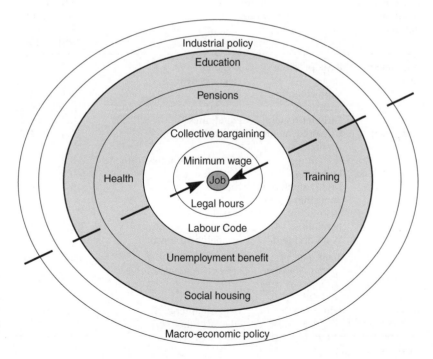

Figure 5.3   State interventions impacting on French employment

Labour Inspectorate, which annually reports about one million infringements but mounts only about 13,000 successful prosecutions. In 1993, 36 per cent of these were cases of employing illegal workers or foreigners and just 21 per cent were about health and safety. About 5 per cent concerned breaches of the laws covering the requirement for daily rest periods (Timbart and Serverin 1995). Labour legislation is therefore not so much a strict universal law, but more like a strong moral guideline. Often it is only implemented in full where there is a sufficiently strong trade union presence to insist upon it, and not always then.

Beyond the inner 'rings' of employment intervention come the state's organisation and partial provision of *individual* (pensions, health, unemployment, access to training) and *collectively* focused (education, housing) welfare. These interventions support entry into and exit from jobs, and often subsidise the employer by helping workers remain in work at lower pay rates than they would otherwise have to charge. The evolution of the shares of different welfare elements within GDP are presented in Table 5.5,

Table 5.5   Welfare programmes and expenditures, percentage of GDP, 1981 and 1996

Relationship to labour market	Welfare programme		Transfers as % of GDP	
			1981	1996
Permanent exit	Basic pensions	Retraites régimes de base	7.3	8.6
	Supplementary pensions	Retraites régimes complémentaires	2.1	3.3
	Early retirement	Préretraites	0.5	0.2
Temporary exit	Unemployment benefit	Chômage	1.4	1.7
	Retraining	Inadaptation professionnelle	0.2	0.5
Reproduction	Maternity	Maternité	0.5	0.4
	Family (including housing)	Famille	3.7	4.2
Maintenance	Sickness	Maladie	6.5	7.7
	Invalidity	Invalidité	1.5	1.8
	Work accident	Accidents du travail	0.8	0.5
	Total share of Social Protection transfers as a part of GDP	*Part des prestations de protection sociale dans le PIB*	*25.9*	*30.0*
Entry	Education*	Dépense intérieure d'éducation	6.4	7.3

* Data for 1980 and 1995.

Sources: André-Roux and Minez 1999: 23; Plaisance 1998: 102.

broken down by their principal thrust in terms of the employment relationship: aiding permanent exit, temporary exit, reproduction of the labour force, maintenance of the labour force and entry.

State interventions affecting the price, availability and quality of jobs have increased in volume and scope considerably since the end of the 'golden years' in the mid-1970s. Whereas in the past the poor would have been left largely defenceless, the democratic advance created by the 30 post-war years of near full-employment persuaded voters that everyone had a basic right to a decent lifestyle. Political pressures then mobilised behind demands for both *égalité* and *fraternité* and pressured governments of both right and left to extend welfare to take account of the gaps left in what was previously an essentially occupationally-based system. It is in this context that these new benefits tend to be subject to means testing. Table 5.6 provides a list of some of the most important welfare measures introduced since 1981.

The fiscal consequences of these extensions of welfare are that French taxes and social security contributions together rose from 35.1 per cent of GDP in 1970 to 41.7 in 1980; by 1990 they stood at 43.7 per cent before rising again to 46.1 per cent by 1997 (Bordes and Gonzalez-Demichel 1998: 119). The rise in unemployment and increase in the proportion of part-time and temporary jobs led to the proportion of social security funded by employee's contributions falling from 83 per cent in 1990 to 69 per cent in 1999, with the balance being paid by the state (up from 4 to 17 per cent) and by individual users (as in the health service where users or their insurers generally have to pay one-fifth of the costs of treatments) (Montalembert 2001: 174). The principal way the state made up this gap was through the compulsory deduction made to workers' monthly pay packets known as the general social tax (*CSG*).

The issue of whether it is the individual who funds their own social security insurance or whether it is the state that does so from general taxation is important in France where, as we saw in Chapter 3, the compromise creating the mass welfare state after 1944 was on the basis of the establishment of a large number of self-funding and jointly (employer–trade union) managed schemes. At the end of the 1990s there were, for example, 120 basic pension and more than 180 supplementary insurance schemes corresponding to individuals' different jobs and status.

The importance of this large number of schemes can be judged by the fact that in 1997 while 55.1 per cent of retired people were pensioned from a single base insurance scheme (topped up by supplementary schemes) throughout their active life, the rest received pensions from a variety of different funds. Among single insurance pensioners, 70 per cent are private sector employees who subscribe to the General Scheme (*Régime général*) which is then topped up by one or more supplementary insurances through *Association des régimes de retraites complémentaires* (ARRCO), or subscribe if they are *cadres* (qualified managers and professionals) through their special scheme, *Association générale des institutions de retraite des cadres* (AGIRC).

Table 5.6   Evolution of French welfare state, 1981–2002

	Benefits		Total benefiting in 1996	Monthly value (francs) Jan. 1998
1981	Widow(er) benefit	*Allocation d'assurance veuvage*	17,000	3187 in first year
1983	Pensions paid from 60			
1984	Long-term unemployment benefit (after exhausting all insurance)	*Allocation de solidarité spécifique (ASS)*	516,000	2434
	Uninsured unemployment benefit	*Allocation d'insertion (AI)*	18,400	1714
1988	Minimum working income	*Revenu minimum d'insertion (RMI)*	1,010,000	2429 single
1993	Social housing benefit extended to all low-income individuals	*Allocation de logement à caractère social (ALS)*	2,119,000	816
1994	Secondary school allowance	*Aide à la scolarité*	700,000	
	Parental encouragement to stop work on birth of second child	*Allocation parentale d'education (APE)*	448,000	3006
1995	Early retirement and younger worker job substitution	*Allocation de remplacement pour l'emploi (ARPE)*	49,500	
1996	Adoption allowance	*Allocation d'adoption*		
1998	Economic insertion subsidy (part of Anti-exclusion law)	*Insertion par l'activité economique (IAE)*	250,000	
1999	Free access to health service for low-income families	*Couverture maladie universelle (CMU)*	6,000,000	
2002	Dependency allowance	*Allocation personalisée d'autonomie (APA)*	800,000	600–7000

Sources: André-Roux and Minez 1999; Ambler 1991; *Le Monde*, 30 December 2001, 5 February 2002.

Only 16.6 per cent of all pensioners only receive one pension and no top-up pensions (Dangerfield and Prangère 1999: 424–5). Here we will look briefly in turn at individual- and collectively focused welfare provisions.

Individually and collectively focused welfare

The French welfare state provides protection to individuals against the risks of living in a market economy through a range of insurance schemes, funded largely through contributions and through several direct programmes financed through general taxation. It has frequently been described as representing a cross between the Bismarckian (occupational insurance) and the Beveridgian (universal flat rate) systems. Palier and Bonoli (1996) suggest that the former dominated up to the end of the 1970s, targeting principally the maintenance of the individual's existing income (*égalité* of treatment) rather than the ending of poverty (which required more *fraternité*).

Insurance-based systems are notoriously unfair towards those with short or incomplete employment records. Thus, in 1993 while 65 per cent of retired men had an unbroken employment record, this was only true of 35 per cent of women. They also discriminate against those on lower incomes. But nonetheless, French pension levels are quite high. They averaged 9,234 francs per month in 1997 for former employees with one base scheme, although within that figure there were private sector women workers on 6,702 francs and male civil servants on 13,219 francs a month. Pensions of between 60 and 70 per cent of final earnings levels are common (Dangerfield and Prangère 1999: 425).

High levels of protection are also initially provided to insured workers who become unemployed. During their first year such unemployment workers in 1996 received on average 64.7 per cent of their former net salary (André-Roux and Minez 1999: 58, 73).

With high unemployment in the 1980s and 1990s, more flexible working patterns and a growing proportion of women workers, increasing numbers of people were 'excluded' from the benefits of an occupationally based system. Thus the proportion of people registered as unemployed receiving benefits (through the UNEDIC unemployment insurance scheme or the state-run ASS and AI schemes) fell from 62 per cent in 1992 to 54 per cent in 1999. Greater emphasis started to be placed on what were called 'solidarity' programmes. These emerged, however, in the context of government attempts to reduce levels of state expenditures and lower the social costs on employers, and thus also meant more targeting of recipients (through an extension of means testing) and a development in the logic of insurance from 'social' towards 'personal' (Palier and Bonoli 1996: 32).

If pensions and health costs are still mainly financed through insurance-based individual contributions, the more collectively-focused state interventions providing education and housing that help to ensure entry to the labour market or render it more stable, are met out of direct and indirect taxation. Education, for example, is largely free, with nominal fees payable only in Catholic schools or for access to state universities. By 1995, there were 12.7 million at school in France (including 2.6 million in nursery classes), 306,000 apprentices and 2.2 million students of higher education, a number that had nearly doubled since 1980 (Plaisance 1998: 102). Housing aid is provided both through means-tested housing benefits and through access to social housing. Altogether about a third of all households are aided.

The numbers receiving housing benefits rose from 4.5 million in 1990 to six million in 1996 (including both renters and home buyers), while the HLM (*habitation à loyer modéré*) social housing sector share rose from 13.3 to 15.7 per cent between 1978 and 1996 (André-Roux and Minez 1999: 86; Bordes and Gonzalez-Demichel 1998: 51).

Despite the gradual advance of neo-liberal ideology insisting on *individual* rather than *collective* responsibility for welfare, French provision has remained strongly collective. Concern about the industrial relations and political consequences of making the poor pay for the economic slowdown of the 1980s and 1990s led governments of both right and left to respond to the economic crisis by extending collective protections. Probably about an additional ten million adults have received protection under new measures introduced since 1974 that they would not have received if these choices had not been made. This has been possible because of the strength of political commitment to inter-generational social solidarity, where 15.64 million contributors to France's compulsory insurance schemes paid the pensions of 10.86 million retired people in 1996 (André-Roux and Minez 1999: 74). This solidarity is partly structured through the institutional mechanisms running much of social security, where those who administer the schemes have an in-built interest in maintaining the values of solidarity rather than of encouraging individual savings in stock market-based pension funds. And it is partly generated through a political emphasis upon *solidarité/fraternité* that is embraced not only by the French left but also by the Catholic components of the Gaullist right and political centre – to the great annoyance of the large insurance companies, who since 1998, as we shall see in Chapter 7, have been campaigning to change the system.

5.5   Conclusion

State interventions in contemporary France represent a mixture of continuities and discontinuities from the 'thirty glorious years' of economic growth after the Second World War. Change has been considerable, but choices have been made by different actors coming from different social classes within a context framed not only by the economic pressures of globalisation and liberalism, but also by the realities of a dense network of institutions and considerable political support for *fraternité*, the ideology of social solidarity. These realities have limited the choices available to those in the French capitalist elite who wished to advance more rapidly towards a neo-liberal future; but they have also limited the choices available to the those on the left who wished to advance towards significantly greater worker rights and protections.

The presence of the Socialists in, or near political power, for most of the years between 1981 and 2002, has meant that the state has played a stronger role as defender of workers' rights and opponent of 'commodification' than in Britain. In the area of workplace rights the PS modernisers seem to have largely 'gone with the crowd' in enabling quite major reforms to be negotiated (and often imposed) increasing task and temporal flexibility. Nonetheless, many core parts of the old industrial relations system still survive, in particular in the guise of a democratic workplace representative structure.

In the area of welfare, change has been less far-reaching: 'collective' welfare has ceded little to 'individual' welfare since the 1970s, and the use of 'targeting' has generally been restricted to new protections rather than to undermine the older ones. The system is still criticised by the employers as imposing too great costs on French competitiveness, and by others as a Machiavellian construct aiming to 'trap' the working class into co-operation with capitalism that in any case fails to deal with remaining poverty. Poverty has continued to affect very large numbers. Between 1996 and 2000 there was virtually no change in the 1.6 million households and the 4.2 million individuals who were defined as living in poverty (with half the income of the French median household equivalent). Poverty is experienced most strongly by young adults and by France's Arab population, of whom one in four households lives in poverty (INSEE study of *'Revenus et patrimonie des ménages, 2000'* quoted in *Le Monde*, 23 March 2001). Yet in face of the mounting pressures for reform a combination of political inertia and the strength of worker mobilisation has led to the retention of the core insurance-based schemes alongside an extension of means testing.

This welfare settlement is another result of the failure of the French neo-liberal right to take and secure political power in France in the 1980s and 1990s. The shift towards the new global 'norms' of American capitalism coincided with the left being in government for a longer period than ever before in French history. In turn this meant that the left's agenda, and in particular the Socialist Party's ambivalent but continuing commitment to social democracy, remained an important element shaping the construction of contemporary employment relations. It is not the only element. The employers, too, have had their own agenda and have mobilised vigorously as we shall see in Chapter 7 to achieve political power and influence independently of the political parties. In Chapter 6 we stake out the ways French capitalism and management have been affected by this distinctive political-economic context.

6
Contemporary Capitalism and Management: Change Amid Continuity

What is new in terms of French capitalism and management at the start of the twenty-first century compared to the 1970s? Most obviously, a more rootless financial capitalism and professional American managerialism are both much more widespread. At the same time the influence of the past is still very strong. As Serge Weinberg, the chairman of the Pinault-Printemps-Redoute group reminds us: 'We still live in France with the idea of the divine right of the boss' (*Le Monde*, 19 July 2002). While weakened, family and close-knit educational elite networks still hold the keys to doing successful business in product and financial markets. Equally, while American managerialism continues to spread, it is still being cherry-picked for those aspects that build upon existing managerial behaviours. Overall, change and restructuring of aspects of capitalism and management only marginally outweigh the experience of continuity. The market-driven world view of the centrality of individual *liberté* has become more influential, and ideas of fraternal social responsibility and egalitarianism less so. Yet, the strength of the two latter ideological perspectives continues to provide both a myriad of restraints upon French capital, and poles of resistance to the 'inevitability' of France's complete adaptation to the American model.

Many companies have been forced to take management strategy more seriously to cope with a more competitive marketplace and accelerating pressure from American and British investment funds to conform to American stock market norms. Research and development, sales and marketing have all become more significant parts of firm organisation than previously. In much of French business product variety has increased, along with sub-contracting and specialisation. Generally, delivery times have fallen and product quality has risen. Establishment and firm size have fallen. Rapidly rising numbers of managers have become increasingly educated in American managerial methods. A growing proportion of these are women – whose numbers in private business rose from 125,000 in 1982 to 300,000 by

1994 (Baron 2001: 249). Human resource managers (many of whom are also women) within a substantial section of French industry are applying techniques including employee shareholdings and stock options aimed at motivating their increasingly qualified employees.

At the same time, while these large firms shed employees, their reach into France's small and medium-sized firms has increased through stock participation, the creation of small subsidiaries and sub-contracting. As a force big capital is at least as important as it always has been, and probably more so. At the same time, as we saw in Chapter 5, the French state is as omnipresent as ever, employing nearly one in four, absorbing (before redistributing) nearly half of GDP and still providing a protective neo-corporatist environment for many firms. There also remain huge areas, particularly among small and medium-sized businesses, where management culture has barely evolved. Many of France's best performing firms either retain authoritarian management styles and apply Taylorist organisation, or have applied computer-driven neo-Taylorist control.

Many important changes have and are continuing to take place. But the continued strength of 'family' and 'elite network' capitalism, a background economic stability that derives from the persistence of a high level of state intervention, and the continued weakness on the ground of trade union opposition in small and medium-sized firms, has had two important consequences. Through permitting French capitalism to shed labour, invest heavily in new technology and keep wage inflation low, its mix of change and continuity allowed France to retain its international competivity despite considerable substantial divergences from the American non-regulatory anti-corporatist model. This chapter first sketches the financialisation of large capital, before turning to the declining independence of smaller firms. In Section 6.3 the chapter examines associated changes in the French management.

6.1 Industrial–finance capital

The recent evolution of large-scale capitalism in France has been like a roller coaster. In the early 1980s, as we saw in Chapter 4, there was a huge extension of nationalisation and profitability was low. By the millennium year privatisations had more than reversed that wave of nationalisations, there was a stock market boom, and profitability rose to historically record levels. Just ten of the country's biggest firms announced profits for 2000 equivalent to those of the profits of the 30 biggest firms in 1999 (*Le Monde*, 1 March 2001). Then in 2001–2002 a new downturn set in, amplified by, but predating 11 September.

Despite this macro-economic instability, the continued presence of a substantial state market sector (including the railways, coal, electricity and gas and Paris transport) as well as high levels of government employment and the employment of half the entire workforce (53.8 per cent) in workplaces with fewer than 50 workers, gave French capitalism an underlying stability (Amossé 2001: 129). Why was this? Our argument stresses three developments. First, the business relations of a majority of France's largest 200–300 firms remained under the control of a loose network of at most a few thousand individuals. Their close and interpenetrating links reach into the top of the state machine (civil servants and ministers) providing advantages of competitive co-ordination. Second, these largest firms down-sized a little, but simultaneously extended their presence and influence among the SMEs, providing advantages of competitive flexibility. French capitalism remains strongly 'co-operative' (Windolf 1999). Third, triggered by financial deregulation and the privatisation process, the stock market has become increasingly important in shaping managerial behaviours and financial targets. *Neo-liberalism* – defined by Dumenil and Lévy (2001: 1) as 'the ideological expression of the return to hegemony of the financial fraction of the ruling class' is again in the ascendant. Far from seeing this last as representing a 'break' with the other two developments, as does Morin (2000: 37), we see them as compatible and continuous.

Network capitalism

French network capitalism links those who acquire wealth at birth to those who acquire power through an elite education. The latter first rub shoulders with the children of the super-rich at a *grande école* and then are given 'practical' experience by being 'parachuted' into the top echelons of a French civil service division, a nationalised firm or a French multinational. If they survive they are welcomed into a dense network of interlocking shareholdings. According to Morin (2000: 38) the average interlocking stake held by the network 'hard cores' fell from over 30 per cent of quoted capital at the start of the 1990s to 20.5 per cent in 1997 as American and British fund managers bought into the French economy. Yet, these levels still remain very high, and well capable of continuing to provide those management teams who need it with extensive protection.

At the core of network capitalism is the remarkable enduring strength of the French family-owned firm. Most large American and British firms appear to have passed from direct ownership, where formal and real control both lay in the hands of an entrepreneur or their family, to managerial ownership, where control is exercised by professional managers on behalf of a multitude of small investors. From there, many of the giant firms have moved on to a form of 'institutional' control, where professional managers exercise control but under the supposedly more watchful eye of a handful of large investment funds, generally insurance and pension companies and banks. In France, by contrast, at the end of the 1980s, 28 per cent of France's top 180 industrial and commercial firms were still under 'active' family control with a further 16 per cent under 'passive' family control (Mayer 1992: 95–6).

By 1995, this concentration had been slightly reduced. Half (48 per cent) of the shares of France's 120 largest firms were owned by up to five principal stockholders (OECD 1997). In that year, too, the founding entrepreneurs or their descendants were running one-third of the largest firms. In 1998, only 29 of the largest 100 firms were clearly under 'pure' managerial control (Windolf 1999: 504–9).

The emergence of the giant supermarket group, Promodès-Carrefour, illustrates the pattern. In 1961, Halley Frères and six other Brittany and Normandy family retail and wholesalers merged to form Promodès. It opened its first supermarket at Mondeville (Calvados) in 1970 and in 1972 the 38-year-old Jean-Paul Halley became its chief executive. When in 1999 it finally merged with France's other supermarket giant, the family-controlled Carrefour, to form a business with 240,000 staff worldwide including 110,000 in France, the Halley family retained 13.5 per cent of the total stock and Halley remained president of the new company's strategy committee, while three sons from the next generation of the family worked in different bits of the business (*Le Monde*, 4 April 2000; Pinçon and Pinçon-Charlot 2000: 74–5).

Although the trend diluting family control accelerated considerably under the plethora of stock market take-overs since 1995, Table 6.1 confirms the relative strength of French family holdings and the relative weakness of financial holdings at that date by comparison with their British counterparts.

Serge Dassault provides an example of the modern French family network capitalist who also practises political paternalism. He was the son of the French aircraft maker and wartime deportee who on his return founded the military aircraft company *Avions Marcel-Dassault* in 1945. Dassault (the elder's) close links with De Gaulle enabled his firm to win the order to equip the French air force with Mirage fighter jets, but under Mitterrand in 1981 it was nationalised. Serge Dassault, who had been running their non-strategic businesses in *Dassault Industries*, inherited the whole business in the year the aircraft business was privatised, 1986. Like his father, he was already active in the Gaullist RPR but he saw himself as a neo-liberal. He implemented a selective and individualised payment system and froze all general

Table 6.1 Ownership characteristics of the 500 largest French and 520 largest British firms, 1995

Owned by (%)	France	Britain
Family holdings of 75+%	15.8	4.9
Financial sector holdings	35.1	73.6
investment funds	*8.4*	*44.6*
insurance companies	*10.4*	*18.8*
banks	*16.3*	*10.2*

Source: Windolf 1999: 514–15.

wage increases. In an atmosphere of fear based on several redundancy pro-grammes that halved employment in the Dassault group, the new methods were successfully introduced. One senior manager spoke anonymously:

> The company is run like a strict father does his family, and we can't chal-lenge this. It isn't Peru. But jobs are saved and people are not as unhappy as is often said. (*Le Monde*, 29 March 2000)

Dassault also placed a new priority on making money through financial investments, increasing these from nothing in 1985 to 11 billion francs by 1994 (the equivalent of the Dassault Group's annual turnover for that year). Chief executive of both *Dassault Industries* and *Dassault-Aviation*, he became the president of GIFAS, the Association representing French aeronautical and space industries, and also a member of the Executive Council of the national employers' association, the *CNPF*, where he was one of its most influential 'hawks' (Contrepois 2001: 145).

All this activity did not mean Dassault gave up politics. In 1995 and 2001, he was elected Mayor of Corbeil-Essonnes an industrial town in the Greater Urban ring around Paris that had had the same Communist mayor from 1959 to 1993. In 1997 Dassault commented that he 'would like to own a daily or a weekly paper to express (his) views and to…be able to answer those jour-nalists who write things that aren't very pleasant' and in April 2000 he bought up three Paris region weekly newspapers (*Le Monde*, 17 July 2001). These included one that covered *Évry*, the adjoining town to Corbeil-Essonnes, where – the French political system allows individuals to be elected for several posts at the same time – he was elected a UMP deputy to the National Assembly in 2002. As mayor of Corbeil-Essonnes Dassault practises the same paternalistic-authoritarian style as he does in his business life. Sylvie Contrepois (*ibid.*: 147–8) describes how Dassault has a reputation as generous and caring, as someone who will place a 500 franc note in the hand of a poor person or settle their shopping bill personally, or who will inter-vene with local employers to try and persuade them to keep people in work. He also negotiated for the last stage of the 2001 Tour de France to leave from Corbeil. At the same time he is hawkishly anti-union, condemning any industrial action in defence of jobs and threatening to evict the trade unions from their *bourse du travail* local offices in council-owned premises.

While large-scale family-controlled firms continue to exercise direct or indirect political power, they have not rejected modern management tech-niques: many have installed the latest American accounting techniques and make extensive use of consultants. Some, like Dassault, also shifted their own focus of operation from product delivery in France to buying and selling potentially profitable investments on the world's stock markets, emulating directly the behaviours of the Anglo-Saxon investment firms. Windolf (1999: 510) argues that the distinctiveness of contemporary French capitalism is that it has incorporated modern forms of financial control and integrated them with traditional property-based forms of authority.

French 'co-operative capitalism' also differs from its British and American counterparts in its continuing reliance upon close personal networks with interlocking directorships as well as the shareholdings referred to above. Windolf found that in 1995 there was an extraordinarily high binary density of 0.87 among the directorships of 15 large French firms – a density of 1 would mean that each firm had at least one director in all other 14 firms. This density of interlocking directorships appears to have changed little through the financialisation of French big business during the second half of the 1990s. Thus *Le Monde* confirmed that 30 current or former top French managers held over 160 directorships in France's biggest firms in 2001. Twenty-four of these top executives (including just one woman) are listed in Table 6.2.

But French top managers did not only sit on the boards of other big firms. Another study, of 470 French firms, found that one-third of them placed directors on boards of companies they invested in even when their holding was less than 10 per cent. The comparative 1995 proportion of 808 British firms was 0.8 per cent (Windolf 1999: 518–20).

The importance of interlocking groups to the wider French economy developed further in the 1980s and 1990s at the same time as the average

Table 6.2 Interlocking large firm directors, 2001

Name	Company origin	Name	Company origin
Bernard Arnault	*LVMH*	Gérard Mestrallet	*Suez*
Patricia Barbizet	*Artémis*	Lindsay Owen-Jones	*L'Oréal*
Claude Bébéar	*Axa*	Michel Pébereau	*BNP-Paribas*
Jean-Louis Beffa	*Saint-Gobain*	Jean Peyrelevade	*Crédit lyonnais*
Daniel Bernard	*Carrefour*	Didier Pineau-Valencienne	*Ex-Schneider*
Michel Bon	*France Télécom*	Badouin Prot	*BNP-Paribas*
Bertrand Collomb	*Lafarge*	Bruno Roger	*Lazard*
Therry Desmarest	*TotalFinaElf*	Edouard de Royère	*Air liquide*
Michel François-Poncet	*ex-Paribas*	Ernest-Antoine Seillière	*Wendel investissement–Medef*
Jacques Friedman	*ex-UAP*	Serge Tchuruk	*Alcatel*
Henri Lachman	*Schneider*	Marc Vienot	*ex-Société générale*

Source: *Le Monde*, 19 July 2002.

Table 6.3   Assets, turnover and numbers employed in financial and industrial consolidated groups, 1991 and 1994

Numbers employed in consolidated group	Number of groups		Employees (in thousands)		Turnover ex. taxes (francs bn)		Capital assets (francs bn)	
	1991	1994	1991	1994	1991	1994	1991	1994
Micro groups (0–499)	1,631	4,909	273	627	538	962	520	672
Small groups (500–1999)	854	1,006	847	968	1,126	1,445	674	1,025
Medium groups (2,000–9,999)	261	291	1,018	1,106	1,374	1,835	866	1,879
Large groups (10,000+)	80	80	3,260	3,179	3,562	4,116	3,517	4,959
Total	2,826	6,286	5,398	5,880	6,600	8,358	5,577	8,535

Source: INSEE, *Annuaire statistique de la France* 1994: 407; 1998: 450.

numbers employed by the very largest groups declined. Table 6.3 shows that the top 80 firms lost some direct employment between 1991 and 1994 while the numbers employed by France's 'micro' groups more than doubled.

The process of forging strategic network alliances among small firms, and the splitting off by medium and larger firms of subsidiaries developed enormously. Over a longer period than shown in Table 6.3, between the end of 1980 and the end of 1995 the total numbers of all linked groups operating in France rose from 1,300 to 6,700, of which one in five were non-French owned. Among firms with under 500 workers the numbers of network groups went up eight times as firms responded to tightening competition through mergers, demergers, take-overs and product specialisation (Bordes and Gonzalez-Demichel 1998: 449).

Concurrently France's giant groups set about systematically extending their influence over the medium and small-firm sector. One form this took was through the creation of their own small and medium-sized wholly or partially owned subsidiaries. In 1980, large groups with 10,000 employees or more had just 3,000 subsidiaries; by 1995 they had 10,300. But other forms in which this influence was expressed included buying minority shares in SMEs; establishing joint ventures; developing dominant sub-contracting relationships; and through co-operation agreements (Duchéneaut 1995: 228–34). Overall, between 1980 and 1995 the numbers of non-independent firms increased five times to 44,700 (Bordes and Gonzalez-Demichel 1998: 426).

This internal reordering of business activity towards subsidiary status and sub-contracting allowed greater local autonomy while simultaneously maintaining the personal presence (or voice) as a controlling and coordinating mechanism. Thus although senior managers articulate the values of open and 'free' competition, the reality is somewhat different. Much business is done between men who know and trust each other. The success of French 'co-operative capitalism' has been largely based on the capacity of this elite to control the market, competition and the state. The procedures for recruitment to this elite continue to rely on three long-standing institutions: inheritance, the *grandes écoles*, and the shuffle (*pantouflage*) of meritocratically successful top civil servants (and their networks) from government or nationalised firms into private business.

This last process has become much more influential since 1986 with the full or partial privatisation of large parts of the nationalised market sector. The importance of the state-owned, formerly nationalised firms and family-controlled or influenced firms can be seen among France's 30 largest industrial and non-finance service groups shown in Table 6.4.

Three tendencies are worth noting. First, with 12 of these 30 being either current or former state-owned firms it is clear that large-scale French industry retains close organic links with the state. This occurs through state shareholding participation or recent experience of it, through the continuing exchange of top administrators, or more indirectly, through remaining a major client (particularly in the defence sector but also in transport). The close links between top civil servants and industry work both ways: while the industrialists promote unitarist solutions within government, the weight of the huge state enterprises or of state interests continues to exercise considerable pluralist influence over private sector management.

A second tendency concerns another 13 of these 30 non-finance sector firms – those either still dominated by family holdings or partly protected by extensive cross shareholdings. Adding these firms to those which continue to have a direct state shareholding means that the direct influence of the shareholder value, stock market mentality is mediated for roughly three quarters of these big firms. Of course there are still internal pressures on their managers to emulate 'normal' performances elsewhere, pressures, above all, for companies to maximise their stock market value and to secure high short-term dividends (if necessary by merging, taking over other asset rich companies, or being taken over themselves). But the point is that other calculations linked to the influence of the state or the key shareholding family may also be taken into account.

The third tendency observed is that the presence of network capitalism has clearly not deterred foreign, and particularly Anglo-Saxon investors. Compared to the one-third non-French ownership of *all* French publicly quoted firms, the flagship French groups are on average even more exposed to non-French shareholders, and this exposure is increasing. A 2001 study found that the share of the top 40 quoted firms on the French Bourse held by non-French residents was 41.29 per cent or 45.57 per cent excluding

Table 6.4   Share ownership of 30 largest industrial and non-financial service groups, 1997 and 2002, ranked by 1998 turnover

Group name	1998 Turnover (FF. bn)	1997 Non-French shares (%)	1996 Employer (in thousands)	1998 Type of control	2002 Non-French (%)	2002 Anglo-Saxon (%)
Renault	243.9	18	141	P-S	30	14*
Peugeot	221.4	38	139	F	41	23
Promodès	213.5	13	55	F		
Carrefour	179.7	11	109	F	30.5	12
Elf-Aquitaine	211.6	47	85	X-s		
Total	159.6	50	58	P-s		
TotalFinaElf					65	35*
Vivendi	208.0	38	217	X	23	18
Suez Lyonnaise des Eaux	203.0	20	190	X	52	21.5
EDF	185.0		120	S		
France Télécom	161.7		165	P-S	11	3
Alcatel–Alstom	139.5	38	101	X-s		
Alcatel					50	40
Alstom					51.5*	47*
Saint-Gobain	116.9	34	112	X-s	51	22*
Pinault-Printemps-Redoute	108.3	25	63	F	35	n.a.
Bouygues	96.0	30	92	F	30	22
Casino Guichard	92.8	20	55		8	5
Rhône-Poulenc	86.8	40	75	P-s		
Danone	84.8	30	82	P	44	24
Michelin	81.9	23	120	F	50.7	24*
L'Oréal	75.4	43	43	F	20	6.5*
Usinor	71.8	30	57	P-s		
Lagardère	70.1	33	47		42	32
Eridania Béghin-Say	64.8	73	19	SUB		
Pechiney	64.5	n.a.	36	P-s		
Lafarge	64.3	38	35	P	58.5	31
Aerospatiale	54.9	n.q.	38	S		
Schneider	50.0	33	63	P	34	26
LVMH	45.5	23	21	F	17	5
Thomson CSF/Thales	40.5	23	65	P-S	13.9*	11*
Air Liquide	39.9	22	28	P	34.9	15.5*
Valeo	39.5	47	75		35*	19*

* = 2001 data; n.a. = not available; n.q. = not quoted; P = Public company, no dominant share holder; s = Significant state holding; S = Formerly state owned; X = Cross holdings significant; F = Family holding significant; SUB = Partly-owned subsidiary of a non-French MNC. Firms named in italic no longer existed in 2002.

Sources: *Le Monde*, 23 March 1999: 20; 8 November 1997: 17; 15 June 2001: 22; 22 June 2002: 20; OECD 1997b: 141; Bordes and Gonzalez-Demichel 1998: 135.

France Télécom and its affiliate Orange. The same Georgeson Shareholding study found still higher levels of foreign ownership among certain French finance giants. Thus, Dexia was 74 per cent foreign owned, AGF (54 per cent owned by the German giant Allianz) was 73 per cent, AXA 52 per cent, BNP-Paribas 40 per cent and Crédit Lyonnais 35 per cent (*Le Monde*, 15 June 2001). By June 2002, despite the slide in the world stock markets, the trend continued. Of 32 of the stocks that make up the CAC 40, the Paris Bourse index of prices, a slightly higher 42.6 per cent were foreign-owned, and the Anglo-Saxon share had risen from 20 per cent a year earlier to 24 per cent (*Le Monde*, 22 June 2002).

Far from being anathema to non-French institutional investors, French network capitalism was identified as a source of strength and as an investment opportunity. While the relatively high values of the dollar and sterling compared to the French franc and the euro after 1995 may have rendered French stock comparatively cheap, the external shareholders appeared satisfied by French management style and profitability. In the notable case of Vivendi in 2002, the American pension fund nominee directors only finally pulled the plug on Jean-Marie Messier's opaque financing and self-allocation of stock options after Vivendi's share values fell more sharply than the CAC average for several months.

Financial deregulation

The growth in the numbers of French firms significantly 'exposed' to stock market influence, and particularly to Anglo-Saxon pension and insurance fund investors, reflects the retreat of the state described in Chapter 5 and the near revolution in business financing since the mid-1980s. The cumulative changes were dramatic, as shown in Table 6.5.

Whereas in the 1970s firms had financed themselves principally by borrowing from the banks (55 per cent), by self-financing out of cash flow (39 per cent) and share issues comprised just six per cent, the average for the three years 1995–1997 showed self-financing had risen to 65 per cent, with share issues making up 23 per cent and bank borrowing had fallen to just 12 per cent of company financing (Duménil and Lévy 2000: 156). The financialisation of French capitalism was well under way.

There are several aspects to this evolution. There was the turnaround from a state-dominated banking system to a privately-owned one where family-ownership plays a less significant part. There was the emergence from nowhere of a powerful new financial institution, the stockbroker, which has become a major vehicle for holding liquid assets. There has been a huge shift in bank business from providing loans to share dealings. Borrowing was overtaken by shares as the main mechanism besides self-financing for raising company finance – although share issues still only constituted five per cent of all new investment in 1997. There is the increased activity of companies in buying and selling shares – much in line with the financialisation

Table 6.5   Structure of business financing, 1980–1997

	1980	1984	1992	1995	1997
Numbers of credit organisations:					
Publicly-owned banks		112			30
Privately-owned commercial banks		0			57
Mutual banks		5			28
Controlled by family or independent shareholders		34			14
% of French liquid assets held by:					
All banks (commercial and mutual)	61.1			45.0	
State savings banks and Post Office	34.6			28.4	
Share brokers	0			21.9	
% of deposits held by top 5 banks			59.3		68.6
% of commercial bank business as:					
Loans to customers	84.2				50.9
Share placements	4.8				34.6
Cheques as % of all banking operations	77.6				46.9
Credit card as % of all banking operations	2.4				24.9
% of international activities by credit orgs.			39.9		48.0
Shares as a % of external company finance	27.2				80.0

Source: Plihon 1998.

of contemporary American capitalism. Then there is the internationalisation of finance activities, and the emergence of the credit card as a major financial instrument.

However, elite network capitalism survived. France's very largest banks actually increased their hold over the whole economy and an interlocking web of financial and industrial interests survives at the heart of the system. This system is shown graphically in Figure 6.1 reproduced originally in *Le Monde* from the OECD (1997b: 136) and Plihon (1998: 35), and updated by me to take into account the outcome of the big bank take-over battle of 1999 between Société Générale and the Banque Nationale de Paris (BNP), in which the latter's successful take-over of Paribas has reduced the numbers of major financial groups to five.

The interlocking web confirms the extent of the mutual interests of the French financial and industrial elites. Cross-holdings are the traditional way by which French managers protected themselves from hostile take-over bids and short-term stock market pressures. In 1994, 58 per cent of all quoted shares were held in this way, compared to 39 per cent in Germany, 25 per cent in Japan and 3 per cent in the United Kingdom (OECD 1997b: 125).

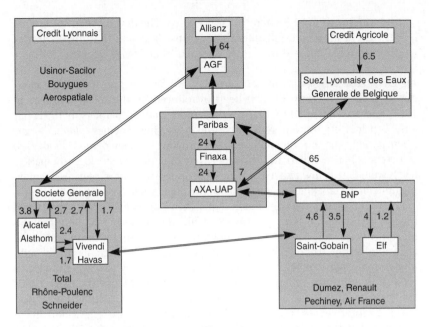

Figure 6.1 Major financial groups in 1998–1999
Sources: *Le Monde*, 17 June 1998, 25 August 1999.

The purchase of AGF by Europe's second largest insurance company, the German firm Allianz, in 1998 also underlines the importance of two major discontinuities: the merger and hostile take-over bid, and the increasing adoption of the Anglo-Saxon emphasis upon transparent reporting of company results and shareholder value (Coutrot 1998: 226–8). These intrusions have not been altogether welcomed by the doyens of French 'network capitalism'. In 1998, the financial director of Lagardère argued that too strong a presence of foreign investors on the Paris Bourse created an artificial volatility, a view shared by the then Socialist Minister of Finance, Dominique Strauss-Kahn. While British and American pension funds traditionally invest in long-term stock in their domestic markets, they are considered to be much more predatory and ready for short-term gains in overseas stock markets (Renault 1998). In June 2001 the managing director of Schneider, Henri Lachman, expressed a similar desire to retain some sort of protective 'French' safety net:

Firms are a collectivity that must take account of their clients and their markets, and also of all those who work within them. They must not, either, be subjected to the dictatorship of short-termism that too often dominates the financial markets. So it is important that, through capital investment, we root French firms in France. The development of French pension funds would facilitate that rooting. It is vital that the centres of decision remain based in France. (Quoted in *Le Monde*, 15 June 2001)

An employee saving scheme encouraging workers to save through investing in their own company had been introduced by the social Gaullists in 1967, and was extended to all firms with more than 50 workers in 1991. But although in 1995 there were 6,500 company saving schemes (*plan d'épargne d'entreprise*) in place, principally in larger firms where they owned on average somewhere between two and three per cent of company stock, participation levels were far too low to act as a real brake on the relocation of decision making or to create any kind of substitute for the huge Anglo-Saxon pension funds.

The result of the growing French dependence upon share placements and inward investment is that, whether they like it or not, the recipient companies are forced to respond to the demands of the Anglo-Saxon investors. Lachman argues that French businesses benefit considerably from such investments, particularly in an increase in transparency towards shareholders and in 'an improvement in business governance'. Since the early 1990s French companies have increasingly established formal audit and remuneration committees to try and indicate greater transparency, and have accepted that capital has a cost that must be repaid through higher rates of return. All France's major companies have now adopted target rates for returns on capital employed of between 10 and 15 per cent a year, and in order to deliver these have increasingly embarked on programmes selling off less profitable subsidiaries. In 1997, for example, Danone, under pressure from the Agnelli family, its major Italian shareholder, sold its underperforming pasta (Panzani) and Carambar businesses before seeking a listing on the New York stock exchange (*Le Monde*, 8 November 1997: 17). By the summer of 1999 with the bids and counter-bids between Total and Elf, and Paribas, the Société Générale and BNP, pension fund and other private company shareholder demands for either higher share prices or higher returns or both, were increasingly determining industrial policy. Decision-making with considerable consequences for employment relations was taking place with significantly fewer social constraints than had existed under the different configuration of class mobilisation that had existed 20 years earlier. This evolution can be traced in the series of large-scale redundancies announced by Michelin in September 1999 and by Danone in 2001.

6.2   Medium and small capitalism

How have medium and small-scale French firms been affected by the changes of the 1980s and 1990s? Much of the medium and small-scale French industry remained partly insulated from the trials and tribulations facing the survival of big network capitalism. It remained small-scale and unphased by much of the public attention given to Anglo-Saxon investment funds and globalisation. Of France's 2.3 million firms, only 110,000 were involved in exporting goods in 1998. In that year independent firms (not the subsidiaries of larger firms) with fewer than 500 staff provided only 25 per cent of all exports, compared to the ten per cent provided by just four giant firms (Renault, Peugeot, Citroen and Airbus Industrie) (*Les Échos*, 18 February 1999). Half of all exports are made by just 250 firms (Duchéneaut 1995: 477).

This is not to argue that the small independent firm sector is disconnected from the medium and the large. The 1980s and 1990s saw a dramatic increase in the power of large French firms. They extended their majority or minority shareholdings in small firms and increased their control through sub-contracting and demands on product quality. In 1994, one representative survey of France's 137,000 small (10–49) and 22,600 medium (50–499) firms in commerce, building and industry quantified these 'network' relationships. More than half of their capital was owned by another firm in 12 per cent of the small and 39 per cent of the medium-sized firms; while of all the independent firms, 37 per cent were fully or partly dependent on sub-contracting, particularly (and traditionally) in the construction sector. But even in industry, transport and services, between a fifth and one-third of 'independent' SMEs were either fully or partially integrated sub-contractors (Duchéneaut 1995: 233–4). A 1990 government study of small and medium-sized industrial businesses, found only one in five firms (two-thirds of which had fewer than 50 staff) without any practical form of alliance or co-operation with other firms (cited in *ibid.*: 186). Subsequently, with the emergence of flexible-specialisation, the role of the personal (education or local friendship) network of contacts of small and medium-sized business proprietors became still more important through the 1990s.

Co-operation between small firms may range from membership of an information exchange network to, more commonly, agreements to co-operate on sales. In agreements between firms, one study showed that nearly half the firms most often relied upon shared norms and values to secure adherence, a quarter referred to confidence and experience, and one in six relied on individual trust (Duchéneaut 1995: 190). About one in six small firms also belong to one of France's wealthy 153 Chambers of Commerce and Industry. Given a legal status in 1898 their contemporary role is to provide information on markets, to offer firms advice and support, to train managers and to help develop the local economic infrastructure. In the course of time these last two functions have led them to become a major player in higher and adult education (with roughly half a million students) and in facility management (e.g. they manage 110 of France's 121 airports). In 1990, the Chambers of Commerce directly employed 26,000 staff and had a FF21bn annual income, of which roughly a third was the receipts of a special training tax imposed by the state (Duchéneaut 1996: 118–27).

While the influence of large capital over small makes the very definition of an SME more problematic than it already is (should it be by numbers of employees or by turnover?), the weight of this sector in the French economy remains considerable. Mainly shops or other commercial businesses, transport businesses and industrial firms, an estimate of the numbers involved and their contribution to the French output in the early 1990s is shown in Table 6.6.

With something like four out of five small firms with less than 50 workers independent of larger firms, and with 52.5 per cent of French employees (outside the state sector) working in firms with less than 50 workers, it appears that somewhere between 40 and 45 per cent of all French employees work in completely 'independent' very small businesses. And these are overwhelmingly family affairs. In Duchéneaut's 1994 survey of SMEs with 10–499 employees, 84 per cent of their managing directors controlled directly or indirectly the majority of capital in their firm (Duchéneaut 1996: 41).

What does the experience of a small family firm entail? Three arguments are put forward to suggest that the experience is generally positive. Working for small firms is held to offer a more convivial family atmosphere. The ideal goal for up to half of small French entrepreneurs is to pass their firm on to their children, rather than to seek growth for its own sake. Growth often entails greater risk and borrowing money threatens their independence, so they prefer to retain a family, extended 'family' or 'clan' atmosphere. A second argument is that these firms are less bureaucratic, with workers more easily 'lending a hand' to others when required. There is less paperwork and greater access to the boss (or bosses) is claimed to permit workers to feel more involved in the decision-making process. A third argument is that small firms are more culturally attuned to French traditions than are larger firms. When a representative sample of adults was asked in 1994 where they

Table 6.6   Employment and company turnover by size, 1991 and 1993

Number of employees in firm	1991		1993	
	Workers (in thousands)	Employment share (%)	Turnover (francs bn)	Turnover share (%)
Micro (0–9)	3,351	25	2,325	19
SME	*8,074*	*59*	*5,706*	*45*
10–49	3,755	27.5	2,446	19
50–99	1,494	11	1,018	8
100–199	1,398	10	1,038	8
200–499	1,427	10.5	1,204	10
Large (500+)	2,215	16	4,593	36
Total	*13,641*	*100*	*12,624*	*100*

Source: Duchéneaut 1995: 53, 59.

would rather work, if they had a choice, over half replied in a small rather than a large firm (Duchéneaut 1995: 76–9).

However, other evidence provides a different perspective. Many small employers continue to believe in their 'divine right' to manage (Préel 1989: 199). Even those who are less paternalistic often focus most directly on the most urgent issues of production, sales and finance, and either remain untrained and ignorant of person-management or just do it badly. When it comes to informing workers about a whole range of issues on which they have increasingly been seen as having a right to knowledge (the economic situation of the firm, employment and salary trends, training, promotion procedures and so on), very small firms (10–49 staff) are less likely than those slightly larger and much less likely than large firms (1,000 plus staff) to provide employees routinely with this information (Duchéneaut 1995: 85). A further illustration of this managerial unitarism is the evidence that one in four of the firms (particularly the single-owners but also where large firms still had a high number of hierarchical levels) which gave management interviews to the 1999 *Réponse* researchers then denied their request to distribute questionnaires to the employees (Zouary 2002: 7).

The small firm and non-union environment is also, arguably, commensurate with greater individual risk taking at work, perhaps being one factor in helping to explain why France's average annual fatal accident rate in manufacturing over the six years 1990–1995 was 51 per million compared to the United Kingdom's 16 per million (calculated from data in Vernon 2000). What is certainly the case is that workers in SMEs work longer hours than those in larger firms and that the staff turnover rate in firms with 10–49 workers is double that of firm with 500 or more (Duchéneaut 1995: 118–19). A national survey in 1992 found that just 7 per cent of workers in the 10–19 employee firms had undergone some planned external training, compared to 12 per cent in firms with 20–49 workers rising to 55 per cent in firms with 2,000+ workers. Not surprisingly the same survey found that managers and skilled professionals made up just 10 per cent of those in firms with 20–49 workers, compared to 15.3 per cent of those in the 2,000+ firms (*ibid.*: 128–31). What is the evidence about differences in management practices between big and small firms?

6.3 Changing management behaviour

The evidence that management practices have significantly changed since 1980 is contradictory. On the one side there is some cultural evidence (admittedly from less rigorous surveys than that analysed by Hofstede) suggesting continuities with past. But there is also a more weighty suggestion from the French workplace industrial relations surveys conducted in 1992 and 1998, involving in each case over 3,000 face-to-face interviews in different companies with managers and often with employee representatives. Their evidence suggests that Taylorist and neo-Taylorist organisational strategies remained deeply implanted. On the other hand, there is evidence that some sections of French management have implemented several components of HRM as well as company accounting procedures. Bob Hancké's detailed examination of Renault, EDF and Moulinex management between 1985 and 1995 also concludes that having faced 'a dramatic productivity and profitability crisis' in the early 1980s, French large firms re-organised their 'governance arrangements' to give them 'free rein to restructure'; 'a critical condition for readjustment was the autonomy of management' (Hancké 2001: 239, 205).

The cultural evidence of continuity comes from Hampden-Turner and Trompenaars (1993: 339–44). In the early 1990s, they found that their French management respondents were much more likely to see a business as a 'web of social relations with the dilemma of Profit versus Stakeholders' well-being' than were American managers, who were more likely to see it as reducible to a system of tasks and functions. Equally, when asked to choose between individual freedom and improvement and collective improvement, while the Americans chose the former the French were much more likely to choose the latter. Hampden-Turner and Trompenaars then cite other research by INSEAD's André Laurent, who surveyed the different nationalities of the aspirant managers who went to study there, confirming also that considerable differences remain between American and French managers. Laurent's findings are reproduced in Table 6.7.

Table 6.7   Franco-American management attitudinal differences, around 1990

	Agreement (%)	
	French managers	US managers
The manager of tomorrow will be, in the main, a negotiator	86	50
An organisation structure in which certain subordinates have two direct bosses should be avoided at all costs	83	54
Through their professional activity, managers play an important political role in society	76	52
Today there seems to be an authority crisis in organisations	64	22
Most managers seem more motivated by obtaining power than by achieving objectives	56	36
It is important for a manager to have at hand precise answers to most of the questions that his subordinates may raise about their work	53	18
The main reason for having a hierarchical structure is that everyone knows who has authority over whom	45	18

Source: Hampden-Turner and Trompenaars 1993: Chapter 13.

French managers were still more likely to see managerial activity as being about power and political influence, and they continued to focus more on the need to appear all knowing. They were also more concerned about their authority and their position within their company's hierarchical structure than were the surveyed American managers. The picture drawn is not greatly dissimilar to Hofstede's predictions about the consequences of high power distance and uncertainty avoidance cultures drawn from research conducted two decades earlier (see Table 3.2). The influence of Cartesian rationality among French managers, cultivated by an educational system that exalts success in mathematics, remains strong. In his exhaustive study of SME managers Duchéneaut (1996: 48) quotes Hervé Serieyx as describing Cartesian logic as being a method of simplifying complex problems into a series of clear linear steps capable of logical resolution, and comments:

> The French manager is certainly a man of power, but he is also very marked by a Cartesianism that prevents him from seeing situations other than from a rational perspective.

Providing a perspective that suggests greater real change in management practice is the evidence of the first major national workplace employment relations study conducted in France. The 1992 *Réponse* Survey (Coutrot and Paraire 1996) found that one in five organisations with more than 50 employees claimed to practise 'just-in-time' production, working without in-house production stocks, and one in three used multidisciplinary project work teams. Slightly over one in three companies claimed to practise 'total quality management', but only 8 per cent indicated their compliance with the ISO quality norm. A total of 11 per cent reported having established in the previous three years 'autonomous work groups' of multi-skilled employees who organised their work themselves on the basis of objectives determined by their line managers. Considering all four of these innovations half of all French organisations had not implemented any, a third had introduced one, 12 per cent two and 5 per cent three or all four. Contrary to the researchers' expectations, the innovating firms were distributed across all sizes of firms, although those who had implemented three or four innovations did tend to be the 1,000+ size organisations (Coutrot 1996: 175–6). Different innovations, too, appealed more to different industries: 'just-in-time' was more concentrated in the industrial sector, while multidisciplinary project teams were more likely to be found in the predominantly process sectors, commerce, health and banking (Coutrot 1996: 210).

Not only, however, did these innovating organisations take on board these largely American-originated or recycled ideas, they also changed their structures. In the three years prior to the survey, 46 per cent established new departments to deal with sales and marketing, one-third closed old functionally-structured departments, and 37 per cent reported having changed the old job classifications of their employees (Coutrot 1996).

Table 6.8 Organisations practising participative management, 1993

Workplaces with %	Shop meeting	Quality circle	Suggestion box	Company charter
Establishment size				
5–19	64.4	29.3	18.6	23.6
20–49	70.3	31.0	17.4	26.6
50–99	73.0	34.7	23.3	26.3
100–199	77.9	37.4	21.6	28.7
200–499	80.1	44.0	25.7	34.0
500–999	88.0	64.8	24.3	40.0
1000+	81.7	67.8	28.2	51.5
All organisations	70.2	33.1	20.2	26.2

Source: Coutrot and Paraire 1996.

The first *Réponse* survey also found, as shown in Table 6.8, that a significant proportion of these 50+ employee-sized organisations, often operating units with many different sized workplaces, had introduced formal participation processes.

Shop (or office or section) meetings were more common in 1992 than in 1990, when only 59 per cent of organisations held them; when they were held, more than half had held seven or more in 1992. Quality circles started appearing in the early 1980s, but then surged forward in 1985 and again between 1990 and 1992, when one-third of those existing in 1992 were set up. Although perhaps one in five of these were no longer meeting, in half the organisations where they did exist they met at least five times a year. They were particularly strong in those 500+ employee workplaces with well-established personnel or HRM (*Gestion des ressources humaines*) teams, where the influence of France's approximately 50,000 HR professionals (varying between one and 3.5 per cent of total employment) was strongest (Cazal and Peretti 1992: 76–7). These, too, were the workplaces which, especially since 1988, were most likely to have developed Company Charters aimed at forging a strong company culture, and where organisation 'open days' were most likely to be held (in one-third of the 1000+ group) (Coutrot and Paraire 1996). The evidence appears clear: by the mid-1990s around 20–30 per cent of French organisations were implementing both the restructuring and the HR practices associated with the new American managerialism.

Thus, at the time of the 1993 *Réponse* survey French management was living a contradiction. Some firms had been thoroughly 'modernised' and had brought or were bringing their organisation and its control systems into line with international 'best practice' by genuinely seeking to win the co-operation of their employees. This 'choice' has most frequently been exercised where these employees bring high value to the process of production or service delivery, and where the quality of the output or of the company–client relationship must be of the highest level.

At the same time, other managers were consciously using the rise in unemployment to exercise their traditional levers of power, to reinforce the military managerial model, and to impose rather than seek to win unitarist control of the workplace. For many, particularly in smaller firms, paternalism has remained virtually unchallenged. Thus the *Villermé* Association of Labour Inspectors reported between 12,000 and 15,000 employee representatives being fired or made redundant each year in the 1990s in a continuing 'massive, direct or disguised repression' (Garcia and Monnot 1999). This implementation of 'hard' HRM, or 'numerical' flexibility, is what Coutrot calls 'forced co-operation' (Coutrot 1998: 217–51).

Another group of managers, particularly those in France's large firms where the trade unions remain well implanted (and especially in the public sector or recently privatised companies), have not even had the luxury of 'choice' about their approach. They have had to accept the political and legal obligations of a pluralist work environment that has restricted considerably their room to manoeuvre.

From the mixture of experiences that made up French firms in the early 1990s, Thomas Coutrot identified the five main types of French firms shown in Table 6.9.

Roughly 40 per cent of firms continued to work along traditional hierarchical lines and exercise control over their workers through paternalistic and/or authoritarian methods. They were largely small-sized businesses. A further third (largely medium-sized) had embraced new technology to control the work process, and exercised numerical control over their

Table 6.9 Typology of firms and management regimes (in 50+ workplaces), 1993

Firm type	Size	Market	% of firms	% of workforce	Work regime	Employee relations
Post-Fordist	Large	National	17	15	Controlled autonomy	Conflictual, soft HRM
Neo-Fordist	Large	Gobal	10	20	Controlled autonomy	Conflictual, hard HRM
Computer-assisted Neo-Taylorist	Medium	European	29	33	Limited autonomy	Passive, hard HRM
Traditional	Small	Regional	33	26	Hierarchical control	Paternalist, authoritarian
Traditional and incompetent	Small	Local	7	7	Hierarchical control	Direct, authoritarian

Source: Adapted from Coutrot 1998: 41–61.

employees without any significant resistance. Among the larger firms there were two main work regimes: about a fifth of all workers were subjected to a 'neo-Fordist' work process, where their degree of autonomy is structured by the production system. Within the HRM literature these firms would generally be qualified as implemented 'hard' HR strategies, focusing essentially on numeric flexibility. Only around one in six workers was offered a 'post-Fordist' work environment with some real degree of albeit still controlled autonomy – for short, a 'soft' HR strategy.

What additional evidence is brought to bear by the second *Réponse* survey that interviewed managers and employee representatives between December 1998 and May 1999? From the results published so far it appears as if the divisions noted above, between a majority exercising 'hard' HR control strategies and a minority 'soft' have persisted. Table 6.10 compares the presence and evolution of management techniques divided by me into whether they were 'soft' or 'hard' HRM or concerned greater participation, between the two survey periods of 1993 and 1999.

Table 6.10 Developments in organisational and operational management, as a percentage of *Réponse* survey respondents, 1993 compared with 1999

Measure	1993	1999	Change
'Hard' HRM			
ISO compatability (lean)	12.4	33.8	+21.4
Just-in-time (lean)	28.9	35.2	+6.3
Contraction of managerial hierarchy (lean)	29.7	30.1	+0.4
Job elimination	35.0	33.7	−1.3
Use of numerical controlled machines/robots	21.6	16.3*	−5.3
Development of sub-contracting	28.3	19.2	−9.1
New job classifications	39.3	24.7	−14.6
Participation strategies			
Company Charter	29.6	32.7	+3.1
Suggestion box	22.0	24.9	+2.9
Departmental meetings	76.1	77.3	+1.2
Workplace newspaper	35.4	34.2	−1.2
Company open days	15.5	13.0	−2.5
'Soft' HRM			
Project team working (team)	39.1	63.1	+24
Autonomous work teams (team)	11.9*	35.0	+23.1
Quality circles (team)	42.3	53.6	+11.3
Computer-assisted production	37.8	38.6	+0.8
Repatriating sub-contracted work	16.6	10.3	−6.3
Job specialisation	30.8	24.2	−6.6
Direct expression groups	32.9	21.5	−11.4

* Questions not directly comparable between the two surveys.

Source: Coutrot 2000b: 2, 5.

There was a major jump forward in the proportions of firms with ISO certification and of those who were implementing team working, although given that 'project team working' became a major managerial fad in the 1990s, and that its name was subsequently given to virtually any group of people who met more than two or three times to discuss a particular problem, it is probably wrong to herald this as a major change in work organisation. With stability in the use of many other techniques and decline in the use of some others, the overall conclusion still appears to be one of little overall change in the proportions of firms divided between Coutrot's 'post-Fordist' and 'neo-Fordist' or 'neo-Taylorist' categories, while the proportions of firms that had not innovated at all, or only a little, also remained constant. One significant change did, however, occur between the two surveys. Whereas in 1993, there was no statistical association between the most organisationally innovative of firms and economic growth, by 1999 that association was clear. Without being able to distinguish the cause and effect, the highly innovative firms, which implemented more frequently both the 'lean' and the 'team' elements flagged up in Table 6.10, were the firms that grew fastest, were most exposed to international competition, had the highest proportions of skilled workers, made the most use of individualised pay increases and stock options, and had the lowest turnover, despite also shedding labour more often than the less innovative firms (Coutrot 2000a: 11; 2000b).

Two important points emerge from this research. First, the nature of the market does appear to be a key element in shaping the kinds of ways firms are changing. Second, it seems clear that in the 1990s there is no single 'new productive model' dominating France. Even in the 15 per cent of firms where 'post-Fordist' attempts at employee involvement have been taken the furthest, the 'autonomy' that has been given is strictly controlled and industrial relations are often conflictual.

Perhaps the safest conclusion to draw is that there is both continuity and change in work organisation and management employment relations strategy, although it is clear that the change is more concentrated in the larger firms. The findings can be sketched (see Figure 6.2) to indicate the presence of these different, overlapping but also often complementary tendencies in contemporary French management.

Unitarism and pluralism are present in roughly equal proportions among the largest firms, which bargain both through their employers' association and at the level of the firm. Pluralist firms are divided, with the ideology of bargaining and rights of representation being increasingly challenged in large firms by a form of 'soft' HRM, where, while continuing to co-operate with formal bargaining procedures, managers also aim to win 'unforced' co-operation from their employees. Among small firms pluralism is virtually non-existent, although the legal extension procedure for collective agreements means that it continues to have some formal relevance in establishing national minimum pay scales and maximum hours.

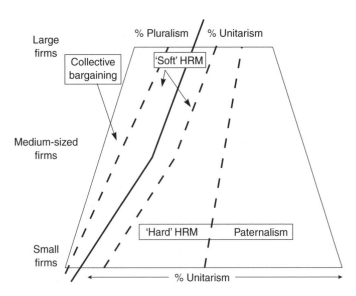

Figure 6.2   Unitarist and pluralist business cultures around 2000

The unitarist managerial perspective, by contrast, remains the dominant one in both large and small firms. It is present both as paternalist unitarism and unitarist HRM. Paternalism exercises undiluted personal authority in traditional ways, while the HRM approaches do so either through 'forced co-operation' ('hard' HRM) where the dominant logic is resource constraints, or through 'voluntary co-operation' (some forms of 'soft' HRM). When asked by the 1999 *Réponse* survey whether they would like to change the representation system in their workplace, the divisions among the employers became apparent. Only 15 per cent of employers responded that there was no problem while a further 43 per cent found the existing situation satisfactory although it could be improved. But on the other hand one in four (23.7 per cent) was either opposed in principle to employee representation or believed it served no useful function (Malan and Zouary 2000: 3).

6.4   Making managers

Managers are changing in France, but less at the very top than in the layers below. Thus the three main mechanisms of entry to the very top are still in place. They are either via inherited wealth, or from a *grande école* via an industrial career or through *pantouflage* from the top echelons of the civil service. Between 1985 and 1993, while the proportion of chief executives of the top 200 firms who were founding entrepreneurs or who had inherited wealth remained around 30 per cent, those who had previously had careers in the top civil service rose slightly to about 45 per cent (Duchéneaut 1996: 57). The others are professional managers recruited either very young, and who then stay in the firm throughout their careers, or are recruited from other firms. Here we first look at two examples of these manager careers and then discuss in greater detail recent experiences of French *cadres*.

Claude Bébéar joined France's Rouen-based 17th largest insurance firm directly on leaving the elite *École Polytechnique* at the age of 23. In 1974, at the age of 39 he became its managing director and in 1982 began the construction of AXA, one of the world's largest insurance companies, by taking over a larger competitor. In 1991, he bought up the failing Equitable Life insurance company, and in 1996, UAP. He retired in 2000 and handed AXA's reins on to his chosen successor, Henri de Castries, but continues to exercise huge influence both through his directorships and personal networks. During the 1990s Bébéar, a Christian liberal, played a leading role among French employers, founding an employers' club, *Entreprise et Cité*, and pushing his neo-liberal protégé, Denis Kessler, to the number two position in the Medef (*Le Monde*, 15 June 2001). Bébéar's career is traditional with his educational starting point at a *grande école*, in his effectively staying in the same business and firm throughout, and in his high public profile as a representative of the collective French employer class. He exemplifies the *grande école* 'home-grown boss' (*patron maison*), who make up nearly one in three of the chief executives of France's top 100 firms.

More recently there is a growing acceptance in top management posts of experienced senior managers whose careers span more than one large firm, and whose elite membership does not come from birth or *grande école*. They made up about one in six of the biggest 100 in the late 1980s (Duchéneaut 1996: 56). Noel Goutard, Valeo's chief executive from 1986 to 2000, provides an example, although on the way he did a stint at the top of a then nationalised firm. Initially having a legal training at Paris and Bordeaux universities, Goutard retrained as a financial analyst and entered management. In a mobile career he worked his way up through Pfizer, Gevelot, Schlumberger, and Chargeurs and then was a managing director (*directeur générale*) at the nationalised firm Thomson, from 1983 to 1986, before taking the top job at the then loss-making Valeo. Having taken it into the ranks of the world's top ten automobile components' makers in 1993 Goutard was nominated 'manager of the year' by *Le Nouvel Économiste* (*Le Monde*, 4 April 2000).

While representative of some increase in meritocratic recruitment to the elite, Goutard remains representative of the gender domination of top jobs by men. The lack of change in the gender composition of recruitment to France's top business jobs is another continuity from the 1970s. One analysis of the top 5,000 French firms in 1996 found that women made up only two per cent of presidents, 4.7 per cent of managing directors and 7.6 per cent of directors. Even where women were in these top posts, they still tended to be tightly pigeon-holed. In 500+ firms one in four women directors was director of communication and one in six a director of HRM (Baron 2001: 250–1). While the 'class ceiling' privileging wealth or educational background is beginning to show signs of erosion, the 'glass ceiling' keeping women out of these top posts is still in place (Pigeyre 2001).

Change among lower management layers

There are several complex changes occurring among managers who are below board level. The most obvious is the continuing vast growth in the numbers of those whose work consists essentially of communication and co-ordination, as shown in Figure 6.3.

Unlike the wholly masculine level of top management, this new weighty class of managers includes a growing proportion of women. As many as two-thirds of the increase in those classified as 'company administrative or sales managers' since 1980 have been women (Baron 2001: 24). The consequence of this growth in an economic context in which large firms have been shedding staff (including managers) has been to erode much of the distinctive privileged status of the *cadre*. Thus more managers were made unemployed, numbers rising from 2.8 to 4.5 per cent between 1985 and 1998 (Frickey and Primon 2001: 170). In the 1999 census, 129,000 private, state and voluntary sector managers declared themselves unemployed compared to 86,000 in 1990 (Amossé 2001). In the ten years from 1984 there was also a 52 per cent increase in the numbers of managers who took cases to Industrial Tribunals (*conseil de prud'hommes*), with 25,095 cases being recorded in 1994. This disputatious trend is continuing. In Lyon alone the number of cases rose 40 per cent between 1989 and 1999 (Baron 2001: 52).

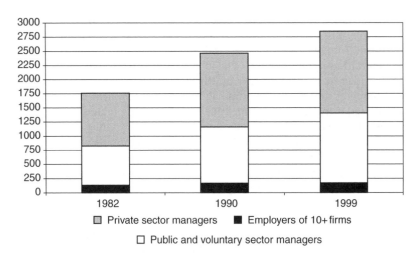

Figure 6.3   Numbers of managers, 1982–1999
Source: Amossé 2001.

Contemporary France is thus witnessing both continuities and discontinuities in the evolution of the management layers that separate the ruling
elite from the workers. The old layer of higher managers, *cadres supérieurs*,
remains in place but is being diluted by the growth of 'normal' university
entrants and women into its ranks and by changes in the nature of its work,
which is becoming increasingly subject to computer monitoring and control.
Originally, giving them a *status* that allowed them a 'certain freedom in
organising their time and movements' was one way of obscuring their subordination and securing their co-operation. But today's firms have less and
less need for people whose tasks are largely to order the activities of others,
and require more and more committed experts who can contribute directly
to raising productivity (Baron 2001: 121). The *cadres* have even been subjected to legal control over their working hours in the Aubry Law of 2000.

Historically the term *cadre* has been much narrower than the much looser
term 'manager' has become in the English language. *Cadres* are defined as
those whom collective agreements designate as eligible to vote in the 'Third
Electoral College' in elections to company Works Councils, and who in principle have higher education (*grande école* or university) training or equivalent professional experience. Thus, in 1997, 61 per cent of *cadres* have
degrees. Their status as an 'officially recognised' manager provides them
with certain privileges, particularly in their pension arrangements and if
they are made unemployed.

In addition, however, there are huge numbers of *assimilés cadres*, 'made-
up' managers, who also pay into the AGIRC management pension fund but
who do not meet the basic criteria for a *cadre*. One quarter of these had the
baccalauréat, and one in six had left school without even that (André-Roux
and Minez 1999: 141). Their being 'made-up' was permitted by Article 4 of
the national collective agreement of 1947 that allowed their assimilation
provided they met at least one of three criteria: having an equivalent training to other company managers and carrying out functions requiring the
application of acquired knowledge; being in a position of authority; or carrying out functions requiring initiative. Management numbers were further
expanded by a 1982 law that placed foremen in the management electoral
college for industrial tribunal elections (Bournois 1991: 38). Many made-up
managers are found in firms too small for managers to be entitled to separate representation or where firms ignore the law, but sales managers and
general business managers across all sectors and organisation sizes outside
the strictly controlled public and recently-privatised companies are nearly
all automatically 'made-up', sometimes to 'cadres' but often also as 'engineers'. Ever since 1934, when the right to award the professional status of
'engineer' was legally given to the *Commission du titre d'ingenieur*, companies
had the right to give that title (and the status of *cadre technique*) to anyone
doing the job. This status has been increasingly diluted in the 1980s and
1990s as firms found they needed to strengthen the ranks of intermediary

staff who would co-ordinate complex business processes and communicate both upwards and downwards. By 1996 of France's 670,000 'engineers and technical *cadres'*, two-thirds did not have an engineering diploma, and of those who did, one-third did not do any technical work (Bouffartigue 1998).

Driven by the greater number of distinct business organisations, by their smaller average size, and by their growing specialisation, the growing needs for commercial and technological cooperation have led to the numbers of French employees exercising co-ordination functions increasing more rapidly than total employment. This managerial expansion is reflected in the growth of the ranks of the higher-grade *cadres*. Between 1982 and 1997 numbers were up 17 per cent to 285,000 in the public sector, up 46 per cent to 801,000 in private firm administrative and sales functions and up 77 per cent to 660,000 among professional engineers and technical managers (Baron 2001: 68). Growth was especially strong, Paul Bouffartigue (2001) argues, among those who have some form of specialism and among women managers. The Baron (2001) data shows that between 1982 and 1997 women *cadres supérieurs* in the public sector increased from 24 to 31 per cent, among company administrative and commercial *cadres* their share rose from 20 to 33 per cent, and among professional engineers and technical *cadres* feminisation rose from 6 to 11 per cent.

Other sources confirm this pattern. In the ten years from 1984 among privately-owned and state market sector organisations with 20 or more employees the proportions of *cadres*, professionally qualified and technically qualified staff in total employment increased by 25 per cent, as shown in Table 6.11.

In the service sector, however, where average organisation size was smaller, the proportion of employees in these three categories rose from 32 to 39 per cent, that is to just over 1.5 million women and men compared to the just under one million men and women 'managers' employed in industry. If only three out of four of these actually had supervisory responsibilities this is

Table 6.11   Managers and qualified staff in 20+ market sector firms as a percentage of their total employment, 1984–1994

	Cadres		Professionals and sales managers		Professional and technical staff		Total cadres and qualified staff	
	1984	1994	1984	1994	1984	1994	1984	1994
Men	11.8	16	19.1	20.6	1.3	1.5	32.2	38.1
Women	4.3	8.1	11.9	15.6	4.8	5.8	21.0	29.5
All	9.2	13.1	16.6	18.8	2.5	3.1	28.3	35.0
Service sector	11.1	15.4	17.2	17.9	3.8	5.9	32.1	39.2

Source: Bordes and Gonzalez-Demichel 1998: 95–6.

a total of nearly two million in the commercial sector, to whom should be added the near 300,000 public sector employees who also had *cadres* status in 1997 and the 1.7 million individual employers in commercial and industrial organisations: a total of about four million managerial workers out of a total labour force of 25.5 million (André-Roux and Minez 1999: 141; Marchand and Thélot 1991a: 188).

By the end of the 1990s roughly one in six in the French labour force were employers or managers. Their education and the generalisation of American managerial approaches to France, therefore, has been at the centre of the expansion of higher education noted in Chapter 4. It also underlay the trend improvement in managerial professionalism.

Educating French managers

Three-quarters of France's most senior managers continue to be largely educated within the elite *grandes écoles* system. Table 6.12 compares the elite recruitment experience of Oxford and Cambridge in Britain with the way in which diplomas from the most exclusive of these elite universities shape the background of the CEOs (*présidents*) of France's top 200 firms in about 1995.

While Oxford and Cambridge delivered just one-third of British Chief Executive Officers, around one in four was produced by each of two post-graduate schools, the École Polytechnique and by ENA, with a further one in four coming from the other *grandes écoles*. Another analysis of 2,500 top appointments found that besides the Polytechnique, HEC and ENA, the nearly as elitist *Institut d'études politiques de Paris* (*Sciences Po* as it is known colloquially) had even more of its graduates appointed company director in 1993 than did the Polytechnique (Duchéneaut 1996: 49). Sciences Po was the university attended by the aristocrat Baron Ernest-Antoine Sellière, the future founder of the Medef, before he went on to the ENA (in the same year

Table 6.12 Educational background of top 200 company CEOs in France and Britain around 1994

		France %		Britain %
Grandes	Polytechnique	27	Oxford	15
Écoles	ENA	23	Cambridge	17
	HEC	7		
	Other *Grande école*	16		
Others	University	4	University	28
	Abroad	6	Abroad	4
	Self-taught	17	Self-taught	36
Total		100		100

Source: *Entreprise et Carrière*, 18 July 1995; reproduced in Duchéneaut 1996: 59.

as Lionel Jospin), started a diplomatic career and then returned to run his family firm, the Wendel financial conglomerate (*Le Monde*, 15 January 2002).

However, there were also changes. More intense international competition, a rising number of non-French multinationals located in France, the growing weight of non-French shareholdings and demands for higher quality outputs stepped up pressures on firms to learn about and adhere to 'best practice' in financial, organisational and HRM practices. Managers as a whole became more highly qualified. Between 1985 and 1998 the proportion of private business *cadres* who were qualified to the level of *Bac + 3* years of study rose from 37 to 46 per cent (Frickey and Primon 2001: 169). Even for professional engineers there has been an increase in post-18 business-oriented diplomas and degrees, as graphed in Figure 6.4.

While the share of the *grandes écoles* has remained just under 40 per cent, the proportion of engineering *cadres* who have been to the university or another technical school for at least two years has increased from a combined 42.4 per cent in 1990 to 50.3 per cent by 1997.

Management is thus now taught in much wider variety of higher education institutions. At the beginning of the 1990s the highly technical engineering-related areas of research, manufacturing and production remain dominated by graduates of France's prestigious engineering schools (in particular those of the first and most famous of Paris' *grandes écoles*, the *Polytechnique*, but also by regional schools). But the universities now compete strongly in the provision of lower class 'engineers' in computing, communications and company logistics (Bouffartigue 1998: 171). In these last two areas the *grande école* for business, the selective HEC and the other

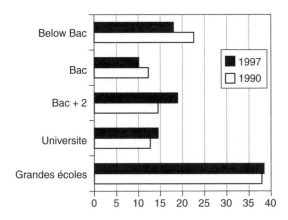

Figure 6.4   Educational level of professional engineers (percentage of total) 1990 and 1997

Source: Baron 2001: 137.

commercial schools established and run in France's major cities by the Chambers of Commerce from the receipts of a national training tax provide the core of recruits into *senior* management. This national training tax is also used by companies to sponsor employees, particularly 'made-up' managers, on adult post-experience education and training courses. In the 1990s, the state has increasingly pressed higher education to play a greater part in providing management training and retraining, particularly on short courses directed specifically at small and medium-sized businesses.

Many 18–24 year-old business students are often required to undertake (frequently unpaid) 'work experience' in firms as part of their studies (providing some firms with not insignificant savings) and then create a pool of mass recruitment to junior manager positions. The pull of American business schools has become strong, too. Not only is there quite intensive advertising for MBA programmes, but senior career patterns are beginning to change. Thus the latest member of the Michelin family to head up the (family-owned) tyre multinational was educated at American business schools and the management education now being offered as standard fare to these growing numbers of students is also structured firmly around the case study approach and content of American MBA programmes. Virtually everywhere a significant part of the teaching is conducted in the business language, English. As long ago as 1988 virtually one-third of Grenoble University's business school library consisted of American textbooks.

Today's dominant managerial paradigm is a more critically reflective American managerialism than the triumphalism of the 1960s and 1970s. Its core message stresses the key role of senior managers in mapping out change, in exercising greater levels of control and in extracting new levels of commitment from employees through more effective motivation. As competition intensified in the 1990s, American management further taught that managers must take on greater and more flexible responsibilities, while simultaneously responding more sensitively to customers. Mauro Guillén argues that the new HR paradigm is a blend of the American organisational models of scientific management and human relations:

> The business firm is seen as a community, almost to the exclusion of all other possible group memberships that workers may have. The buzzwords of the organizational culture paradigm include *sense of belonging, integrative leadership, organizational climate, involvement, participation, loyalty, commitment, harmony, interdependence, cohesiveness, and team spirit*…The echoes of the human relations paradigm could not resonate louder. The overall tone is strongly paternalistic. (Guillén 1994: 289–90) (*original emphasis*)

This tone helps explain why HRM took over so rapidly as it has in France. Starting from human relations theory, people's needs and motivations are put at the centre of organisational structure and business strategy. Bureaucratic management must be uprooted and replaced by a common culture of commitment to wider organisational goals. From this viewpoint managers are essentially inspirational leaders, and firms they lead thus have the option of adopting a 'quality scenario'.

This is very close to the technocratic and paternalist core values that we suggested in Chapter 3 have consistently characterised French management unitarism. Goff (Goff 1995: 50) makes the interesting point that this new management discourse is full of military phrases, citing extracts from French management guru books called *Mobilise for success* and *The Third Type of Firm*, such as 'Managers cannot win these battles alone', '(quality) circles allow commando action', and the need to congratulate managers for 'showing the company flag'. The paradigm's idealism also made it particularly attractive to the modernising Catholic wing of French management, helping advance the speed with which the managerial fashions of management-by-objectives, quality circles, just-in-time, lean production, re-engineering were implemented in France. In about 1988, the human resource department of the giant family-controlled Bouygues company produced the classic management catechism reproduced in Table 6.13 as a Charter for its *cadres*.

Another link between the 'traditional' Catholic-paternalist ideology and HRM practice lies in the encouragement of employee shareholding. In 1959, De Gaulle announced a profit-sharing scheme and in 1967 a new law made it possible under the scheme for workers to receive shareholdings in the companies for which they worked. This approach was then made concrete in Chirac's privatisation law of 1986, when up to 10 per cent of the stock of the privatised firm was to be reserved for the employees, who could buy them at a discount of 20 per cent below the offer price. As a result about three-quarters of the employees of the firms privatised bought stock, and they now hold an average of between three and four per cent of their capital, as shown in Figure 6.5.

Table 6.13   A modern management catechism at Bouygues, around 1988

Anticipate	Have the person you need, where and when you need them
Identify	Know how to bring on and conserve ability
Choose	Recruit fairly
Welcome	To win over new colleagues
Appreciate	So that everyone knows where they stand
Reward	In order to encourage personal effort
Give direction	In opening up perspectives for advancement
Train	To improve professionalism and bring out potential
Lead	Through participation to get more involvement
Communicate	Listen and dialogue to succeed together

Source: Reproduced in Cazal and Peretti 1992: 75.

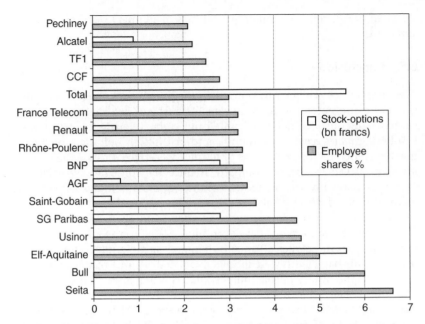

Figure 6.5   Employee shareholding in 1999 (in per cent) and stock options at 30 June 2001 (in billion francs) in fully or partly privatised French firms

Sources: Le Monde, 2 March 1999, 9 July 2001.

Several private sector firms also adopted this practice in the 1990s in order to try and stabilise their management and professional staff, making stock options more widely available than simply to their most senior directors. Thus between 1996 and 2000, the number of holders of stock options in the CAC 40 list of firms on the French stock exchange rose from 8,841 to 33,125. In 1999, the *Réponse* survey found stock option schemes present in three per cent of all workplaces, annual appraisals present in 44 per cent and individual bonuses in 52 per cent (Coutrot 2000: 7).

Yet, the recession of the early and mid-1990s also required many French companies to undergo major downsizing, often with repeated 'social plans' making employees redundant and reorganising the work of those who remained. Under these circumstances it was the 'harder' version of American HRM that was often embraced. This was much closer to 'neo-Taylorism', with an emphasis on the manipulation of inputs and outputs to engineer higher productivity and competitive advantage. It stresses 'resource' efficiency allocation as being the most critical element within the term 'human *resource* management'. In this efficiency paradigm managers are essentially inspired controllers, and competitive advantage is achieved on quality and price. The new managerialism taught in France's higher education system thus had the advantage of offering all things to all men (and they were still a majority).

6.5   Conclusion

This chapter has sketched the current principal features of French capitalism and management. At its heart remains a web of personal contacts that we have described as 'network capitalism': contacts made largely through family or *grandes écoles* backgrounds, and/or through holding senior positions in French nationalised firms or in the civil service. Despite the increasing part played in French company finance by 'foreigners', particularly by Anglo-Saxon investment funds, continuing cross-holdings between big finance and industrial capital still bed these personal contacts in place. Paradoxically, the mutual support and protection these continuing networks provide, are in many ways even more suited to the era of financialisation than to the earlier alliance of banking and manufacturing. This is because while bank loans were ultimately related to some real form of assets or product, the beauty of shareholder value is much more in the eye of the beholder. Policies that deliberately enhanced share value and distributed stock options widely to senior managers required exactly the particularly compliant form of corporate governance that the contemporary French network capitalism provides.

It is certainly true, as Hancké (2002) argues that managers have greater autonomy from the state than before the mid-1980s; and it is also true, as Morin (2000) argues, that shareholder value has become a major ideological weapon used by senior managers to maintain or seize power and against which to measure performance. But the developments of the last 20 years require a broader view than a focus on single explanatory factors or arguments about a 'revolutionary' transformation.

Big French capital has become more powerful gradually, although it still protests to the contrary. The political turning point was the Mitterrand U-turn and the abandonment of Keynesianism that we discussed in Chapter 4, but this itself was partly forced by the French bourgeoisie's investment strike and its removal of capital form the country. In a context where the Socialists talked *solidarity* and *market*, where the racists talked national betrayal and the traditional left workers' party, the Communists, could barely talk at all being so compromised by the negative attachment of the PCF to Russia, world views began to change. The new disciplines of economic restructuring and high unemployment on the workers, and of financialisation on the large employers, altered their dominant discourses and helped demobilise the former and mobilise the latter.

At big capital's periphery there is now a myriad of small and medium-sized firms that are increasingly subject to their beck and call, either through minority or majority shareholdings or through sub-contracting or through quality control and just-in-time production schedules. What is emerging for most manual and white-collar employees is no autonomous idyll. Management practices in many firms have evolved in the 1980s and 1990s, but far from using the new technologies to liberate workers from stress, what appears to be happening is that most are retaining their traditional hierarchical and Taylorist or neo-Tayloristic organisations, while only a minority offer some form of largely 'controlled autonomy' to their employees.

Organising these developments has required the growth of a huge class of co-ordinators and communicators. This class is no longer the especially privileged *cadre* of the 50 years from 1930. Today this group is more feminised and more broadly educated in American managerialism than before. It is also much more subject to the ebb and flow of cyclical capitalism. In 1999, the major employers' association, the Medef initially proposed putting the rigidity of the *cadre* status in France on the bargaining table to be renegotiated along with the total revisions it planned for all the other social institutions that were established at their major moment of class weakness in the aftermath of the Second World War. They would dearly like the flexibility of the Anglo-Saxon system where many low-grade employers take on the 'manager' title without it raising any expectations at all about this giving them access to a higher status and improved working conditions. But even for the ideologues behind the *Medef* strategy this proved a bridge too far. Better, they considered, to focus on dividing the unions and then emasculating them, while publicly campaigning for a neo-liberal political agenda, than to risk distancing themselves from the nearly three million *cadres* who normally without hesitation can be expected to put *liberté* before *égalité*. In Chapter 7 we examine how French employers' organisations mobilise to exert power over the state and the working class.

7
Liberté: Employers on the Move

The winning recipe that the French employers have relied on since 1950 for higher than average European levels of productivity growth has three core ingredients: their individual authority in the workplace; their enduring family and interlocking social networks covering both industrial and finance capital; and their ability to collectively exercise influence over the state through the employers' associations. The first ingredient continues to serve them well, aided by the near-complete route of the trade unions in small and medium-sized firms, while the second still serves more than adequately, despite the adaptation to financialisation we traced in the last chapter. Here we focus on the contribution to the continued accumulation of income, wealth and power by France's ruling elite of the third ingredient, employers' organisations.

French employers' organisations are particularly interesting because, in playing a key overt role in mobilising employer power they open a window on collective strategising within the ruling financial–industrial elite, as well as illustrating a corporatist continuity with the past. Christian Dufour (2001: 3) is wrong to suggest there is little 'exceptional' about the French employers' associations. Not only do key leading business figures lead or participate actively in the deliberations of the Medef, its biggest collective organisation, but quite uniquely in Europe this association has regularly taken to the streets in face of the resistance of the French *pluralist-dirigiste* state to the liberalising forces of globalisation.

The world of French employers is changing fast and in ways that challenge much of their traditional corporatism. Old family firms and traditional networks of influence are being weakened by the rapid increase in the proportions of non-French stockholders. The nation state's capacity to protect *national* employers' interests has been weakened by France's participation in the creation of a greater Europe, where many of the new rules opening up competition worked against the French 'insider' ways of doing business. Employer power in the workplace has ebbed and flowed over the last 60 years, but if it is in many ways at a new high, the nature of much work is also changing, often rendering their traditional paternalistic, bureaucratic and authoritarian management styles less effective and even counterproductive. Finally, while intra-firm competition is starting to cast doubts on the viability of its employers' associations continuing to conduct national collective bargaining, the downsizing of the biggest firms, coupled with their growing influence over small ones, is beginning to lead to a convergence of interests between big and small firms.

On top of these challenges – many of which are common to other European employers' organisations – French employers are also faced by a trade union movement with an acutely discomforting national presence. Although numerically weak and chronically divided, it remains comparatively strong in mobilising potential. This derives in part from the legitimacy given to it directly by an omnipresent state that has been much more positively pluralist since 1980 than it ever was before. In part, it derives from French trade union history, where an explicit ideology of class struggle has played and still plays a central role.

If union mobilising power needs to be undermined, then the problem is how to do it. Direct attacks on the unions are a dangerous strategy, creating union unity and leading to 'responsible' elements being rapidly overtaken by 'irresponsible' ones. An indirect attack is therefore preferable, operating along two parallel lines. First, by offering the CFDT confederation the possibility of a 'special' relationship and privileges if it supports the employers' 'modernisation' agenda. Ernest-Antoine Seillière, Medef president, who has described the CFDT as a 'great reforming union' (*Le Monde*, 18 July 2001) explained:

> We need representative, credible and modern (social/labour) partners. It is their current weakness that is directly at the source of the recent rapid appearance of new radical unions coming from a logic of (class) rupture, that are based entirely on protest and conflict and are almost exclusively rooted in the public sector. (*Le Monde*, 15 January 2002)

The Medef's second line of attack is to try and roll back the state's artificial protection of the unions. Ideally it wants them to be only allowed to represent their actual members, and not as at present, *all* employees, whether union members or not.

This chapter first sketches the evolution of the central employers' association, the *Medef–CNPF*. Next, it focuses briefly on the experiences of small and medium-sized firms and that of other employer organisations. Finally it examines the Medef's attempt to remould French employment relations and welfare in its *refondation sociale*.

7.1 The making of the Medef

The embrace of a centralised pluralist strategy by the CNPF, in the face of the huge explosion in industrial conflict in the decade following 1968, did not survive the return of Mitterrand in 1981 and the new socialist government's intensive programme of nationalisation. Appalled, the CNPF's membership rejected another pluralist candidate as its new president and elected Yvon Gattaz, a prominent medium-sized employer, who had promised to campaign and mobilise resistance. In the autumn of 1982, as deficits on the UNEDIC unemployment insurance scheme rose, the CNPF proposed to keep employer payments into the scheme at their current level and to return the UNEDIC to balance by excluding a quarter of a million unemployed. If this 'rescue plan' was rejected Gattaz threatened to withdraw from the agreement altogether, and to leave it in the hands of the state. The government called his bluff, and introduced increased charges by government decree. The CNPF then mounted a massive campaign against additional charges to business. In December 1982, it organised a mass meeting at Villepinte of 15,000 employers who were then joined by a further 6,000 building industry employers (Weber 1986). The mobilisation had some success. The CNPF outflanked the more militant oppositions being mounted by two smaller national employers' organisations, and forced the government to make several concessions to the employers across a wide range of business issues. In March 1983, the government announced its austerity plan and its conversion to monetarism. Gattaz drew the lesson that the time was ripe for the employers to strike. He told a public meeting of 500 employers that they should profit from the presence of the left in government by 'lowering workers' purchasing power' (quoted in Weber 1986: 341).

In 1986, the head of Unilever France was elected to replace Gattaz. The Socialist U-turn and the election of a right-wing government allowed the CNPF to distance itself from Gattaz' confrontational SME leadership style. In 1988, when to many commentators' surprise Mitterrand was narrowly re-elected and a new socialist majority was installed in the National Assembly, the resumption of confrontation risked further isolating the CNPF from the state at precisely the moment in which the Socialists were being extremely effective in holding down industrial conflict and in marginalising the trade unions. Another factor, too, was coming into play: the impact of the increasing links between big business and government that followed the nationalisations of 1981–1982 and the subsequent privatisations of 1986–1988. More than even before the individuals who were at the top of formerly nationalised and now privately-owned companies were top civil servant graduates from the ENA or from the other elite *grandes écoles*, who had only recently 'shuffled' across to business sector (private or state owned). They knew France's top politicians personally and were ready to use their new influence within the CNPF to moderate its oppositional tone.

Another factor in the CNPF's shift back towards a pluralist social dialogue was the 1991 law introducing state funding of political parties. These banned companies and employers' associations continued to fund deputies and (generally right-wing) political parties. In arguing that its members should comply with the law (some did not), François Perigot had to propose other ways in which the employers could influence employment regulation. His solution was through having more 'soft' social dialogue and less 'hard' law. This corresponded with the turn towards HR strategies taking place in his own Unilever France, as well as in many of France's other big firms. Over the next few years a new leadership was installed at the CNPF that was much more prepared to negotiate. The culmination of this process occurred when Jean Gandois, the head of the recently privatised Péchiney steel giant, was elected Périgot's successor at the end of 1994 on a platform openly calling for a renewal of social dialogue with the unions. In 1994 and 1995 the CNPF embarked on a new series of meetings with the national unions and signed up to four new multi-sector agreements including one on incentives for early retirement (ARPE) that was signed by all five representative unions.

The veering of the top CNPF leadership between strident neo-liberal unitarist appeals to its SME base and the advocacy of pluralistic social dialogue with unions and the state that appealed to its largest members over the half century of the association's existence is shown in Table 7.1.

By the time of the 1997 National Assembly elections, this 'social dialogue' turn was already being criticised by the rising generation of neo-liberal managerial executives. There had been no new national collective agreements since 1995, and those that had been signed before that year's strike wave appeared to have had no impact in averting it. The criticisms were supported, too, by the growing presence of non-French stockholders, particularly American and British pension funds, on the French stock exchange. In particular, Bébéar's AXA protégé, Denis Kessler, now head of the insurance employers' federation, was frequently quoted as identifying the business opportunities available if the French welfare system was restructured around

Table 7.1 CNPF presidents and policies, 1946–1998

President	Elected	Background	Dominant CNPF policy
Georges Villiers	1946	Deportee, SME	Free enterprise
Paul Huvelin	1966	Resistance, Polytechnique X	Pluralism and social dialogue
François Ceyrac	1972	PoW, UIMM and CNPF official	Modernisation and social dialogue
Yvon Gattaz	1981	SME entrepreneur CNPF outsider	Free enterprise Resistance to the state
François Périgot	1986	Unilever France	Modernisation and Europeanisation
Jean Gandois	1994	State-owned Péchiney	Social dialogue
Ernest-Antoine Seillière	1997	Sciences Po and ENA, Wendel family	Free enterprise Resistance to the state

an individual insurance- and pension-capital funds basis rather than on its continuing self-financing redistributive basis. Known as 'DK' in the American fashion to his close associates (Mouriaux 2001: 8), Kessler is an intellectual with a doctorate in economics and a passion for big ideas. Central to these was a major shake-up of the *paritarisme* (joint management) system that administers much of the French welfare state. This argument was now more likely to fall on receptive ears. The shock of experiencing the 1995 strike wave meant that larger employers were more open to ideas that might successfully mute the minority but still damaging trade unions (Roger 2001). And if such ideas also involved successfully 'privatising' much social welfare, thereby reducing externally imposed wage costs, then all to the good.

The tripartite meeting chaired by Jospin on 10 October 1997 on the 35 hours was decisive. The CNPF was outraged that its total opposition to the 35-hour week did not carry more weight. It had expected significant concessions in terms of the distant postponement of the final date of implementation, or widespread exclusions, and an agreement to proceed by negotiations between the social partners rather than by law. Jean Gandois, a close friend of Martine Aubry, felt publicly humiliated. He immediately resigned, saying that the CNPF needed a replacement with a 'killer' instinct. The successful candidate for the contract then told *Le Point* a month later: 'National labour negotiations, I say very calmly but very clearly, are over for me' (cited in Béroud and Mouriaux 2001: 53).

The Medef

The new CNPF president, the Baron Ernest-Antoine Seillière, closely reflects the financialisation of contemporary French capital. He is the chief executive of the huge Wendel family-owned investment fund, an aristocrat and a *Sciences Po* and ENA graduate. His civil service career began as ministerial adviser to Pompidou's first prime minister, Jacques Chaban-Delmas. His right-hand man and ideologue is Denis Kessler, who was promoted to the post of Deputy President and given overall responsibility for the day-to-day running of the CNPF as well as policy formulation. Together they decided to use the sense of crisis following 1995 and the 35-hour debacle to build a 'new CNPF'.

One year later, on 27 October 1998, the new *Mouvement des entreprises de France* (Medef) was launched in Strasbourg in front of an audience of 1,700 employers. Flanked by two of the most well known names in French business, Francois Michelin and Martin Bouygues, Seillière declared:

> We are changing the world.... Taboos, forbidden issues, statutes, certainties about acquired rights, laws and peremptory decrees no longer suffice to exorcise reality. It is our task, we the entrepreneurs, to bring back French society to the reality. (*Le Monde*, 29 October 1998)

Seillière went on to outline the Medef's aims: to 'promote an entrepreneur-ial spirit by reiterating the messages, aspirations and ambitions of business people on the ground'; to campaign for a reform of the state 'as an absolute priority'; and to turn some areas of social welfare over to the private sector. The Medef's new aims were closer to the 1965 Liberal Charter than to the pluralism preached and practised by the CNPF between 1966 and 1981 and between 1988 and 1997 (Roger 2001). The key difference with 1965 is that the change drivers have changed: now it is French big business that is lead-ing the call for entrepreneurial freedom rather than the Medef's small firm members.

The Medef's new structure includes a larger national executive (up from 36 to 45), stronger regional representation (up from 8 to 12) and the stipu-lation that three quarters of the monthly executive council must be serving company heads. Among those elected to this Executive in 2000 were the Presidents or Vice-Presidents of Shell Europe, Schlumberger Europe, Coca-Cola France, Philips France as well as top managers from TotalFinaElf and Delachaux (Medef *Website*, 26 January 2002). The Medef's structure in 2001 is shown in Figure 7.1.

At its base between 500,000 and 700,000 affiliated firms (Seillière's esti-mates, *France Europe Express*, 9 December 2001) pay subscriptions through

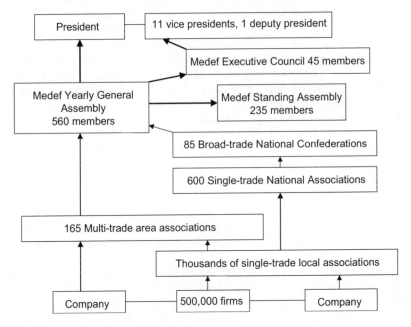

Figure 7.1 Medef membership and structure, around 2001
Sources: Jacquier 1998: 36; *Le Monde*, 15 January 2002; Medef *Website*, 26 January 2002.

three different routes. Depending on which trade they are in and their extent of localisation in a particular region and their size, they may affiliate to a local area or regional general employers' association (*union locale* or *union territoriale interprofessionnelles*), which in turn will affiliate to the Medef. Or they may affiliate to an area or regional association of employers within their own narrowly defined trade (*syndicat professionel local*), which itself may either affiliate to the area association or to a national association for employers in the same trade (*syndicat professionnel national*). The latter may either affiliate directly to the Medef or form a Federation with other trades, or even subsequently to a Confederation that will ultimately be the direct Medef affiliate. Many firms, therefore, are affiliated by several routes, and may even be additionally affiliated to some of the non-Medef associations discussed in the following section. Seillière and Kessler, who in the light of the right election victory of 2002, announced their intention to stand for office again in January 2003 also indicated that they will then undertake a major review of the Medef's internal structures to increase efficiency and focus more on effective political lobbying (*Le Monde*, 10 July 2002).

The new 1998 Medef constitution returned to the pre-1969 constitutional situation by making national intersectoral agreements the exception rather than the rule: just one of the 22 sectoral federations on the executive that can insist on a two-thirds majority of the whole executive before the Medef can be mandated to negotiate nationally. Another key change is that firms can now join the Medef directly, rather than being only eligible to do so through sectoral federations (Bilous 1998).

Could Seillière and Kessler not have changed the CNPF without changing its name? The Medef now considers the term *patron* (the nearest equivalent in English is probably 'guvnor' or 'boss'), first used in the 1861 census (Zarca 1993), an anachronism. The selection of the term *Mouvement* reflected a desire to modernise its image and to have an independent political impact. Roger (2001: 84–5) suggests that the new title also seeks to emphasise that the Medef is the sole legitimate representative of the whole of business life, in a way that was impossible when the CNPF's use of the *patronat* or bosses also focused attention on 'the workers'. In addition, in the absence of reliable political allies in the National Assembly, the Matignon Palace (home of the prime minister) or the Elysée Palace (residence of the president), the name gave the politicians a warning that an inner cabal of employer hawks were prepared to mobilise on their own, even, if necessary, in defiance of a parliamentary majority.

This was not a warning to be ignored lightly. The Medef's disclosed annual budget is about 180 million francs, enough to run a staff of around 200. About 40 million francs of this comes from payments for its participation in the joint management *parity* organisations, about 130 million francs comes from the national trade associations (the engineering employers' UIMM pays over 26 million francs), and about 10 million francs comes from the

Area-based associations (*Le Monde*, 3 April 2001). But the Medef's resources are much greater than this. It claims that roughly 7,000 employers and senior managers participate in its various policy study groups (Medef *Webpage*, 26 January 2002). In addition, some 4,000 Medef–CNPF members are elected to run the hugely wealthy Chambers of Commerce, and a further nearly 10,000 members are nominated by it to help run the principal remaining *paritarisme* organisations (3,400 in supplementary pension schemes, 4,300 in unemployment insurance and 1,800 in social housing committees), even after it pulled 4,500 members out of jointly administering the Social Security (Duchéneaut 1996: 68, 122). In total it claims to mandate 35,000 employer representatives to one body or another (Medef *Webpage*, 26 January 2002). This is a substantial body of foot soldiers but far from being the full tally of French employer activists.

7.2   Other employer associations

The heterogeneity of French capitalism and each fragment's interest in making their own distinctive representations to the arbitrator-state is amply reflected in a wide variety of other employers' associations alongside the encompassing Medef–CNPF. There are thus as many organisational divisions on the employers' side as among the trade unions.

The core division is between large and small firms. The CPGF, the CNPF and the Medef have been consistently viewed with suspicion by most micro and small French firms. Thus, the CGPME, although founded immediately after the Liberation in 1944, originated in 1936 as a protest against the 'big employers' of the UIMM and CGPF for signing the Matignon Agreements that significantly extended workers' rights. In 1948, the reality that only large firms could second managers to run the CNPF, who then took all the leading roles and decisions, led the first CGPME president, Léon Gingembre, to resign from the CNPF executive, although most of his members continued to subscribe to CNPF affiliates, as do about 60 per cent today to the Medef (Pichot 1996: 82). The CGPME claims to represent more than half of all French SMEs through the affiliations of 310 confederations and federations that group 3,200 single trade associations, and 112 regionally-based multi-trade associations. It claims as many as 1.6 million member firms (*Le Monde*, 15 January 2002). In periods when, as in the 1970s and from 1988 to 1995, its overshadowing alter ego, the CNPF, played a pluralist hand, the CGPME increasingly stressed its independence. But when, as at present, the Medef mobilises against state intervention and for free enterprise, the CGPME tends to be relatively quiescent. Thus, it has passively gone along with the Medef's proposals to reshape social security in France, and meekly abandoned its management positions within the Sécu (Social Security) in October 2001, when the Medef told it to.

A third employers' association that is legally recognised as entitled to sign national and sectoral collective agreements that can be given the force of law is the *Union professionnelle artisanale* (UPA). It organises firms with fewer than ten workers, and in 1997 had three confederations, 50 federations and other single trade associations, 23 regional associations, 91 departmental associations and 4,500 local associations (Jacquier 1998: 37). In total it claims to bring together 820,000 small businesses of which 430,000 employ an average of four staff (*Le Monde*, 2 April 2001). The UPA also lives in the shadows of the Medef–CNPF. Much more so than the CGPME, it is currently very concerned that the Medef's populist rejection of continued tripartism would prove attractive to its own membership base. If small craft businesses then ceased to organise separately, the UPA believes that it would only be a matter of time before the big businesses that dominate the Medef would sell the small ones down the river, as they argue its predecessor, the CNPF, did only too often. In response to the Medef's threats to pull out of the *Sécu* Social Security organisation, Robert Buguet, the UPA's president, therefore took the opposite tack. He called for the Medef to stop being 'a political organisation' and to 'return to be being a great employers' organisation, representative of large business and the general interest' (*Le Monde*, 24 July 2001). On 1 October 2001 when the Medef finally carried out its threat the UPA was left alone as the only employers' organisation still participating in social security management (*Le Monde*, 2 October 2001).

Several other employers' organisations are not recognised by the state as nationally representative, but are either viewed as influential within the segment of employers they do represent, or within the Medef itself. Some of these show their influence in the elections for the Employers' College of the Industrial Tribunals. In 1997, the lists involving the CNPF, the CGPME, UPA, UNAPL and FNSEA attracted 88 per cent of the voters who turned out (21 per cent of the 920,000 employers eligible); the SNPMI gained 6 per cent and the militant CID-UNATI under 1 per cent (Jacquier 1998: 37). The dozen most important of these employers' associations or pressure groups are shown in Table 7.2.

Chambers of Commerce and Industry

Alongside these employers' associations and pressure groups there is another important institution that helps give French employers a sense of collective identity. This is the Chamber of Commerce. First established in Marseille in 1599, and invested with considerable disciplinary powers over business by the crown in the two centuries that followed, they were abolished in 1791, only to be revived by Napoleon Bonaparte. In 1898 they were given legal status as official representatives on trade matters of industry and commerce, and in 1960 they took on their present acronym, the Chambers of Commerce and Industry (CCI). A national trade tax on firms provides about a quarter of their total revenues. In 1999 there were 151 independent local

Table 7.2 Employers' associations and forums independent of the Medef, CGPME and UPA, ranked by numbers of affiliated firms, 2001

Group	Founded	Role	Members	Influence
AFEP	1982	Private sector big business club	81	Major pressure group within *Medef*
L'institut de l'entreprise	1975	Big business club (private and state)	100	Discussion forum
Entreprise et progrès	1970	Business and progress	110	Pluralist discussion forum
CID-UNATI	c1960–1964	Self-employed Defence and Action League	n.a.	Extreme right militant group believes in direct action
Ethic	1976	Independent medium-sized firms association	1,500	Ginger group for free enterprise. *Medef* associate
APM	1986	Clubs for management progress	1,800	Forum to exchange best managerial practice
CJD	1938	Young directors centre	2,300	Christian humanism, modernisation *Medef* associate
EDC	1926	Catholic employers and directors centre	2,500	Overlaps with CJD and *L'institut de l'entreprise*. *Medef* associate
SNPMI	n.a.	Small and medium sized trades association	12,000	Far right links Has some employer seats on Industrial Tribunals
UNAPL	1938	Self-employed liberal professionals association	620,000	Sits on social security system management boards
FNSEA	1946	Farmers' union	32,000 local branches	Sits on social security system management boards

Sources: Duchéneaut 1996: 102–17; Jacquier 1998: 37; *Le Monde*, 15 January 2002; UNAPL, FNSEA *Websites*, 26 January 2002.

CCI, 21 regional CCI bodies and a national body, the ACFCI, set up in 1964, co-ordinates their interventions at national, European and international levels.

Altogether some 1.8 million firms are affiliated to one or other of the Chambers. These are run by 4,500 officers who are elected on employer association slates every six years – thus about 4,000 of them are Medef people – supported by a further 26,000 employers and managers in various co-opted roles. Roughly one in five of its members participated in the 2000 elections, compared with twice that proportion in 1974 (Duchéneaut 1996: 118–27; ACFCI 2001: 20).

While fewer firms have participated in the elections held since 1988, the CCI still perform four major functions: they keep local employers informed; they provide consultancy services; they train managers; and they run many important local services, such as ports (32 freight and fishing ports), airports (110), conference venues (55) and industrial zones. They are thus huge employers, with a total of 26,000 staff in 1995, and then indirectly employ a further 110,000 people in airports and 30,000 people in ports. They also play an important part in providing elite managerial university education. In 1999 about 20,000 students attended the 30 *grandes écoles de commerce* they administer, and a further 4,000 attended one of their 16 professional engineering universities. They also provided adult training for 381,000 managers in 214 training centres and provided trade apprenticeships for over 75,000 young workers. In that year alone some 87,000 managers took their language courses. Their total 1999 income of 3.2 billion euros was spent largely on general services (41 per cent) and training (28 per cent), with airport and port management taking the rest (ACFCI 2001: 9–10, 21–2). Aside from the tax income transferred to them by the state, their other sources of revenue come from subscription fees, payment for services, management charges and loans.

The CCI thus play a key role in shaping French business culture. Often very wealthy organisations, they are public actors with a major role in elite formation: they educate a significant part of that elite; they provide the bulk of professional management training; and their full-time consultants service 20,000 firms and answer enquiries from a further 150,000 firms a year. Yet they are not just opinion-formers. They also demonstrate the continuing physical presence of collective business interests in running France's economic infrastructure.

7.3 The Medef challenges the state and *paritarisme*

French corporatism, the regulation by the state of business and the reciprocal involvement of business with and in the state machine, is viewed by the Seillière-Kessler Medef leadership as one of the causes of a significant decline in French international competitiveness in the 1980s and 1990s. While the assumption of such a significant French 'failure' is an ideological construct rather than a reality (Duménil and Lévy 2001; Hancké 2002; Husson 2000a), it does have the advantage of portraying their collective class interests as the victims of discrimination, helping make their mobilisation easier than if the description was more accurate.

The employers' collective sense of loss of influence derives partly from the continuing pluralist agenda of state power, and partly from the sharpening American managerial challenge to their traditional ways of doing business. Their defensiveness is exacerbated by what would have been unheard of before the 1990s: legal challenges to big business practices. Not only was a director of a Thomson factory fined for allowing managerial staff to work without a record being kept of their hours, but in November 2001 the Montpellier Appeal Court fined the HR director and the chief director of the local IBM factory for obstructing the functioning of its Works Committee by not transferring it in full the subsidy of 0.2 per cent of its wage costs (*Le Monde*, 6 November 2001). Several large industrial firms have also been caught up in corruption cases and some big financial firms are suspected of turning a blind eye to money-laundering. After both AXA's founder, Claude Bébéar, and its current president, Henri de Castries, were charged with money laundering through a Luxembourg subsidiary, the head of the French Bank Federation wrote to the Minister of Finance, Laurent Fabius, complaining of an excess of government regulation (*Le Monde*, 15 June, 17 July 2001). Then, Daniel Bouton, the president of the giant bank *Société générale* and a Medef leader, was indicted on another charge of laundering. For the Medef's chief Seillière this proved 'the lack of clarity in the law', and 'showed how far today this penalisation has made the profession of business leader a dangerous one' (*Le Monde*, 17 January 2002).

The Medef goal was to turn the CNPF's defeat over the 35-hours to the employers' advantage through mobilising against the working time laws and then using the momentum gained to radically re-shape French industrial relations and welfare so that they protected workers less from the 'free market forces'.

Opposition to the 35-hour week

The Medef's opposition to the 35-hour laws was based on the argument that it would increase costs and lead to the relocation of jobs outside France. It could not have been more mistaken. In the four years between 1997 and 2001 the French job market expanded by 7.2 per cent, by more than at any time in the whole of the twentieth century. There remain debates about how many of these new jobs, ranging from 65,000 to 500,000, were the direct result of the shorter working week (Pisani-Ferry 2001; Husson 2002b). But, not for the first or last time, the Medef's gloomy predictions were proved entirely wrong. This did not prevent them from opposing and continuing to oppose the laws by all means possible. First, it advised its sectoral associations to seek agreements with the unions that would weaken the previous national framework agreements on working hours by any means necessary, including threats to denounce sectoral bargaining in its entirety if their demands were not met. Second, it counselled individual employers against trying to get the incentive social charges reductions held out by the government by signing 35-hour agreements before the last legal minute. Kessler and Seillière argued that employers should no longer look to the state for handouts. They also objected to the government's intention to pay for the incentives from the improved balance in the social security receipts that would flow from having more employees in work and paying out less in unemployment benefits. Where 35-hour agreements were signed they also advised employers to insist on the maximum concessions through wage freezes or 'pay moderation', increasing job flexibility and extending the agreed total of annually allowed overtime hours. The sectoral agreement signed by the FO trade union (the most ambivalent union concerning the 35-hour law) with the UIMM allowed company-level bargaining to achieve all these things. This sort of agreement, the Medef believed, would ensure the costs of the 35-hour week were recovered as fully as possible, while ensuring that any negative feelings resulting from increased work intensity would be deflected onto the unions (Jefferys 2000).

The third element of the Medef's fight against the 35-hour laws aimed to forge a high degree of employer unity. Seillière and Kessler knew their small and medium-sized members were concerned that the 35-hour week would increase their costs and lower their profitability. They also knew that even if this was not a big consideration for its larger members, these were now more ideologically opposed than in the past to the very fact of government substantive regulation of employee working conditions. Seillière summed up their attitudes:

> Listen, for months, for years, politicians, law-makers, administrators have been coming right into companies to regulate and intervene in their detailed daily lives. Well, businesses are now demanding the right, for them, to tell the politicians in the clearest possible way exactly what they can and can't do. (*Invité d'Europe 1*, 22 October 2001)

On 4 October 1999, the Medef united these large and small groups of members together in a huge 25,000-strong protest meeting at the Porte de Versailles to protest against the '100% old-fashioned Aubry law'. Kessler, its principal organiser, recalled that 'this was the second time in 20 years that we have come together to say "no" to dogmatism, "no" to the seizure of social dialogue, and "no" to an administrated economy' (quoted in *Le Monde*, 6 October 1999). The Medef then successfully threatened to withdraw from the jointly-run unemployment insurance scheme (UNEDIC) if the government went ahead with its plans to use some of the money paid into that scheme by the new jobs created to fund the incentives given to employers to sign 35-hour agreements. One group of employers, the lorry owners, failed to negotiate an agreement with the unions and then took their opposition, to a decree introduced by the government imposing a weekly-hours limit, to the point of organising blockades at major frontier crossing-points on 10 January 2000 (*Le Monde*, 9 January 2000).

The Medef campaign ultimately failed to stop the 1998 and 2000 Aubry laws being enacted, and many of its own members did sign up for the incentives available for coming to agreements before the 1 February 2000 deadline when the law started to apply to all firms with 20 or more workers. But it did subsequently win a reprieve from Jospin for all small businesses (where full enforcement was delayed by a further three years to 2005) and with the victories of the right in the 2002 presidential and national assembly elections, Seillière immediately called for urgent action to modify the law (*Le Monde*, 10 July 2002).

Rolling back *paritarisme* and the state

The employers' new strategy, however, was not just about short-term opposition. It was to use the (perhaps temporary) unity in its ranks brought about by the campaign on the 35-hour week to shift the target to two linked issues. The first was the need to rewrite what they see as the 'archaic' post-war basis of the French welfare state. The second was to significantly reduce the protective role of the state over the labour market as a whole. 'The rules of the game established roughly 50 years ago have shown themselves completely useless,' Kessler told the *Nouvel Economiste* (23 November 2001). 'We need a new social contract'. As a result of nearly continuous *pluralist-dirigiste* political governance since 1968, and despite growing trade union weakness, the state remains a guarantor of last resort of working conditions around which the unions can still mobilise. Kessler frequently hammers home one element of French exceptionalism: '25 per cent (of employees) work in public services, and they are involved in 75 per cent of the strikes' (Medef *Pointe de presse mensuel*, 16 October 2001).

Since the state is their major target this strategy has involved the employers in political interventions with a large 'P'. They openly campaigned against the Socialists before the 2002 elections, and since then have mounted renewed pressure on France's conservative right to abandon Gaullism and *dirigisme* and adopt a fully neo-liberal programme. But the Medef is also exerting heavy political pressure on the trade unions. And not just at the level of rhetoric, as after 11 September 2001 when Seillière denounced those unions pursuing public sector strikes as lacking in 'social patriotism' (*Medef Point de press mensuel*, 16 October 2001).

The Medef strategy is fairly clear. Recognising that some unionisation is inevitable it would like to see one centre-right trade union confederation, the CFDT, fully embrace a partnership-HRM approach to industrial relations and become *the* privileged French employee representative body at all levels. This is not easy to achieve since its primary aim of rolling back the state and weakening *compulsory* pluralist arrangements also involves the Medef making life difficult for the CFDT as well as for the other less favoured union confederations. *Voluntarist pluralism* with the CFDT is what it would like, but not if the price is too high.

Employing the rhetoric of the need to give a *more important* voice to the 'social dialogue' – best interpreted in English as 'consultation with labour' – the Medef's key aim is to give a *less important* voice to the state. Its repeated refrain is the need to prioritise *contract* over *the law* in matters of employment relations. The law should practise subsidiarity: it should not be the prime source of reference, but only apply as a safety net where 'contractural freedom' is absent (*Le Monde*, 11 May 2000, 8 December 2001). The Medef wants workplace rules 'voluntarily' established by the different employment relations actors at the level where the employers are currently strongest: at the workplace and between the company and the individual worker. Their return to 'free' collective bargaining means in practice 'freedom' to go below state-imposed minimum standards and rights.

By taking this indirect approach to reducing trade union influence the Medef cleverly situated itself within a growing right–left rift in the trade union movement itself. Edmond Maire, the influential General Secretary of the CFDT in the 1970s and 1980s, had already attacked the Socialist government's '*dirigiste* and archaic conception of industrial relations', denouncing an 'authoritarian left that puts a Jacobin state into the saddle'. Nicole Notat, the CFDT General Secretary from 1993 to 2002, who was most identified with the union's turn away from conflict, explained her union's distinctive approach:

> The whole of the left today focuses exclusively on action by the state apparatus in the way that it thinks and builds social change. (While) we have for a long time been convinced that the actors and forces of civil society are key in successfully changing labour relations. (*Le Monde*, 14 November 2000)

The CFDT, which by the mid-1990s probably had more members than the CGT, had become a confederation the employers could 'do business with'.

Why attack welfare?

The welfare state was the Medef's initial terrain chosen for its offensive. This is for three main reasons. First, it occupies a huge financial space whose privatisation could open up substantial new opportunities for profit-taking and rent, particularly in the now highly influential finance and insurance sector. Second, welfare's redistributive basis means that the current generation of workers and their employers pay directly through 'social charges' for those who are sick, unemployed or in retirement. The result is that while direct income taxes are very low, French labour on-costs are high. Euzéby (*Le Monde*, 29 January 2002) calculates that on-costs make up 51 per cent of gross labour costs. Thus for every 100 euros that an employer pays his workers, the employer has to pay an extra 37.4 euros in social charges while the employee only receives 86.4 euros after having had 13.6 euros deducted as their contribution. Euzéby argues that if growth continues at between 1 and 2 per cent of GDP then the system can cope both with the growing proportion of the elderly in the population and still maintain workers' existing real purchasing power. This view is supported by Husson (Husson 2000b) whose study of the pension 'crisis' shows that if the current contribution rate increases in line with the increase in the dependency ratio over the next 40 years, then future pensioners will be no worse off than current ones, provided wages and purchasing power rise at the same rate as productivity.

But the financial interests now dominating the Medef want to see the share of national resources going to capital increased, not stabilised or reduced over the next 20 years. Hence they want to reduce social charges (enabling profitability to rise, they argue, so creating more jobs), lower the minimum guaranteed levels of benefit, and encourage the individualisation of responsibility for sickness and old-age care. The Medef has examined the UK and US experiences showing that cutting benefits is more politically feasible where welfare is financed out of direct personal taxation than through retaining separate social charges. The Seillière and Kessler strategy is thus to weaken France's social charge-financed welfare (and its organisations) and to try and manoeuvre the state both into increasing (unpopular) direct taxation and into taking direct responsibility for cutting benefits.

A third reason for the employers' assault on the French welfare state is because it is central in structuring French industrial relations. The French *paritarisme* (shared responsibility or joint management) system is now the cornerstone on which virtually all French welfare and collective bargaining rests. Defining exactly what it means is not easy, since it tends to be interpreted differently according to whose interests are at stake. Thus, three distinct definitions are given in the introduction to a special issue on *paritarisme* of the journal of the major French independent industrial relations research unit, IRES, ranging from a quite narrow interpretation to a highly universal one (apRoberts *et al.* 1997: 7–8). It is defined as an employer-driven bipartite consultation mechanism that operates independently of the state; as the galaxy of experiences describing relations between industrial relations actors where there exists an autonomous arena of regulation distinct from full state or full market control; and finally as an all-embracing political formula allowing capital and labour to work together to produce mutual benefits or write rules, whatever their particular form (tripartite or bipartite with worker majority or with formal equality).

The institutions involved include sickness, industrial accidents, the family and old age, as well as adult training, supplementary pension funds and unemployment insurance. The justification of their joint management, most commonly (but not exclusively) with equality of representation on management committees and alternating presidencies between the employer and union sides, lies in the fact that they are funded both by the employee through deductions from the wage packet and by the employer through social charges.

Contemporary *paritarisme* was largely codified during the two periods of acute employer political weakness that followed the Liberation of France and the events of May–June 1968. With the recovery of employer confidence and growing trade union weakness in the 1990s it has become a target because the employers believe it provides more funds and greater legitimacy to the trade unions than they deserve. This is because the codified *paritarisme* tends to be the broadest of the three definitions listed above, where unions are formally recognised by the state, rather than the much narrower definition preferred by the employers that allows them to decide with whom they would consult. State recognition gives the unions a status and influence, especially at the national level, which is not directly linked to their strength on the ground. If the unions no longer performed such a widely accepted and important task as controlling or influencing the principal organs of the welfare state, then, the employers believe their mobilising capacity would be significantly reduced.

The involvement of thousands of trade unionists in paid part-time or full-time positions jointly running the welfare state also provides the unions with many opportunities for small-scale fraud. One investigation found that many full-time union activists were actually on mutual fund payrolls and, in the case of the Concierge Pension Fund, the late General Secretary of the Communist Party as well as a former General Secretary of the CGT, were both found to be receiving pensions despite never having paid any money in (*Le Monde*, 8 January 2000). This sleaze in the management of part of the *paritarisme* system was not a surprise to the employers, who place their own people in similar ways. But it does render the system more open to criticism.

Trying to write new rules

The Medef leadership wants a completely new system of rules covering the industrial relations actors at all levels. Kessler argues:

> We must have new rules of the game at three levels: between the labour partners and the State defining their respective responsibilities; within firms so that there are negotiators able to contract those they represent; within sectors where the question of the real representativity of the unions has been sharply posed. (*Nouvelle Economiste*, 23 November 2001)

To write the new rulebook the Medef decided to force the pace. After securing the endorsement of a General Assembly on 18 January 2000, Seillière formally announced that the Medef would be withdrawing from all the bi-partite welfare organisations it jointly managed with the unions from 31 December 2000, and from the UNEDIC unemployment insurance scheme (the term of the existing three-year agreement had already expired at the end of 1999) on 30 June 2000. Unlike its previous threats (in 1982 and 1999) this was not made to secure the withdrawal of an unacceptable measure. This time the threat was made offensively in order to force the unions to agree to 'rebuilding the French social system'. Kessler added a warning that 'if the government gets involved in the discussions, the whole exercise will stop' (*Le Monde*, 20 January 2000).

It became clear very early on in the negotiations that began on 3 February 2000 that the Medef negotiators were intent on using the negotiations over the future of UNEDIC as a blueprint for all the others. If they did not get the concessions they were looking for they would withdraw from the *parity*-joint management system. On the unemployment insurance reform there was strong opposition to the Medef's proposals since they proposed to remove the universal right of the insuree to unemployment benefit, and to replace this by a conditional right that could be forfeited if the unemployed person refuses between one and four job offers. 'Punishments' for not accepting an offer could range from benefits dropping by 20 per cent to temporary or permanent suspension of benefits. These benefits are substantial in France ranging from about 70 per cent of their former earnings level for lower wage earners to about 50 per cent for higher wage earners. For many critics this was not only the slippery slope towards the British 'job-seekers' allowance', but it was a major breach in the system of unconditional 'acquired rights' that are the cornerstone of French welfare. An agreement was eventually reached just days before the Medef's self-imposed deadline, but only two of France's five nationally representative trade union confederations, the CFDT and the CFTC, signed initially. They were far from representing a majority of the share of votes cast at the last French Industrial Tribunal elections in 1997 (receiving 25.34 and 7.52 per cent, respectively). It was only four months later when the CGC also signed that the employers could claim to be a majority of the five officially recognised representative unions. This was enough for the government, which then ratified the PARE agreement into law.

After completing the UNEDIC negotiations, the Medef went on to raise the other issues where it believed major reforms were necessary to achieve its *Refondation sociale* – its re-founding of the French industrial relations and welfare systems. However, while the Medef originally gave itself just one year to complete all the negotiations, the length of time taken to reach the PARE agreement, the difficulties involved in persuading the CFDT to break ranks with the other unions, and the time each set of negotiations took, meant that despite its original projections even two years later there was relatively little to show. By the start of the election year of 2002 there was only a partial agreement postponing discussions on pensions, a common 'position' on collective bargaining and a minor agreement on occupational health to boast about in addition to the PARE. The issues under negotiations and outcomes are listed in Table 7.3.

From the outset the Medef leadership appeared to be looking for at least one area in which they could break with the joint management system and provoke a crisis that would require the state taking over. This was the logic of their negotiating tactics. In virtually every set of talks they began by threatening to withdraw from the parity management of that part of the welfare system unless at least one or two of the unions signed up to the reforms the Medef was suggesting.

Table 7.3   The Medef *Refondation sociale*, 2000–2001

Issue	Outcome	Unions signing	Duration
Unemployment insurance	PARE agreement introduces lower charges and adds requirement to take potentially unsuitable work	CFDT, CFTC	5/4/00–14/6/00
Workplace health	Agreement: objectives to be redefined, and local doctors to be allowed to do occupational medicine visits	CFDT, CFTC, CGC	22/3/00–19/12/00
Pensions	Postponement of negotiations to after the 2002 elections	CFDT, CFTC, FO, CGC	3/3/00–10/2/01
Training	No agreement reached		20/12/00–23/11/01
Equality at work	Negotiations not begun		
Management training and qualifications	Negotiations not begun		
Social security: health insurance, industrial injuries	No agreement reached: Medef and CGPME withdrew from jointly managing the 'Secu' system (CNAM)		1/10/01
Collective bargaining	Common position adopted on the ways and means of deepening collective bargaining	CFDT, CFTC, CGC, FO	14/3/00–23/11/01

Sources: Medef *Website*, 26 January 2002; *Le Monde*, various dates.

One of its series of threats backfired in a potentially risky way. On the issue of reforming the additional pensions regimes, the Medef wished to cut the pensions bill by increasing the number of contributions required to 45 years' worth in order to secure full entitlement. When its negotiators failed initially to break trade union unity (they responded by unanimously proposing increasing the amount contributed), Seillière instructed Medef members to stop deducting the ASF contributions that help fund early retirement, and Kessler warned that the Medef might also pull out of the parity systems managing the major supplementary pension schemes, ARRCO and AGIRC. This radicalism was a step too far for the other two legally 'representative' employers' associations. The CGPME's Jacques Freidel protested, 'We are for dialogue, not breaking up everything'; and the UPA's Jean Delmas added, 'We want a solution and don't want to pour oil on the fire or to force a breakdown'. Some 300,000 workers also took to the streets in demonstrations throughout France (*Le Figaro, Libération*, 26 January 2001). Even the large private sector employers in the AFEP held a meeting at which Seillière was openly criticised for going too far in risking a mass mobilisation and in not getting the CFDT sufficiently onboard (*Le Monde*, 28 April 2001). It was not even clear that most employers followed the Medef's instructions to stop forwarding ASF contributions. The Medef then backed down: it reopened negotiations and agreed to postpone its threatened walkout to 31 December 2002, after that year's elections.

Medef finally chose to walk out of joint management of the CNAM on 1 October 2001. This is the biggest tripartite organisation in France, responsible for reimbursing 75 per cent of charges incurred in the health service – the *Sécu*. From its origins until the 1980s the CNAM was essentially bipartite, but since then an increasing share of its budget has been raised directly by the state through the special National Social Deduction (CSG). The state also took powers to decide who should be its national and local directors, thereby largely deciding at what levels benefits and contributions should be set, and *de facto* transformed it into a tripartite body (Jacquier 1998: 87). And it is the area that Medef wants to semi-privatise. But, reflecting doubts about its aggressive tactics, the employers' walkout was not unanimous. While the Medef and the CGPME pulled out, the UPA stayed. The Medef even had to warn individual employers that they would be expelled from the Medef if they agreed to continue to serve in any *Sécu* joint management positions.

Political pressure

What did the Medef's *social refondation* strategy achieve during its first phase under the Jospin government? In terms of the actual changes implemented, very little. But in terms of the Medef's wider aims, it had withdrawn from a major component of the *paritarisme* system, proving that it could be done, and it had consolidated a close working relationship with the CFDT. It then decided to take these achievements into the wider political arena that opened up with the start of the 2002 election campaigns.

While openly admiring both Vincente Fox, the former Coca-cola manager elected president of Mexico, and Sylvio Berlusconi, the Italian prime minister, for having brought businessmen and pro-business policies on to their national agendas, Seillière could not have realistically challenged the incumbent right-wing President and have stood himself. Instead the Medef used all means possible to put its political programme into the public eye. It organised seven large regional meetings followed by a 2,300-strong mass meeting at Lyon in January 2002 (opposed by a 10,000 strong demonstration) to launch its own demands. No longer just demanding tax cuts it spelt out the full neo-liberal election programme shown in Table 7.4.

With right-wing candidates cautious about identifying too closely with them, neo-liberal logic has been given a much higher profile than if the Medef had not been involved. Seillière, when he decided to stand for a second term as Medef president, explained that he was doing so because he now looked forward to 'working with a right that dares' (*Le Monde*, 10 July 2002).

Table 7.4   Medef political programme for 2002 national elections

Issue	Objectives
Taxation	Tax reductions on inheritance; trades tax to be abolished
Social security	System to be divided into two: employment-based insurance to remain as it is; the rest (family allowances and health) to be funded by direct taxation and regulated by the state and to be semi-privatised. The CNAM would be abolished and Individuals would have the right to tell the state to place 'their' health insurance entitlement in a private or mutual insurance fund or savings bank.
Pensions	Duration of contributions to be adjusted upwards along with life expectancy; individualised flexible retirement; optional private pension fund schemes.
Work	Repeal of the 35-hour laws
Collective negotiations	Revision of trade union representation criteria; precedence to be given to workplace agreements; contractual agreements to be given precedence over the law
Education and training	Decentralisation of education and training; compulsory business module in national curriculum taught with participation of employers
Reform of the State	Public sector employment to be linked to private sector wealth creation; a new business-state partnership to be built
Civil society	Improve transport and telecommunications infrastructure; introduce codes of good behaviour

Sources: *Le Monde*, 15 January 2002; Medef *Website*, 26 January 2002.

Whether the UMP majority will now 'dare' to embrace the Medef's election programme is, however, still an open question. When it 'dared' in 1995 it provoked the biggest strike movement since 1968. A great deal will depend, as we argue in Chapter 8, upon the evolution of trade union unity.

7.4 Conclusion

The challenges to French employer organisations at the turn of the twenty-first century are considerable. The state no longer protects them against overseas competition, but remains powerful internally and continues to insist on pluralism in employment relations when the employers believe there is no objective need to maintain it as a method of restraining employee mobilisation. Yet, the employers' collective leverage over the state had been weakened both by the continuing political strength of social democracy and by the resilience of a nationalist-conservative-Catholic Gaullist political current whose historic political mission had been to use the state to save French capitalism. After four and a half years of the Jospin government the Medef president complained that he had only been invited twice to meet the prime minister (*France Europe Express*, 9 December 2001). The employers believe the state no longer automatically gives them the consideration that is their due, and complain that it continues to provide an 'excessive' level of protection to the workers, thus hampering their business performance. *Liberté* is lacking; 'free' market forces are not yet quite free enough.

The discourse is not new. In 1945–1955, 1965 and 1982–1986, when the influence of France's SMES was greatest, the same complaints were being made. What is different today is the greater unity between employers of different sizes. The current neo-liberal rhetoric is being orchestrated by many of France's largest firms. In October 2001, 56 presidents of some of the largest French firms signed a public letter attacking the Guigou 'social modernisation' law increasing the length of the consultation process before workers could be dismissed. The large employers now have a genuine sense of urgency, driven by the financialisation of their capital and the more intense international competition that is summarised in the term globalisation. French employers have witnessed the disarray on the political right over the last 20 years and many conclude that Gaullist *dirigisme* and social paternalism is a dangerous blind alley. At the start of the 2002 election campaign Chirac, as he had in 1995, was again giving out mixed messages to employers, pointing to France's 'social fracture', saying that 'the rich are getting richer and the poor are getting poorer' and arguing that 'globalisation ... must be regulated, humanised' (*Le Monde*, 19 January 2002).

Fortunately for the employers, the collapse of Jospin's first round election vote and the surge in support for Le Pen meant that Chirac was first re-elected and then was handed a large right-wing majority in the National Assembly with one of their own leaders, François Mer, nominated as number two in the government. Even so, the neo-liberal ideologues leading the Medef are not certain the will is there to push the new government as far as they want. The only neo-liberal candidate in the presidential election, Alain Madelin, fared disastrously, although leaving a political marker as one of the possible successors to Chirac in 2007. And on top of that the Medef is aware that a combination of government inertia, triggered by the looming battle over Chirac's succession, and a continuing presence of Catholic social Gaullists and classical *dirigiste* conservatives could encourage political caution rather than 'daring'. They therefore have to decide whether to return to their traditional quiet backroom lobbying, or to continue to up the stakes in threatening and blackmailing their trade union 'partners'.

Their unprecedented struggle for entrepreneurial *liberté* against a social democratic government since 1997 has revealed divisions on the employers' side: some large businesses still have the option of preferring a *clientelist* relationship with the government; many employers have been able to turn the opportunity to negotiate additional flexibility provided by the 35 hour laws to their own advantages; some believe that the risks of provoking a new strike wave are too great; some top executives owe much to the government that appointed them to their high office; and smaller business associations feel threatened by the Medef's adopting a campaigning militant stance. Yet this campaigning has also united large and small employers. Any criticisms from the latter about the costs of transition to the Euro on 1 January 2002 were simply dissolved in the sea of Medef's anti-government political propaganda.

At the same time the Medef 'modernisation' offensive has destabilised and reinforced divisions within the already weak trade union movement. Before the 1990s, the 'natural' major union confederation with whom the employers could 'do business' was the traditionally anti-communist FO. But since 1995, the employers' 'natural' ally has become the CFDT. How it will respond if the Medef decides to provoke a crisis by overturning the whole post-war employment relations and welfare settlement during the lifetime of the current 'sympathetic' government, is unclear. The dilemmas of the French trade union movement are discussed in Chapter 8.

8
Égalité: Trade Unions on the Defensive

Facing France's increasingly focused employers is a divided and much less focused trade union movement. It is a movement that was born later than in Britain and Germany. It was and remains weaker in numbers, in terms of union density and in its degree of feminisation. Whereas 21 per cent of the active working population were union members in 1978 that figure today is about eight per cent. Nor has it ever known organic unity: it is more heterogeneous than the trade union ideological maps of Italy, Britain and Germany presented by Hyman (1996; 2001). The cleavages between the *struggle, market* and *societal* poles in trade union thought go deep. These divisions were to some extent frozen in place by the powerful presence of the Communist Party and its rigid concept of class struggle. But they were institutionalised by the state's decrees of 1948 and 1966 that gave state recognition and privileges to certain targeted confederation centres. The decrees were fashioned to overcome the problem that from 1947 to about 1990 the communist-led CGT usually represented the majority of French trade unionists. The state's solution to this tricky democratic obstacle was to elevate the status of the minority unions so they could sign agreements the CGT would not. These decrees therefore effectively rewarded ideological distinctiveness rather than size. Each pole was occupied by a different and competing trade union confederation. This left little room for stable coalitions involving two of the ideological poles to comfortably dominate the third. French trade unions were and are chronically divided, divisions that are then often cited by workers as reasons for their not wishing to join.

Yet despite, or perhaps because of, this heterogeneity, the French level of strike action has generally surpassed that of the much larger German or British trade union movements. French manual workers held mass factory occupations in 1936 and 1968 and between 1945 and 1980 a majority of them voted Communist. An acceptance of the right to protest and mobilise collectively has continued up to the present. Even excluding French public sector strikes from the count, from 1992 to 1999 there were between six and nine times as many strikes each year in France as in the United Kingdom

(ILO 2000). In France in 2000, 222,000 private and nationalised industry workers were recorded as taking part in 1,556 strikes and as losing nearly 810,000 working days, a level of strike action similar to that a decade earlier. Government workers were much more strike prone even excluding local government and hospital workers: in 2000 they lost a total of 1,650,300 working days – a level only surpassed in 1989 and 1995 in the previous two decades (Merlier 2002). Then in December 1995, more workers demonstrated publicly against proposals to increase by five years the contributions public sector workers had to pay for a full pension, than had demonstrated in the May–June events of 1968 (*Le Monde*, 7 and 14 December 1995). Most of the frequent one-day strikes are also accompanied by street demonstrations: on 25 January 2001, for example, 300,000 demonstrated against the Medef, while just five days later somewhere between 100,000 and 150,000 teachers and civil servants took to the streets for more pay (*Le Monde*, 27 January, 1 February 2001). The French police estimate that altogether between 1993 and 1999 some 6.25 million people participated in 8,591 'political' street demonstrations in Paris alone (*The Observer*, 1 April 2001).

French unions have had to rely heavily on industrial conflict and legal intervention to shape substantive or procedural workplace rules (Goetschy and Rozenblatt 1992). French employers have only rarely offered them the genuine possibility of evolving in a fully neo-corporatist direction. Only a minority has voluntarily embraced full collective bargaining and pluralism. Instead, most employers consistently implemented unitarist strategies to undermine state-imposed pluralism through restricting union growth and influence in *their* workplaces. High levels of labour productivity, of industrial accidents and of victimisations of trade union activists testify to their success and the cost to workers. While Hancké (2002) rightly argues that large French employers regrouped at the level of the firm after 1985, it must also be remembered that historically they exercised nearly unilateral power at that level right up to 1968. Collective bargaining and pluralism was embraced more wholeheartedly by the state than it was by the employers who, as a whole, were not tempted by a containment strategy that involved recognising unions as having rights to challenge their managerial authority.

In this largely hostile context French trade unions found it easier to focus on state intervention to force the employers to provide workers' employment rights, substantive working conditions and welfare provisions than to achieve these goals through 'normal' collective bargaining. They have not done too badly. Despite 20 years of high unemployment French workers still have a constitutional right to take strike action, to elect half the judges in industrial tribunals and to a level of welfare protection that has protected them from the disproportionate growth in inequality and poverty that has occurred in the United Kingdom. Workers also have the possibility of retiring in their 50s on levels of income that keep them well above the poverty line, and many do so: just 30 per cent of those aged 54 to 64 still work in

France, compared with 37 per cent in Germany and 50 per cent in Britain (Cohen 2002). This achievement of early retirement on a living social wage owes much to the decade of struggles from 1968 and to French trade unionism's continuing mobilising capacity. And the wider working class recognises this too. Within the legally imposed employee representation system the trade unions continue to do far better than their membership levels would suggest. While remaining numerically weak the unions remain capable at key moments of mobilising non-members not only to vote for them, but also to participate in mass strike waves and demonstrations that can have major political repercussions. France lives the paradox of a trade union movement with Europe's lowest levels of trade union density, but with a high mobilisation potential.

In Chapter 2 we examined the historical context from which French unions emerged, explaining why such a high proportion of members are activists, why there are seemingly so many distinct trade union centres, and what values divide them. This chapter examines the contemporary relationship of the unions to the wider working class, and then turns to the problems the divided unions face in responding to the renewed employer challenges described in the preceding chapter.

8.1 Representation, membership and union audience

Out of the roughly 19 million full and part-time employees in France about half work for organisations where they are legally entitled to vote in one form or another of workplace election. Roughly two-thirds of these (six million) regularly exercise this right (Jacquier 1998: 31). These workplace elections allow workers to express their trade union preference for a range of positions such as workplace personnel or works council representatives (reps). Since 1954, elections have taken place every other year in private sector workplaces, and they now also occur every three or four years in the public sector, where the equivalent to the works council or the group works council is the 'joint administrative advisory council', the CAP. Sometimes judging union support in the public sector will be through elections for other forms of representatives. In the state-owned National Savings Bank (*Caisse d'épargne*), for example, the only representative elections are for worker side members of the bank's disciplinary committees. A major consequence of this state-imposed workplace democracy is to reinforce intra-union ideological conflict in the regular competitions for non-members' votes, a process that is marked most in the run-up to the biggest elections that occurs nationally on the same December day every five years, those for industrial tribunal judges.

How many employee reps are there in France? In private and semi-public industry there are about 200,000–230,000 elected reps and deputy reps serving on roughly 25,000 works councils (CE – *comités d'entreprise*). There are also approximately 260,000 *personnel* reps and their deputies, a lower figure than the 300,000 counted in the mid-1980s. A slowly increasing proportion of personnel reps (28 per cent in 1994) are women. In addition there are an estimated 39,000 trade union reps (equivalent of senior union reps or convenors) nominated by the unions. With the doubling up of many mandates (most CE reps will also be personnel reps), and the inclusion of joint administrative advisory committee (CAP) reps from the public sector, this means in total there are somewhere between 300,000 and 350,000 workplace reps although only half their number are trade union members (Jacquier 1998: 22; Andolfatto; IRES-DARES 1998: 12, 27). This means that on an average there is about one unionised rep for every 60 workers in workplaces with 50 or more staff.

Do these reps really speak for French workers? Evidence suggests that despite very low membership the answer is yes. The 1999 *Réponse* survey of 10,303 employees in 1,791 workplaces with more than 20 workers found that 59 per cent of their respondents believed the unions were 'irreplaceable' as representative workplace institutions (Zouary 2002: 3). But how is it that with such a low number of members the unions survive to offer representation to both members and non-members?

Union structure and financing

The state obligation on employers to provide representation channels decided regularly by electoral challenges partly explains the continuing union presence. It encourages union activists to underline their ideological and organisational differences with activists attached to other centres. The electoral system also eases unions' financial problems: many workplace rep activists actually work full-time for the union at their employer's expense under firm or sector-level agreements dividing up a total 'pot' of annual hours between the unions according to their electoral scores. Each union can then 'spend' its share of annual hours on whichever union activist(s) and in whatever way it chooses – even if this means that the activist from a particular sector takes up a national union post only very remotely connected to the employer who continues to pay his or her wages.

The representative system may also be viewed as helping bind the unions to their base and as reinforcing the historical pattern equating union membership with union activism. Thus when an employee joins a workplace section, or more rarely a national or local union, it is usually a sign that they wish to become more involved in union activity than before. With the decline in union membership, leaving the existing activists frequently complaining about the shortage of members to take on a growing number of positions, this now means being included very early on upon a union slate for a representative position – or being involved in a some form of consultative role by the union as its eyes and ears into the workplace. With the highest union densities in 200+ workplaces, somewhere between one in five and one in ten of the members of every union present will have at least one representative position. Contrepois (2002) shows how, far from being a decision motivated by an individualistic analysis of the balance of personal advantage, the act of joining today generally involves embracing some sense of collective responsibility. The alternative for workers who are sympathetic and who vote union but who do not want to take their relationship any further is to continue to 'free-ride' the union.

Each union workplace section is a part of an individual union. Where they are big enough the sections join together to create a local union that covers a district or town. If not they simply link together at the level of the *département* (county) or the country where they form a single national union. Each union forwards a proportion of the subscriptions they receive through to the organisations they affiliate to. When it is organised locally or at department-level the union usually affiliates to an *interprofessionnelle* 'trades council', which represents all the local or departmental unions in dealings with the local state (mayors, prefects) and on any consultative committees. Local or departmental union branches also normally affiliate to two specific sectoral bodies: to an area-based body (*union territoriale*) and to their national federation (*fédération professionnelle*). In most cases both the area-based organisations and the national federations then affiliate separately to whichever of the nine national union centres they feel is most appropriate ideologically, industrially and professionally.

Union members pay between 0.5 and 1 per cent of their monthly net wage in subscriptions. In most cases they receive a stamp on their card from the collector of their union section or their local union treasurer. It is illegal for the employer to 'check-off' dues directly from the wage packet system, since this was viewed as a means of giving them too much control over what should be completely independent organisations. Although a growing proportion (particularly of white collar workers) now pay their dues by bankers' order, the need for the others to remember to pay each month leads to most missing a few months' payments each year. Most union branch treasurers therefore calculate their membership on the basis of 'eight stamps = one member', leading to a situation where unions that increase the proportion of their members on bankers' orders (thereby paying 12 stamps a year) almost automatically increase their claimed membership. This technical 'improvement' in dues collection, which has advanced most in the CFDT, was one factor behind the bottoming-out of a 20-year membership decline in the early 1990s.

The combination of low membership revenues and several calls on the dues that are paid (from section, local, area, federal and confederal organisations) mean that French trade unions have very few cash resources compared to their British or German counterparts. The confederations and federations hardly have any full-time officials paid for out of subscriptions. National full-timers are largely activists on paid secondment from their jobs.

This is possible in larger private and public organisations where activists accumulate enough legally permitted rep-time to cover their full working hours, and where they have a sectoral agreement giving them an entitlement to a certain volume of annual hours to release activists for federal or confederal posts. Such secondments are particularly developed in the public sector and so ultimately it is the tax payer who currently pays the wages of all five of the general secretaries of the five officially recognised national centres.

Besides financing public sector activists' time, the state also gives considerable grants towards union training programmes. At department or local level, where *bourses de travail* have been set up, the unions may be given free or peppercorn rent office space and subsidised telephone lines, paid for by local government. Another major source of unofficial subsidy arises at the workplace level through the works councils. Where (as is the case almost universally in the larger ones) the secretary is elected on a union slate, CE facilities are often used unofficially for such things as printing union leaflets, besides works council reps using their CE paid time off for what is really union business. The employers in the larger firms are aware of this and turn a blind eye, partly because to change their attitudes would provoke more open conflict, and partly because their more pluralistic components see them as means of institutionalising industrial relations (Contrepois 2002). Indeed, the most recent enquiry into French works councils found that now where they were still being formed, it was more often at the initiative of the employer in search of some form of legitimate means of dialoguing with his employees than it was as a result of union agitation (IRES-DARES 1998).

Finally, there is the very considerable subsidy provided directly or indirectly through the parity welfare system. The hundreds of different welfare associations that workers pay into generate about 30,000 full and part-time administrative posts for the unions to fill (Jacquier 1998: 87). Naturally they tend to nominate victimised, redundant or retired union activists to the posts and, not surprisingly, the nominees find several ways to return the favour. Sometimes this is simply done by their being available (along with retired activists) to swell the numbers on demonstrations called by their union; sometimes it goes further, to the point of arranging for some activists on the payroll of a welfare scheme to be seconded to work for the union on a permanent basis.

The patronage available from coming to a working arrangement with the employers at national level is maximised through the arrangement where the social partner who presides at national level automatically nominates the chairs of all the linked local joint administrative committees as well. Within the bipartite French welfare system the presidency of the managing committees of each separate organisation is decided by a voting system that requires cross voting. Thus, to elect a president, either one or more of the employers' organisations has to vote with the trade unions, or one or more

Table 8.1 Chairs of selected national welfare parity schemes, 1998

Parity body	English translation	Chair arrangements
ACOSS	Central agency for social security	Medef
AGFF	Investment fund management agency	All signatories in turn
AGIRC	Supplementary pension scheme for managers	CGC/Medef alternating
ARRCO	Supplementary pension scheme for non-managerial workers	FO/Medef alternating
CNAF	National family allowance agency	CFTC
CNAMTS	Workers health service agency	CFDT
CNAVTS	Workers old age pension agency	CGC
OPACIF	Individual training leave joint management body	All signatories in turn
UCANSS	National social security agency	CFDT/Medef alternating
UNEDIC	Unemployment insurance for industry and commerce	CFDT/Medef alternating

Source: Jacquier 1998: 86.

trade union has to vote with the employers' organisations. Since the employers will not vote for the communist-linked CGT the spoils are divided between the other four national centres and the CNPF/Medef, as shown in Table 8.1.

The scale of patronage thus available exerts powerful pressures on the national confederations to reach compromises with the Medef. The change of position of the CGC in 2000 from opposing the PARE agreement on unemployment insurance to supporting it was clearly influenced by the Medef's open threats to withdraw its support from the CGC for its traditional agency presidencies.

Union membership

Evidence confirming that by 1999 the CFDT equalled the CGT in terms of union membership is provided by the second *Réponse* survey. This large-scale Ministry of Labour-sponsored survey involved nearly 1,732 face-to-face interviews in workplaces in 1993 and 2,255 in 1999 in a comparable weighted representative sample of all French workplaces with more than 50 or more workers. It found that the CFDT was present in 47 per cent and the CGT in 45 per cent of workplaces, while in terms of the proportion of workers covered they were exactly equal with 62 per cent (Zouary 2000). The CFDT's high public profile and, arguably, the greater support given to it by the employers have made it more 'visible' in the workplace than the other unions. In 1999, where a CFDT trade union rep (DS) was present some 53 per cent of the respondents to the *Réponse* employee survey were aware of this, compared to an awareness average of just 41 per cent when they

Table 8.2   Estimated average annual trade union membership (excluding retirees) (in thousands), 1950s–1990s

	1950–1959	1960–1969	1970–1979	1980–1989	1990–1999
CGT	2,046	1,321	1,500	768	420
CFDT		507	684	486	500
CFTC	360	150	200	185	160
FO	1,000	800	1,000	500	300
CGC	100	200	300	225	180
FEN/UNSA	200	300	500	300	100
FSU					150
CSL				100	50
G10 (Sud)				250	100
Others	100	200	300	250	140
Rounded total	*3,900*	*3,500*	*4,500*	*3,000*	*2,100*

* Trade union membership is notoriously difficult to estimate in France, where there is no public scrutiny of membership claims, where figures only began being published regularly by some of the Confederations in the 1980s, the employer check-off is illegal, and where the definition of who is a member may vary according to whether a person has paid one month's dues in a year or eight.

Sources: Jefferys 1996a: 515; *Le Monde*, various dates, for 1995–2001.

were not present (Zouary 2002: 3). The CFDT's growth in relative importance against the background of a nearly unremitting decline in CGT membership is clear from Table 8.2.

Although many workers join the union whose local reps are either the first to ask them, or who make the most impression on them (Contrepois 2002), the political culture of each union still has an impact. In national political elections in 1997 and 2002 the members and supporters of the three largest union centrals, the CGT, CFDT and FO, still reflected their distinctive political traditions, as shown in Table 8.3.

CGT members remain far more likely to vote Communist and for the left as a whole than are FO and CFDT members, although these proportions fell by 10 per cent between 1997 and 2002. The CFDT is significantly less likely to vote for the racist *Front National* than the national average or than FO supporters and members, but was significantly more likely to vote for the right in 2002 than in 1997. The triangle of union ideology traced in Figure 2.6 (page 64) that suggested the CGT was closer to the *class* pole, the CFDT closer to the *social integration* pole, and the FO closer to the *market* pole is given some confirmation. The major representative unions still have distinctive political identities.

As a result of this ideological differentation, trade unionists who disagree with the ideological direction being taken by their confederation may decide on these grounds to leave the confederation altogether (or they may be expelled) and either to join the large majority of non-unionists or to form

Table 8.3 Political differences among union voters in the first rounds of the 1997 National Assembly and the 2002 Presidential elections

%	National Assembly 1997				Presidential 2002			
	CGT	FO	CFDT	National average	CGT	FO	CFDT	National average
Right								
UDF-RPR	7	23	33	29.9	12	20	35	26
FN	11	18	7	14.9	13	18	12	17
Other right				6.6				
Right total	*18*	*42*	*40*	*51.4*	*25*	*38*	*47*	*43*
Left								
PS	34	42	37	23.5	24	18	26	16
PCF	39	4	6	9.9	18	3	1	3
Greens	3	7	10	6.4	3	6	7	5
Far left	5	5	7	2.5	20	19	7	10
Other left				2.8	6	5	7	5
Left total	*81*	*58*	*60*	*45.1*	*71*	*54*	*48*	*39*

Source: CSA exit poll cited by Jacquier 1998; Liaisons-Sociales 2002.

a new ideological centre. In the context of the growing intensity of work over the last 20 years, and of the mounting tensions between the available union responses of 'fight' or 'flight', France has seen the further fragmentation of the union movement and the emergence of new centres.

New fragmentation or new horizons? FEN and SUD

Until 1992, the state-recognised teachers' federation, FEN, carefully balanced the different appeals of professionalism and collective bargaining with the state to give education one of the highest trade union densities in France (as elsewhere in Europe). Then, tensions between the separate primary and secondary teachers' unions exploded in a context where the political discipline over their leaders exercised by the Communist and Socialist parties broke down with the collapse of Communism in Russia and in deep disillusion with the Mitterrand presidency. In 1993, the more left-wing *Fédération syndicale unitaire* (FSU) was formally established. Based mainly in secondary education it became the largest union across the education sector as a whole, relegating the FEN to second place with the CFDT in third and FO in fourth place in the 1993 elections for the national joint management advisory council (Mouriaux 1996: 102, 110). As a result, in the representative elections across the whole government sector the FSU narrowly became the largest union, with 19.5 per cent of votes cast, compared to 16.7 per cent for the CGT and 15.4 per cent for UNSA across the three years from 1998 to 2000.

The 1992 teachers' split was not the only sign of trade union fragmentation and repositioning in the 1980s and 1990s. In the election years of 1986 and 1988, and particularly in 1989, several strikes occurred in which grass roots' strike action more or less by-passed the official trade union channels. The activists formed rank and file 'co-ordination' committees involving strikers from several different unions and different areas and even non-unionists to give their movements leaderships with greater 'legitimacy' than could be claimed by any individual official union centre. One of these took place in the strongly unionised Post Office that was still part of the *PTT*, the state-owned combined post office and telephone company. Although CFDT activists and members were among the strike leaders, the CFDT–PTT national union and the CFDT centre denounced it and invited the newly re-elected Socialist government to use the army to break the strike. The CFDT then expelled many of the known strike leaders, accusing them of having embraced CGT 'class struggle' ideology rather than the CFDT path of 'concrete proposals, negotiations and compromise' (Coupé and Marchand 1998: 28).

Those expelled promptly formed a new union called SUD – *Solidaire Unitaires et Démocratiques*. It was immediately boosted by the PTT joint administrative council (CAP) elections of March 1989 for the public sector equivalent of personnel reps. This election put SUD on the map and gave it a distinct identity. Subsequently SUD's vote rose from 4.5 in 1989 to 18.7 per cent by 2000 in *La Poste*, and from 5.9 to 28 per cent in *France Télécom* (Denis 2001: 216–18). SUD–PTT's membership also rose from 1,800 to 10,000 between 1990 and 2000. Table 8.4 shows the growth in its share of the Administrative Board votes during the 1990s in the two organisations.

The expulsion of the SUD–PTT activists weakened the internal opposition to the national CFDT leadership. As a result the union's shift away from the *class struggle* pole and repositioning on *societal integration* values with an increasing stress on *market* unionism has become more marked, leading to more departures and more small SUD unions being formed outside the PTT. By 1998 there were six other SUD national union federations and some 40 independent SUD local unions (Denis 2001: 237–8). While most SUD unions have been formed in the public or semi-public sectors, a handful have emerged in the private sector, such as at Michelin where the national CFDT centre overruled the local branch's opposition to signing a high flexibility 35-hours agreement.

Soon after its creation SUD–PTT approached a loose group of autonomous unions known as the 'Group of Ten' (G10) for observer status and then affiliated in 1992. The founding 'Ten' unions had first met together in 1981. Seven of them had been affiliated to the CGT up to 1947 and had then gone their own ways. The two largest, the autonomous civil servants (FGAF) and the police (FASP) unions, between them represented half the G10's initial 300,000 claimed membership.

What pushed these autonomous unions to start talking together? Partly a common sentiment that with the new Mitterrand presidency they needed

Table 8.4 Board position (CA) election results in La
Poste and France-Télécom, 1991–2000

	1991	1995	2000
La Poste			
(312,000 electors in			
2000)			
CGT	36.9	39.1	34.2
CFDT	26.4	17.3	18.3
FO	26.7	22	18.9
SUD		14.4	21
CFTC	7.1	5	5.2
CGC	2.9	2.2	2.4
France-Télécom			
(163,000 electors in			
2000)			
CGT	35.8	32	28
CFDT	33	18.1	20.4
FO	20	15.2	13.8
SUD		26.7	27.5
CFTC	6.9	4.6	6.3
CGC	4.3	3.3	3.9

Source: *Le Monde*, 27 October 2000.

to make their voices heard by the government, the employers and the major
union centres, and needed to try and make their numbers weigh more within
the representative institutions; partly also they wished to try and overcome
some of their individual resource weaknesses as their memberships declined.
The G10 was hit hard in 1983 when its two largest associated unions merged
and left, and it was only when SUD–PTT became associated that it began to
get re-energised. By 1998, shortly after the G10 had officially registered itself
as a Centre of autonomous federations and national unions, only three of the
original Ten unions were still affiliated. But they had been joined by ten SUD
unions and seven others with a total of about 65,000 members between
them. The G10's largest member, the Tax Staffs United National Trade Union
(SNUI) in the Ministry of Finance, received 44 per cent of the vote in its CAP
elections in 1997 (Denis 2001). Under SUD influence the G10 has become
increasingly associated with the twin ideas of maximum union autonomy
and struggle against the employers and globalisation.

One reason the G10 finally formalised its existence in 1998 was the pressure placed on it by the establishment on its political right of another much
larger centre of independent unions, *Union nationale des syndicats autonomes*
(UNSA). UNSA was formed in 1993 by what was left of the FEN teachers'
federation and four ex-G10 members. By its third congress in 2002 UNSA

claimed a substantial membership of 360,000 and had a still wider audience, despite not achieving its goal of getting the two decrees annulled that gave national representative status only to the five union centres: the 1966 decree and the 1986 Perben law that extended the representation law to the public sector (*Le Monde*, 21 January 2002).

The issue of membership or union 'audience' is at the heart of current debates about the future of the privileged interlocuteur system. In these debates the CGC, CFTC and FO prefer to retain the status quo, which enables them to hit far beyond their weight. The CFDT opposes state financing of unions because as the wealthiest of the existing confederations it feels that such financing would merely sustain its competitors. It is also, therefore, in favour of trade union recognition being awarded only on the basis of a strict headcount of actual members. The CGT, by contrast, also wants to end the present system, but given its smaller dues-paying base, it prefers to have representativity decided by national (industrial tribunal) and/or workplace elections (which it wants to have all on one day to provide a kind of referendum on national union performance). It feels that a higher proportion of workers will vote for it because of its 'militant' image than would ever join it, so it prefers to have its electorate, or 'audience' weighed in to the count in any decision on representativity. This issue of the union 'audience' is quite critical to understanding the relationship between union activists and the wider working class.

Union audience

The finances, daily activities and many union activists are intimately involved with the extensive range of legally-based representative and parity institutions described in the previous section. The elections they give rise to are one of the most effective ways of gauging the unions' real audience. Figure 8.1 graphs the distribution of the 6.4 million votes cast (excluding

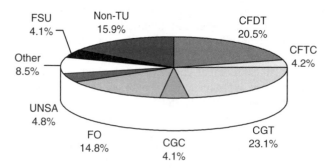

Figure 8.1   Trade union shares of representative votes in public and private sectors, around 1995

Source: Jacquier 1998: 29.

the abstentions) in all the various works council and CAP elections across the civil service and both nationalised and private sectors that occurred between 1994 and 1996.

This picture of trade union influence among the nine million voters in France's 50+ workplaces and organisations makes clear the extent of union influence on employment relations, despite the low overall union membership density of about eight per cent. While the unions only had two million members, nearly three times that number voted for them. A part of this 'audience' are former members or sympathisers, but most are workers who have never joined a union, but who exercise their right to choose a trade unionist to represent them.

An analysis of representative votes over time highlights the changing weight of different unions. The trend in works council elections (private sector only) since 1966 is shown in Figure 8.2.

The growth of the non-union vote up to 1992 partly reflects the increase in the numbers of works councils reported to the Ministry, up from about 8,600 in 1967 to 24,000 in 1978 when it stabilised before reaching 25,000 in the 1990s. At the same time the total numbers of voters also more than doubled. This growth in participation occurred after a 1966 reform that

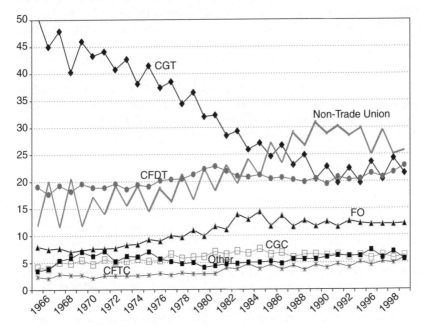

Figure 8.2 Union and non-union shares of works council election results, in percentage, 1966–1999

Sources: Sociales-DARES 1998: 173; Ruelland 1999; 2001.

Table 8.5 Votes cast in elections for all colleges of works councils (in thousands), 1996–1997

	1966–1967	1976–1977	1981–1982	1986–1987	1991–1992	1996–1997
CGT	803	1,561	1,134	909	792	734
CFDT	307	770	796	717	717	706
FO	129	361	385	432	420	403
CGC	67	213	233	225	210	203
CFTC	38	113	104	146	153	160
Other	59	261	155	184	220	218
Non-unionists	240	647	711	759	996	902
Total	*1,644*	*3,925*	*3,517*	*3,373*	*3,509*	*3,326*
% participation	*71.9*	*71.2*	*70.4*	*67.3*	*65.4*	*66.6*

Sources: Labbé 1994: 40; Ruelland 1999; 2000.

made reporting the results compulsory, and after the May–June strike wave of 1968 radicalised many hundreds of thousands of workers. The rise in the non-trade union share of the vote in the 1970s and 1980s, however, testifies to the growing difficulties in putting together union slates. The CGT then lost coverage rapidly while the other unions were virtually only standing still. This can be seen more clearly in the absolute numbers of votes cast. Table 8.5 shows that the CGT vote for CE reps in 1976–1977 halved by the early 1990s to the level it was at in 1966–1967, while the CFDT vote more than doubled in the decade from 1966–1967 before stabilising thereafter. The CFDT maintained its share of a slowly falling total so that it eventually equalled the CGT.

One other national worker election result showed the CGT in 1997 as having the larger audience. This was the election that occurs on the same December day across France every five years for over 7,000 employee 'judges' to sit in pairs alongside two employer elected 'judges' in the private sector industrial tribunals (*Conseils de Prud'hommes*). While there was a big increase in abstentions between the 1992 and 1997 elections, the 1.6 million workers who voted for CGT 'judges' still considerably exceeded those who voted CFDT, as shown in Table 8.6.

While the December 2002 industrial tribunal elections will provide a more accurate guide, it is unlikely that the strong employee support for the CGT will evaporate in the same way as has the working class vote for the Communist Party. Many observers from the trade unions and the employers and from government will be examining the results in some detail to see how far they confirm the continuing presence of a class struggle pole in French employment relations.

At the beginning of the twenty-first century, despite facing a more serious and sustained employers' challenge than any they had faced in the previous half century, French unions are still fragmented and fragmenting in ways that largely reflect historic divisions. How serious is this?

Table 8.6 Industrial tribunal election results, 1992 and 1997

	1992		1997	
	Numbers (m)	%	Numbers (m)	%
Abstentions	8.4	59.2	9.6	66
Voters	5.5	38.8	4.8	33
Union shares				
CGT	1.8	33.4	1.6	33.1
CFDT	1.3	23.7	1.2	25.3
FO	1.1	20.4	1.0	20.6
CFTC	0.47	8.6	0.36	7.5
CGC	0.38	6.9	0.29	5.9
CSL	0.24	4.4	0.2	4.2
Other	0.14	2.6	0.11	2.3
UNSA			0.04	0.7
G10			0.02	0.3

Source: Sociales-DARES 1998: 178.

8.2 The trade union 'crisis'

This section first examines the debate about a 'crisis' in French unionism, and then explores its response to three current challenges. In the 1980s and early 1990s the seemingly unstoppable decline in union membership in a context where rising unemployment reduced labour's bargaining power led to the argument that French unions were living a terminal 'crisis', one that might even lead to the emergence of an institutionally recognised trade unionism without members (Rosanvallon 1988). This argument supports the Tourainian thesis that the trade unions no longer constitute a 'social movement' capable of influencing social change. Ubbiali (2001) summarises five sets of explanations for the union 'crisis':

- it reflects capital's restructuring of labour markets;
- it is the result of changes in the labour force, often accompanied by new employer human resource strategies;
- it reflects the slow death of a manual working class movement with a transformatory agenda;
- it reflects the divisions and fragmentation of the unions;
- it follows from the institutionalisation of the unions that have become cut off from their base.

One school of thought that focuses on the last three of these explanations has been developed by the distant (Weberian) cousins of social movement theory, the researchers grouped around Dominique Labbé in the Cerat research centre of Grenoble University (Labbé and Croisat 1992; Andolfatto and Labbé 1997; 2000). Their analysis focuses on what they see as French workers' growing individualism, where workers allegedly increasingly join unions for 'instrumental' rather than ideological reasons, and increasingly identify with narrow sectional interests rather than broader and more political concerns. To prevent or perhaps postpone an early death, what is needed, they conclude, is for the French unions to become more sectional, narrower, and less political, and to cut free from the institutional props provided by the state, so that they can more 'genuinely' represent ordinary workers. This is the strategy largely followed by the CFDT under Nicole Notat, general secretary from 1993 to 2002.

The strongest evidence for the existence of a crisis lies in the French trade unionism's numerical weakness and divisions. At about eight per cent of the working population French trade union density is the lowest in the advanced industrial world. In whole areas of working life there is absolutely no trade union presence: in the private sector it drops to about seven per cent overall. And where trade unionism does exist its weakness pushes it to rely upon both state financing and state intervention. The *representation* desert is far from as extensive as the trade union desert, but in particular industries it is still huge as graphed in Figure 8.3.

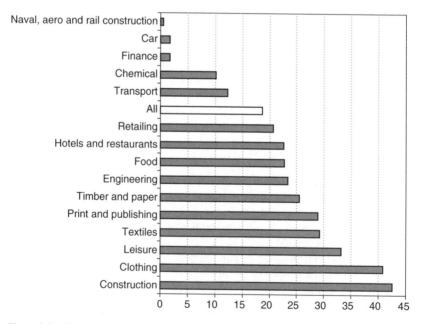

Figure 8.3   Proportion of employees in workplaces with ten or more workers who are not covered by any form of representation, by sector (in per cent), 1999
Source: Ruelland 2001: 3.

'Crisis' or new challenge?

Yet there are several reasons for viewing the 'crisis' analysis with caution. One is the fact that French unions may be viewed as being in permanent 'crisis' virtually ever since the foundation of the CGT in 1895. Writing in 1992 René Mouriaux and Guy Groux identified seven historic 'crises' for the CGT confederation alone, and argued that France's major trade union centre could never really be described as being in a 'natural' crisis-free period (Groux and Mouriaux 1992: 50–65).

A second reason for caution is that the seemingly endless membership decline appears to have halted in the first half of the 1990s and there is some evidence that it has been followed by a certain degree of union renewal. Thus the long-term decline in the proportion of voters participating in works council elections that set in after 1968 ended in 1990–1991, with the rest of the 1990s seeing slightly higher levels of participation (Ruelland 2001). Another recent finding is that between 1993 and 1999 the proportion of workplaces with 50 or more workers covered by a trade union rep (*délégué syndical*) rose from 63 to 72 per cent, while the proportion of workers they covered in these establishments rose from 78 to 84 per cent. The explanations for this improvement lie in part with large firm take-overs of SMEs bringing many of them within the remit of a group: this makes it more likely that they make contact with an existing trade union organisation. But the incentives available to employers under the 1996 Robien and 1998 Aubry laws if they negotiated working-time reductions appear also to have led many employers to facilitate or encourage the nomination of trade union reps (Zouary 2000). Since other research confirms it is the presence of trade union reps that holds the key to the presence of all three other representative channels (Ruelland 2001), if this recovery of the trade union rep is maintained it could even strengthen the 'latticework of organisation' (Shorter and Tilly 1974), so crucial to worker mobilisation.

A third reason for doubting the simple 'weakening trade unionism' thesis is the organisational flux described above. The eviction of the SUD activists from the CFDT, the formation of SUD, the strengthening of the G10 centre, the split in FEN, the creation of the FSU and the emergence of UNSA can only with great difficulty be assimilated into a linear analysis of union decline. These organisational initiatives, certainly involving hundreds and possibly even a few thousand union activists in conscious choices about their personal time cannot be dismissed simply as being irrational acts. Although multi-unionism is systematically encouraged by the French state-imposed representative framework, the flurry of such activity in the 1990s is testimony to the identification of the presence rather than the absence of trade union opportunities. Thus one study of union recruitment in the late 1980s and early 1990s found simply that more members would join if the activists only made the effort to ask them (Piotet *et al.* 1992).

Finally, the stronger versions of the 'trade union crisis' argument are challenged by considerable evidence of continuing union mobilising capacity. Comparing the periods 1990–1992 with 1996–1998, the French workplace industrial relations survey *Réponse* found that as many workplaces were touched by industrial action in the later period (32 per cent) as in the former, but that where it occurred it was 'harder', more likely to involve either very short stoppages or strikes lasting two days or more. The actions that were less common were demonstrations, petitions and refusals to work overtime (Zouary 2000). Figure 8.4 also shows the numbers of market sector strikes that have risen slightly from the historic lows of 1996 and 1998, and days lost through strike action in the market and public sector were higher in the five years after the special year of 1995 than they were in the five years before.

It would be wrong to exaggerate the significance of the combination of the 1995 mini-strike wave and the rise in both private and public sector combativity since 1998. Over a longer time scale the 16 years between 1985 and 2000, experienced an annual average of 1,519 market sector strikes, compared to 3,245 a year between 1969 and 1984 and 1,857 a year between 1952 and 1967 (Shorter and Tilly 1974; Simon 1981; Merlier 2002). Yet in the late 1990s and early 2000s there appears to be more confidence in and a greater readiness to exercise the right to strike than before 1995. And this

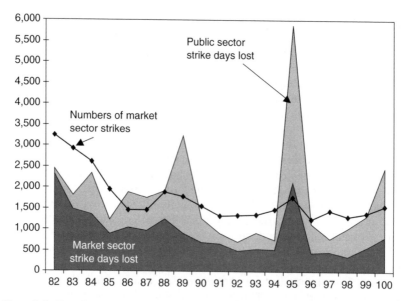

Figure 8.4   French market sector strikes and strike days (in thousands) lost in the market and public sectors, 1982–2000

Sources: Jefferys 1996; Merlier 2002.

is born out in opinion surveys. CSA, one of the principal French polling organisations, suggests the presence of greater popular support for strikes in the second half of the 1990s than a decade earlier. During the winter 1986–1987 public sector strikes only one-third of the general public either supported or were sympathetic to the strikers, yet in the six years from 1995 to 2000, an average of 40 per cent 'supported' the 26 national strikes that occurred and a further 28 per cent had 'sympathy' for them (*Le Monde*, 7 March 2001). Supporting poll evidence from *Sofres* shows the proportion of all French employees expressing 'more or less confidence' in the unions rising from 41 per cent in 1990–1991 to 51 per cent in 1996–1997 (Jacquier 1998: 30).

Thus, the suggestion behind much of the emphasis on its 'crisis' that French unionism in the 1990s is significantly less representative of the interests of the majority of workers than it was in the earlier decades is doubtful, although the picture is complex and still evolving. Rather, from the viewpoint of a ruling elite that sees flexibility, competitivity, American-style managerialism and even an Anglo-Saxon pension-funds dominated stock market as the only route for national economic survival, it is the continuing capacity of the minority unions to mobilise a seemingly recalcitrant core of workers in defence of their workplace and welfare rights that is the cause of whatever employment relations or managerial 'crisis' there is. This was made clear in the second half of the 1990s when three major challenges were made to the employment relations status quo: to the 'pay as you go' pension system, to inflexible restrictions on working time, and to tripartism. Each of these challenges met with considerable resistance from a majority of the trade union movement as a whole, but as we show in the matrix in Table 8.7, each of them exposed growing disagreements between the major union centres.

What were these disagreements between the unions about? We now look briefly at each of these challenges in turn.

State re-regulation of pensions: 1995

In 1995, the government proposed a pension reform that would have cut public sector workers' average pensions at retirement by an estimated

Table 8.7 Union confederation positions on major employment relations reforms, 1995–2001

	CGT	CFDT	FO
1995 Juppé pensions reform	Opposition	Partial support	Opposition
1998/2000 Aubry 35-hour week	Partial support	Partial support	Opposition
2000/2001 Medef welfare reform	Opposition	Partial support	Opposition

5–15 per cent and would have significantly reduced the numbers who could afford to retire aged 55. The result was a strike wave between October and December 1995 that was the largest since 1968. This movement was largely responsible for the evidence found by the OECD that while strike days lost per 1,000 employees in the United States fell from 61 to 39 between 1988–1993 and 1994–1999, in France they rose from 80 to 92 (Coutrot 2001). In 1995, not only were some six million strike days lost (excluding local government and hospital workers), but more people actually mobilised on the streets than occurred in 1968: even the police figures admitted that nearly one million demonstrated on Tuesday 12 December 1995 alone. The strikes marked a reassertion of collective resistance and recalled the strike upsurges that have punctuated French employment relations history (Jefferys 1996a,b).

The possibility of any further such 'strike explosions' in France had previously been written off by many employment relations academics, most of whom had also ignored the earlier signs of renewal. These signs – the union restructuring, the bottoming out of membership decline, the higher level of participation in works council elections, the greater presence of trade union reps – suggested either a more positive assessment of the trade union potential in defending wider working class interests, or a growing awareness of the need to defend those interests. Whichever, the outcome was that within months of Chirac's 1995 presidential victory, his government found itself forced to retreat from its full state sector pensions reform programme because of the breadth and depth of a strike movement that received unprecedented support from the public.

Several factors helped legitimate the strikes: despite the huge right-wing majority in the National Assembly Chirac had lost considerable political credibility through his decision to resume French nuclear tests and through reversing his electoral emphasis upon tackling the 'social fracture' in order to meet EU public sector spending targets; a display of unity in action between the CGT and FO occurred at the first joint October one-day strike when for the first time since the 1947 split, their two general secretaries shook hands in public; on the railways the image of union unity was reinforced by a united front of all three federations, the CGT, FO and the CFDT; a student strike had broken out at the beginning of October that gained considerable public sympathy and focused attention on the government's intention to ram through public spending cuts. At a more mundane level the prime minister, Alain Juppé, a cultivated intellectual elitist *énarque* (as indeed are Chirac and Jospin), had just fired eight women ministers for dissent, and was widely viewed as arrogant and aloof. Under these conditions the grievance – the proposal to extend by five the years workers would have to put in before they could achieve their maximum pension – was easy to generalise. It was seen as being the first major attempt to reduce the costs to the state and employers of the whole welfare settlement of the 1940s and 1970s, to impose

Maastricht discipline on France, and it generated a class response. It was as if workers had been waiting for an opportunity to express their anger about the high levels of insecurity they felt about both jobs and welfare. Across the public sector there were weekly protest stoppages while minorities of from 10 to 40 per cent of workers in the railways and public transport, parts of the post office and France Telecom, French electricity and gas staged indefinite strikes lasting between one and three weeks; in the private sector workers sent delegations to the demonstrations but above all expressed their support for the strikes, and anti-strike protests collapsed.

The principal importance of 1995 for French employment relations and management was its underlining the potential of collective resistance to stand up to policies introduced as neo-liberal imperatives. However, the three main national centres responded differently. The FO talked a very strong oppositional line at national level, even being prepared to participate in joint demonstrations with the CGT. The CGT moved slowly at first to build and spread the strike, but then used its pre-eminence among the railway workers to try and give the movement leadership. In 1998, the young CGT–SNCF union leader, Bernard Thibault, who came to prominence during the strike, took over as the confederal CGT general secretary. The CFDT, however, nationally adopted a 'realistic' approach, ready to accept some reforms and to compromise.

This tweaking of CFDT ideology by its national leadership back towards its 'societal integration' origins interrupted but did not destroy the relations between it and the CGT. During the previous few years the CGT had been more or less openly courting the CFDT. Aware that the two centres were now more or less equal in size, and in a context where the tearing down of the Berlin Wall in 1989 had weakened the PCF and disoriented its activists in the CGT, the CGT had adopted a more genuine position in favour of greater trade union unity and cooperation than at any time in the past. The CGT's approach was not innocent. On the one hand it wanted the CFDT's backing in order to be accepted as an ETUC member, and so to become liable to EU funding. On the other its leadership believed that with the old PCF discipline, if it did ever come to a CFDT–CGT merger, it would not be long before the 'CGT' bit of the partnership would come out on top. The CFDT's leadership, meanwhile, was not unhappy to go some of the way with this project. Thus, in exchange for CFDT backing for CGT entry to the ETUC, the CGT effectively undertook to deny any support to the anti-Notat CFDT minority or to 'poach' dissidents seeking a new home, despite the proximity of the class struggle CFDT minority to the CGT majority.

Ultimately, the 1995 strike created such a degree of disillusion with Juppé and Chirac that when Chirac called a general election one year earlier than required in 1997, the right lost control of the National Assembly. The Socialists had been largely silent or absent from the 1995 strike movement, but the 1997 Socialist manifesto had restated the 1981 promise of a 35-hour week as one part of the answer to high unemployment, and their election – secured largely thanks to the divisions of the right – nonetheless confirmed a small swing in public opinion away from a more neo-liberal approach to modernising France. It is difficult to interpret the decision to legislate the 35-hour week over the objections of the employers, other than as an attempt, however weak, by Jospin and Martine Aubry, the Minister of Labour, to reward those who had resisted neo-liberal de-regulation in 1995.

State regulation of working time: the 35-hour laws

The 1998 and 2000 Aubry Laws implementing the 35-hour week remain controversial (see Chapter 5 for a more detailed account). The employers' organisations opposed them as anti-competitive through increasing labour costs and lowering output, and for having negative macro effects on employee purchasing power (by reducing overtime earnings) and on taxation (which must be raised to help incentivised firms to make the transition). They also opposed the laws on principle. They favour individual contracts, not systematic recourse to the law; and if they are forced to draw up rules they prefer for them to be by agreement and not by the state and civil servants.

However, it is not only the employers who opposed the Aubry laws. FO was also highly critical, and not merely because its macho general secretary Marc Blondel has had legal action taken against him for working his chauffeurs to the point of exhaustion (*Le Figaro*, 1 December 2001). FO's opposition is essentially on the grounds that by encouraging workplace-level negotiations and agreements that can undercut the national sectoral agreements the Aubry laws will neutralise the labour code and leave workers exposed to agreements and contracts decided at a level where the employers are at their strongest. The annualisation of working hours will, FO argues, restrain recruitment while simultaneously reducing overtime opportunities and workers' earnings. It is also equally opposed to the device of unions 'mandating' non-members to sign agreements in firms where they have no membership. This it sees as encouraging non-unionism and situations where non-trade unionists agree to terms that reduce living standards and worsen working conditions, undercutting unionised workplaces.

The CFDT and CGT are more positive on both of these two issues, partly because they are much more present than the FO at local level. Thus for them 'mandating' non-members to negotiate could be a way of increasing their contacts with potential members, while an increasing volume of local negotiations would be an opportunity to demonstrate to more workers the relevance of trade unionism. This very much follows the defence of pluralism in employment relations made by Jospin and Aubry in justifying the measure. In this sense it can be seen as the latest in a long line of interventions developing 'modern' collective bargaining procedures prompted by substantive measures on working time (Jefferys 2000).

Within both the CFDT and CGT, however, there are also many who are openly critical, arguing that the way the laws were drafted opened the doors unnecessarily to an intensification of work. This argument is particularly strong from manual workers who, often, gaining just one half-day a week or one hour a day, have also had to bear not only the reorganisation of working patterns and work intensification, but also wage restraint and reduced overtime earning opportunities. Those who have benefited by having as many as 17 days' extra holidays a year, such as managers, professional workers and some clerical and technical workers, are much more positive.

There is also a debate about the overall effect of the measures on jobs. In early 2002, the government estimated that outside the public sector 128,200 firms employing 8.8 million workers had already signed 35-hour agreements, leaving 7.4 million workers in a further 1.4 million firms uncovered. Those who had not signed were mainly smaller firms that under the 2002 right government are no longer required to move to the 35-hour week at all. In those firms with more than 20 staff that legally should have implemented the 35 hours on 1 February 2000, however, 49,000 firms employing 2.8 million staff still had not done so. These figures compare with a slightly smaller total of 46,800 firms with 20+ employees whose 8.3 million workers were working 35 hours and where, since June 1998, agreements had been reached to create an additional 307,000 jobs (Ministry of Labour 35-hours web site, 27 February 2002). However, there are two big unknowns: whether all the jobs supposed to have been created or maintained as a result of 35-hour agreements actually were; and how many of the roughly one million new jobs created since Jospin came to power should be attributed to the 35-hour week and how many to the economic recovery. Some suggest that the new jobs created is much lower than the Ministry of Labour estimate (Pisani-Ferry 2001), while others argue it is much higher (Husson 2002).

There is thus a continuing debate within the trade unions as to the precise function played by the 35-hour laws within the French employment relations system. Some activists see them as a definite restraint upon the employers, requiring them to treat their staff better, forcing them to the negotiating table and making them employ more workers. Others see the laws as being a clever managerial mechanism for blackmailing the unions to negotiate much greater temporal flexibility than would otherwise have occurred, and in so doing, helping to weaken the ties between the unions and a sceptical workforce. Whichever analysis is made, the initiative not only introduced a new division among the main union centres, but it also led directly to the employers issuing a third challenge to the unions.

Employer re-regulation of welfare

The Medef's *Refondation sociale* of 2000–2001 (discussed in detail in Chapter 7) is in many ways the most significant of the three recent challenges faced by French unions. By attacking tripartism and any state intervention in regulating employment conditions that are linked to exit or entry from the labour market, the employers are quite consciously and deliberately attacking the Achilles heel of French trade unionism. This is, as we have shown in detail above, its reliance upon the state for legitimacy, for cash and a cadre of full-time officers, and most important of all, for a detailed framework of workplace employee representation that literally provides the life-blood of the trade union movement.

The three main union centres responded to the first phase of this attack in a fairly predictable way. Despite several brave words they all finally agreed to attend the Medef's invitation to start talks – the risks of isolation being greater, they felt, if they kept away than if they took their seats. Then, having taken their seats, they effectively fell into the employers' negotiating trap. Since the Medef constantly threatened to walk out of the parity system if they did not make concessions, rather than walk away, the unions continued to talk until some concessions were made.

The CFDT essentially accepted the Medef's argument that it was the state that was now holding back the emergence of a healthy pluralist, zero-sum collective bargaining relationship between unions and employers. Nicole Notat recognised the dangers of 'over-reliance' upon the state and argued that the unions should stand on their own two feet, thereby adopting wholeheartedly the recommendations of the Grenoble Cerat researchers discussed at the beginning of this section. If trade unionism is to have a future, the CFDT centre suggests, it will be dependent upon the employers finding an acceptable union partner with whom they can feel comfortable 'doing business'. Hence to become such an acceptable partner the CFDT will distance itself as far as possible from expressions of its earlier dalliance with *class struggle* and workers' control ideologies, relying instead increasingly on employer recognition and membership services, and less on actively pursuing grievances to recruit new members. It was thus prepared to sign up to the PARE reforms of the unemployment insurance system transforming a service hitherto viewed as an entitlement to benefit for those who had paid into it into one requiring the unemployed to fulfil certain job-seeking obligations. It was also ready to pay what it believes will be short-term political costs. Among these was the breakaway of the *Syndicat national unitaire* (SNU) from the CFDT–ANPE union in the National Employment Agency (responsible for the new compulsory assessments). In 2002 the SNU came top in the agency's joint consultative committee elections with 29 per cent of the poll. The rump of the CFDT won only 12 per cent and was in fifth place compared to the 40 per cent it had received in the 1998 elections (*Le Monde*, 21 January 2002).

FO, by contrast, feels highly threatened by the breadth of the Medef attack. More present in the public than in the private sector, where it is largely dependent on its state-representative recognised status for any presence at the negotiating table, FO's leadership believes its very survival is at stake. Blondel thus spoke out as loudly and publicly as possible against the *Refondation sociale* and, of all the proposed agreements with the Medef, FO only signed the 2001 'position paper' on collective bargaining. This Blondel interpreted as pledging the Medef to maintain the *status quo* until the issue is raised again.

The CGT believed it was better to be present at the negotiations to try and build a majority trade union opposition than to exercise the protest option of an 'empty chair'. It also hoped to be able to use the negotiations as a shop window to help air and popularise a series of alternative proposals that would have increased workers' rights and benefits. Yet in part because it had not fully mapped out its alternatives, in part because the constant ultimatums from the employers helped keep the union side divided, and in part because of the relative lack of experience of its new general secretary Bernard Thibault, the CGT was never really able to take the initiative. Nonetheless its consistent opposition did eventually pay off, with a temporary period of trade union unity finally delivering demonstrations across France totalling some 300,000 people against the Medef on Thursday, 25 January 2001.

By the start of the 2002 election period, when the Medef put its *Refondation* offensive on ice until the electorate decided the future political environment, it was clear that the unions had survived these three challenges without experiencing a major defeat either at or outside the negotiating table (as argued in detail in Chapter 7). Precisely because they are so closely bound to the state representation framework and collective welfare provision, these neoliberal attempts to 'modernise' French employment relations have, paradoxically, given the unions greater rather than lesser mobilising appeal.

Following the 2002 elections, however, the union future did not look quite as positive. The employers took enormous heart both from the victories secured by the right in the presidential and National Assembly elections. It was not just that Chirac had been re-elected on a tax-cutting programme without having given too many promises to the centre-left. It was also that the Socialist 'regulators' against whose policies the Medef had campaigned vigorously for five years were publicly humiliated. Not only was Jospin cut down to size by failing to make the second round of the presidential election, but both Martine Aubry (the former minister most associated with the 35-hour laws) and Robert Hué (the Communist Party's presidential candidate) failed to secure election to the National Assembly after a specific appeal by Jean-Marie Le Pen for FN voters in a handful of key constituencies to vote for the UMP candidates against them. The result was that the Medef was now arguably stronger and closer to the ear of government than at any time since the war, while the unions were arguably weaker and more divided and with the possible exception of 1995–1997 further away from influencing the government than at any time since De Gaulle was in office.

While the government will tread very cautiously to avoid a repetition of the events of 1995 there will be little restraint on the part of the Medef. If it is able to separate the CFDT under its new general secretary François Chèraque from the CGT and FO, and to successfully secure a deep and permanent division, it believes it can pursue its full neo-liberal agenda without facing a major mobilisation.

8.3   Conclusion

What is the future of the French trade union movement? In view of its low membership, its lack of growth in the expanding private service sector, its renewed splintering and its divided response to the Medef offensive since 1998, it is easy to argue that it could have very little. Yet my answer is 'considerable'. This answer rests partly on the evidence that the decline in trade union numbers appears to have halted in the early 1990s and that many French workers still follow their lead, particularly when they have a strong case and demonstrate some form of unity. The argument also builds on the approach taken in an important ethnographic study of trade unionism in the mid-1990s in a small number of both well and poorly unionised factories by Sylvie Contrepois (2002). She finds that despite quite low levels of membership the unions remain key representatives of the wider French working class – in all its diversity and with all its current lack of focus. I apply this approach more widely, arguing that the divided and sometimes inconsistent sectoral federations, national confederations and groupings – as well as their partial retreat from *égalité* and *class struggle* unionism and a growing interest in *market* and sectional (*catégoriel*) unionism – are also reflections of working class experience since the 1970s.

The French 'working class' is not merely a helpful concept in explaining social change. It still has a real presence that extends from some managerial, professional and technical workers, through clerical and service staff to manual workers. While economic growth has raised living standards hugely, the majority of the population who make up this wider working class continue to live as differently from the ruling elite as they did 30 years ago. This class certainly does not now have the 'class for itself' political consciousness that an earlier overwhelmingly manual, male-led working class succeeded in generating at particular moments in its history. But what one of Tourraine's criticisms of the absence of a current holistic project misses is that those famous moments were often short-lived, were far from unanimous, and with the exception of 1968 generally occurred when the working class was a minority of the working population.

Today the trade union 'movement' remains the only independent representative voice of white collar and manual collective working class interests, both in reality and as a potential. Unionised workers live within a network of contacts and relationships with other non-union workers which, despite being in some senses 'artificially' dependent upon state arbitrations and concessions made in an earlier era, are real and sustaining in themselves. And this 'latticework of organisation', to use Shorter and Tilly's (1974) term, imperfect and divided a network as it is, retains some capacity to respond to employer challenges. The structural weaknesses of union organisation, in particular its disappearance in medium and small sized firms and the low numbers of women, ethnic minority and immigrants among its members and leaders, are clear. Equally, the absence of a unifying common transformatory project shaped for and by the wider working class, means that the trade unions tend to define themselves largely only in reaction to the 'movement' of the employers.

However, despite its divisions and the absence of a defining project, the wider French working class does not yet see its interests as having been defeated in a major confrontation with the ruling elite. Historically, the unions have also found it easier to mobilise under right rather than left governments, and if the Medef has its way the period of right-wing government that opened in 2002 will 'dare' to take a further huge step taken in the direction of individualism, *liberté* and neo-liberalism. French trade unions face the early twenty-first century with the values of *solidarité* and *égalité* on the retreat both on the national political arena and at work, but with the potential for further mobilisation in their defense largely intact.

9
Changing French Employment Relations and Management

It is impossible to summarise a study of the richness of the experience of change in French employment relations and management in just a few pages. This concluding chapter therefore seeks first to remind the reader of the aims of the book, and then touches on a few of its key arguments, bringing them together into what is hopefully a reasonably clear whole.

The book was written as a contribution to the comparative employment relations literature. The selection of evidence made is thus through 'foreign' eyes that are particularly sensitive to the causes of differences between the experiences of France and those with which I am most familiar, Britain and to a lesser extent the United States (Jefferys 1986). The selection is also made with the deliberate intent of testing several of the main theories of comparative employment relations. This is not always made explicit, for fear of slowing down what in any case is an already dense text, but it is always there.

The first thing *Liberté, Egalité and Fraternité at Work* does is to challenge the view that the concepts of ideology, class and class interests are no longer helpful tools of analysis in explaining employment relations and managerial behaviours. Its narrative shows how a shift in the employment structure has helped refashion and broaden the attitudes and interests of the French working class. This has been liberated from the political domination of a narrow and undemocratic male manual worker Communist fragment. Yet, in the ideological trajectory it has pursued, ranging between the world views of individual freedom, collective struggle and of social responsibilities and duties, this broader working class has been left with a mobilising potential but no clear alternative transformatory project. Meanwhile, the ruling class, whose mobilising capacity was severely compromised by what could be described as a 'double whammy', the military defeat of Vichy and the hegemony of Gaullist *dirigisme*, has recovered enough of its sense of direction, organisation and confidence to both launch a frontal attack on French workers' employment and welfare rights and to adapt to American financialisation and managerialism without entirely shedding its identity – or its ambiguities.

The book develops the argument that most people's ideological identities are a mixture of *liberté, égalité* and *fraternité–solidarité*. This mix often makes their own interpretation of their class situation and of their class interests confused or ambiguous. Applying a class analysis tries to cut through this ambiguity to make sense of the full range of changes in contemporary French employment relations and management. It provides a thread explaining the choices made by the different human actors, and in particular how they mobilise for change. A class analysis links together the ways the banking–industrial capital network has adapted to financialisation and has mobilised behind 'innovative' management organisation to the Medef campaign to effectively 'privatise' the solidaristic and egalitarian elements of the French welfare state. A class analysis also helps us understand how trade union disunity and employee demobilisation can coexist with the context of greater worker industrial and political protest against the increased 'commodification' of social life that has been a feature of the second half of the 1990s. Despite state encouragement of a 'partnership' discourse, the reality is that among both the bourgeoisie and the sections of the wider working class the sense of 'us' and 'them' has remained strong, providing alternative ways of seeing the world.

Another aim of the book is to critically discuss the helpfulness of three of the main theories introduced in Chapter 1. Touraine's social movement theory is shown to have allowed its impatience with the absence of a clear radical project to dismiss what is unquestionably a lengthy process of working class change, whose direction and future remains uncertain and undetermined. The Regulation School is shown getting perilously close to the trap of a narrow economic determinism. Not only does their presentation of a web of 'required' social rules and institutions emanating from a particular 'Fordist' production regime underplay human agency, but the reality of the continuation and indeed extension of 'Fordist' workplace regimes into the present suggests a major flaw in their somewhat mechanical periodisation of 'production regimes'. Finally, the book's narrative also challenges aspects of Societal Effect theory. The Societal Effect School offers many helpful but fragmentary understandings of employment relations. It is certainly the case that employment relations institutions and management traditions are strongly influenced by 'culture' and 'society'. They fulfil mediating, mid-level roles in rule-making and are shaped by a very wide range of interlinked elements, among which the education system is certainly important. But, as we suggest in the course of this book, population movements, urbanisation, industrial structure, war, politics, welfare and international capitalism, all also play important parts, and these elements can best be interpreted through a framework that identifies the motivating impulse derived from collective conflicts over resource allocation.

One example of such a collective conflict is traced in Figure 9.1.

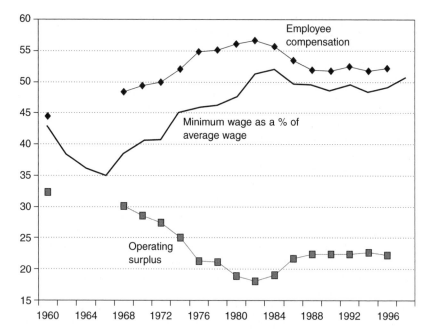

Figure 9.1   Employee compensation and capital's operating surplus as a percentage of GDP, national minimum wage as a percentage of the national average salary, 1960–1996

Sources: OECD 1998b; INSEE 2000.

This graph shows the tension between levels of operating surplus going to capital and the level of employee compensation (including both wages and pensions). There is no zero sum game here: only relative winners and relative losers. From 1968 to 1982 the operating surplus at the disposal of French capitalism was squeezed as the resources allocated to wages (income equality) and pensions (social equality) rose. But in the 1980s there was a clear reversal of fortunes. *Égalité* gave ground to individual *liberté* in the allocation of resources. Capital recovered some of its share and Labour lost some of its, before the balance stabilised in the 1990s.

Figure 9.1 also shows a strong relationship between the rise in the state-regulated minimum wage as a proportion of the national average wage from 1966 through to 1982 and the growth in the overall share of employee compensation. Subsequently, with the minimum wage stabilising at a rate close to 50 per cent of the average wage, employee compensation also stabilised, leaving the bourgeoisie concerned that their operating surplus was still significantly below the average levels of the 1960s and early 1970s, and also still below those of their British neighbours.

In presenting employment relations and management from a perspective that sees exploring the nature or the absence or presence of such conflicts over the allocation of resources as crucial to understanding the nature of working lives in France, the book is thus also arguing for the evolution of comparative employment relations theory. Much of the current debate about convergence and divergence in a world increasingly subject to a dominant American capitalism limits itself to descriptions of mounting globalising pressures on nation states balanced by accounts of greater or lesser institutional resistance to change. The book's thrust could be interpreted in this way, but this is not its intent. Its aim has been to show that what is taking place in France is not predetermined and inevitable, but rather a real series of human choices over the exercise of power, a struggle over the allocation of resources between different social groups.

French history should not be interpreted as moving forward in an inevitable way. French managers are not simply adapting their management styles to some 'normal' neutral behaviour. The trade unions and employers' organisations are not acting 'exceptionally' in comparison with a universal 'norm' for employment relations. French managers and employment relations are not 'converging' or 'diverging' from some pre-determined pattern. Instead, what I have been trying to demonstrate is that behaviours and outcomes are being shaped by the ways different collectives of human actors access and mobilise in the pursuit of the power to constrain others to recognise or serve the interests of the powerful. Rather than comparing a country's degree of convergence or divergence with some abstraction, this book stresses the merit of an approach that seeks to compare and understand different countries according to the effectiveness of key collectives in gaining power, the conflicts involved and the resultant distribution of resources and changes in their distribution over time.

Such an approach inevitably involves taking a long-term view, and Chapters 2 and 3, did precisely that. They point to early divisions among the ruling elites leading to a toleration and expectation of state intervention, while the early strength of rural industry and the survival of a small peasantry into the second half of the twentieth century ensured the instability of both industrial workers' organisations and influence. When workers' strength increased after the Second World War, the state intervened more clearly both to limit the exercise of worker power and to forge closer cooperation and co-ordination with capital. In the context of a working class politically won over by the values of class struggle, state-imposed pluralism was seen as a 'modern' fig leaf to cover the potentially destructive effects of naked employer unitarism. The contemporary employment relations system was thus consciously constructed by the state, with different governments adding little pieces to it over time in response to worker or employer pressure. Paradoxically, then, as both working and the ruling classes became more homogeneous in the 1960s and 1970s, the state became increasingly vital to both. It could simultaneously implement a major extension of welfare rights and spread professional American managerialism in industry. Ideologically, too, employment relations reflected this evolution. Between the 1930s and the 1970s the state's economic discourse moved from a dominant liberalism to a wholehearted and embrace of Keynesianism: while its political discourse abandoned unrestrained individual *market liberté* in favour of a changing balance between the mixed Christian democratic message of partnership and *fraternité*, and the more explicit Socialist concept of *égalité*.

Chapter 4 considered the major political and societal changes of the last 20 years that are important for understanding the current context of employment relations and management. Chief among these was the nearly continuous period of 'left' participation in government. The left's continued electability (often because the extremist National Front effectively split the right vote) made it particularly difficult for the Gaullist right to openly and consistently adopt a fully neo-liberal programme. In theory this should have been easy since the Socialist Party was veering all over the place, implementing monetarist measures after 1983 and then legislating the 35-hour week in 1998, while the Communist Party ended up securing only one third of the votes in the first round of the 2002 presidential elections of the two main Trotskyist candidates combined. But French voters retain considerable attachment to the collective benefits available through the state, and proposals to radically roll it back have rarely been politically rewarded. *Liberté* and neo-liberalism are mobilising more effectively, but have so far only reduced the influence of the ideological perspectives of *égalité* and *fraternité–solidarité*, without getting to the stage where they can ignore their continuing presence.

Against this background the book examined in detail the roles of the state (Chapter 5), French capitalism and management (Chapter 6), the employers' organisations (Chapter 7) and the unions (Chapter 8). Each chapter not only provided a narrative describing the recent evolution of each of these actors and institutions. They also develop four major arguments concerning the changing processes of employment relations and management.

First, the book stresses the continuing role of the state in employment relations. The French state is not just a huge employer and it is not just the guarantor and provider of one of Europe's most generous welfare provisions. It is also the direct legislator of a whole series of substantive and procedural workplace rules from the national minimum wage to the level of overtime pay. It is the combination of these elements that permitted hourly full-time income inequality in France to decline between 1979 and 1998 compared to the increase that occurred across Europe as a whole over the same period (Glyn 2001).

Second, the book argues that French capital has colluded with a high level of state intervention because it remains under the leadership of a small interlocking network of wealthy families who gain access with nearly equal ease both to the highest levels of business and of the state. Strategically this ruling bourgeoisie uses the weakness of working class organisation in the workplace to bolster French productivity while seeking to reinforce its competitive edge by pressing the European state to raise the cost of entry through generalising the French level of statutory control of working conditions. This explains the paradox of the French employers opposing further domestic regulation while simultaneously going along with the German employers in Brussels in terms of accepting further EU-wide regulation.

But this is not the end of the story. Faced with an increasingly intrusive international presence demanding significantly higher rates of return from French capitalism than in the past, the book argues that the ruling elite has both implemented American management techniques on a much wider scale than in the past and has finally decided to cut back the level of protection afforded to French workers by the state. The employers' association, Medef, is now involved in a major attack on tripartism. The outcome of this offensive is by no means guaranteed. There are divisions among the large employers about how far to go in risking a major social conflict, and between the large and the small employers about the extent to which a fully 'free' market should be established. There will also be some resistance from within the state apparatus to any de-regulation that effectively diminishes the role of the law in employment relations by comparison with unilateral or bilateral rule-making.

A key factor in deciding the success or otherwise of the Medef offensive, however, is the trade union response. Will the unions remain divided when the offensive is relaunched in 2003 and 2004? The Medef's gamble is that it can persuade the CFDT that it will be the substantial winner in an employment relations environment from which state props will have been largely removed. Yet, it is by no means certain that there would be any winners if this happened. The argument here is that the trade unions remain influential solely because of their organic relationship to the wider working class. This relationship is a strong, vibrant but unpredictable one, rooted partly in the ideological commitment by small minorities of activists to the class struggle or social integration (principally), but more generally in the legitimacy provided by the state-created representative positions and regular elections both in the workplace and in the 'parity' welfare system. If much of this was undermined, in particular through the co-option of a significant part of the trade union movement, French workers might indeed move into a battle that might deliver them a defeat of the same scale as British workers received with the miners' strike of 1984–1985. Yet, for the moment at least, any sense of an imminent major defeat appears remote. Indeed, if anything, the few small signs of union renewal that have been noted over the last few years, point the other way. What is certainly the case, as was shown by the 1995 strike irruption, is that nothing is inevitable.

Do the arguments advanced here mean that France's particular forms of state-influenced capitalism, its employment relations and management and the ways they are changing are 'exceptional'? In one reading the answer is 'yes': the closer you get to each country's experience the more it differs from that of its neighbour.

In a deeper reading, however, the answer is 'no'. French employment relations and management are only viewed as 'exceptional' because for historical political reasons the underlying conflictual dynamic that exists *everywhere* within capitalist employment relations is just a bit more exposed to view. The human choices that individuals within different social classes make to influence the allocation of resources have led recently in France to major public worker protests, and may well do so again. Yet, while the context elsewhere is different, the processes of weighing up the costs, benefits and possibilities of 'fight' or 'flight' are also everywhere quite similar.

Bibliography

ACFCI. 2001. Chambres de commerce: Annual report. Paris: Assemblée des Chambres Françaises de commerce et de l'industrie.

Ambler, John S. 1991. Ideas, interests, and the French Welfare State. In *The French Welfare State: Surviving Social and Ideological Change*, edited by J. S. Ambler. New York: New York University Press.

Amossé, Thomas. 2001. L'espace des métiers de 1990 à 1999: Recensement de la population de 1999. *INSEE Première* (790) Paris: INSEE.

Andersen, Torben, Sylvie Contrepois, Steve Jefferys and Carole Thornley. 1999. *Country, Sector and Company Effects on Employee Commitment: A Tale of Three Banks in Britain, France and Denmark*. Aarhus, Denmark: Aarhus Business School.

Andolfatto, Dominique. 1998. Le plus faible taux de syndicalisation des pays industrialisés. In *L'Etat de la France 1998–99*, edited by S. Cordellier and E. Poisson. Paris: La Découverte.

Andolfatto, Dominique and Dominique Labbé. 1997. *La CGT. Organisation et audience depuis 1945*. Paris: La Découverte.

——. 2000. *Sociologie du syndicalisme*. Paris: La Découverte.

André-Roux, Valérie and Sylvie Le Minez. 1999. Dix ans d'évolution du chômage des cadres: 1987–1997. In *Données Sociales: La société française*, edited by P. l'Hardy, C. Galant, C. Guével and J. Soleilhavoup. Paris: INSEE.

apRoberts, Lucy, Christine Daniel, Udo Rehfeldt, Emmanuel Reynaud and Catherine Vincent. 1997. Formes et dynamiques de la régulation paritaire. *La Revue de l'IRES* 24 (Printemps-Été):19–42.

——. 1997. Le paritarisme: de l'analyse historique aux enjeux actuels. *La Revue de l'IRES* 24 (Le paritarisme: institutions et acteurs):5–17.

Auer, Peter and Sandrine Cazes. 2000. The resilience of the long-term emploment relationship: Evidence from the industrialized countries. *International Labour Review* 139 (4):379–408.

Azémar, Guy-Patrick, ed. 1992. *Ouvriers, ouvrières*. Paris: Éditions Autrement.

Babeau, André. 1991. La consommation de masse. In *Entre l'État et le marché*, edited by M. Lévy-Leboyer and J.-C. Casanova. Paris: Éditions Gallimard.

Baron, Xavier. 2001. Penser la productivité du travail immatériel et qualifié. In *Cadres: la grande rupture*, edited by P. Bouffartigue, A. Grelon, G. Groux, J. Laufer and Y.-F. Livian. Paris: La Découverte.

Bergounioux, Alain. 1982. *Force ouvrière, Que sais-je?* Paris: Presses universitaires de France.

Berlanstein, Leonard R. 1991. *Big Business and Industrial Conflict in Nineteenth Century France: A Social History of the Parisian Gas Company*. Berkeley: University of California Press.

Béroud, Sophie and René Mouriaux. 2001. Le triangle des Bermudes. *Critique Communiste* 162 (Printemps-Été):51–7.

Béroud, Sophie, René Mouriaux and Michel Vakaloulis, eds. 1998. *Le mouvement social en France: Essai de sociologie politique*. Paris: La Dispute.

Besset, Jean-Paul. 1999. La population est en hausse dans les grandes métropoles régionales. *Le Monde*, 7 Juillet, 6.

Bessy-Pietri, Pascale and Yann Sicamois. 2001. 4 million d'habitants en plus dans les aires urbaines: le zonage en aires urbaines en 1999. *INSEE Première* (765).

Bilous, Alexandre. 1998. Change in the employers' camp – CNPF becomes Medef. Dublin: European Foundation.

Birck, Françoise. 1998. Training Engineers in Lorraine, 1890–1956. In *Governance, Industry and Labour Markets in Britain and France: the modernising state in the mid-twentieth century*, edited by N. Whiteside and R. Salais. London: Routledge.

Boëldieu, Julien and Catherine Borrel. 2000. La proportion d'immigrés est stable depuis 25 ans. *INSEE Première* (Novembre).

Boltanski. 1987. *The Making of a Class: Cadres in French Society*. Cambridge: Cambridge University Press.

Boltanski, Luc and Ève Chiapello. 1999. *Le Nouvel Esprit du Capitalisme*. Paris: Gallimard.

Bordes, Marie-Madeleine and Christine Gonzalez-Demichel. 1998. *Marché du Travail: Séries longues*. Paris: INSEE.

Borgetto, Michel. 1993. *La notion de fraternité en droit public francais: Le passé, le présent et l'avenir de la solidarité*. Paris: Librarie générale de droit et de jurisprudence.

Bouffartigue, Paul. 1998. Les ingénieurs: un groupe professionnel de plus en plus diversifié. In *L'état de la France, 98–99*, edited by S. Cordellier and E. Poisson. Paris: La Découverte.

——. 2001. *Les cadres: fin d'une figure sociale*. Paris: La Dispute.

Bouilloud, Jean-Phillippe. 1998. Introduction. In *L'invention de la gestion: Histoire et pratiques*, edited by J.-P. Bouilloud and B.-P. Lecuyer. Paris: L'Harmattan.

Bournois, Frank. 1991. *La gestion des cadres en Europe*. Paris: Eyrolles.

Bouvier, Jean. 1987. Introduction. In *Le Capitalisme Francaise XIX–XX Siècle: Blocages et dynamismes d'une croissance*, edited by P. Fridenson and A. Strauss. Paris: Fayard.

Boyer, Robert. 1987. Rapport salarial, croissance et crise: une dialectique cachée. In *La flexibilité du travail en Europe*, edited by R. Boyer. Paris: La Découverte.

——. 1995. Aux origines de la théorie de la régulation. In *Théorie de la régulation: L'état des savoirs*, edited by R. Boyer and Y. Saillard. Paris: La Découverte.

——. 1998. Hybridation et modèle productif: géographie, histoire et théorie. *Actes du Gerpisa* (24):7–50.

Branciard, Michel. 1990. *Histoire de la CFDT: soixante-dix ans d'action syndicale*. Paris: La Découverte.

Braudel, Fernand. 1986. *L'identité de la France: Espace et Histoire*. Paris: Arthaud-Flammarion.

——. 1991. *The Identity of France: People and Production*. London: Fontana.

Bréchon, Pierre. 2000a. L'univers des valeurs politiques: permanences et mutations. In *Les valeurs des Français: évolutions de 1980 à 2000*, edited by P. Bréchon. Paris: Armand Collin.

——, ed. 2000b. *Les valeurs des Français: Evolutions de 1980 à 1999*. Paris: Armand Colin.

Briant, Vincent de. 2001. Les politiques sociales: évolution, évaluation. In *La protection sociale en France*, edited by M. de Montalembert. Paris: La documentation Française.

Brizay, Bernard. 1975. *Le patronat: histoire, structure, stratégie du CNPF*. Paris: Seuil.

Bulard, Martine. 2000. Les syndicats n'ont pas la fibre. *Le Monde diplomatique*, June, 18–19.

Cailluet, Ludovic. 2000. McKinsey, TOTAL-CFP et la M-Form. Un exemple français d'adaptation d'un modèle d'organisation importé. *Entreprise et Histoire* (25):26–45.

Bibliography 245

Caire, Guy. 1996. Forces et faiblesses de l'approche française des relations indus-trielles: mise en perspective historique. In L'État des Relations Professionnelles: Traditions et perspectives de recherche, edited by G. Murray, M.-L. Morin and I. da Costa. Toulouse: Octares.
Carew, Anthony. 1987. Labour under the Marshall Plan: the Politics of Productivity and the Marketing of Management Science. Manchester: Manchester University Press.
Carpenter, Mick and Steve Jefferys. 2000. Management, work and welfare in Western Europe: An historical and contemporary analysis. Cheltenham: Edward Elgar.
Cassis, Youssef. 1997. Big Business: The European Experience in the Twentieth Century. Oxford: Oxford University Press.
Castel, Robert. 1995. Les métamorphoses de la question sociale: Une chronique du salariat. Paris: Librairie Arthème Fayard.
Catrice-Lorey, Antoinette. 1997. La Sécurité sociale en France, institution anti-paritaire? Un regard historique long terme. La Revue de l'IRES 24 (Printemps-Été):81–105.
Cazal, Didier and Jean-Marie Peretti. 1992. L'Europe des ressources humaines. Paris: Editions Liaisons.
Conseil de l'emploi, des revenus et de la cohésion sociale. 1999. Presque un quart des intérimaires sont des immigrés. Le Monde, 23 avril, 2.
Chambaz, Christine, François Guillaumat-Tailliet and Jean-Michel Hourriez. 1999. Le revenu et le patrimoine des ménages. In Données Sociales: La société française, edited by P. l'Hardy, C. Galant, C. Guével, J. Soleilhavoup and S. Tagnani. Paris: INSEE.
Chardon, Oliver. 2001. Les transformations de l'emploi non qualifié depuis vingt ans. INSEE Première, Juillet (796).
Charle, Christophe. 1991. Histoire sociale de la France au XIX siècle. Paris: Éditions du Seuil.
Cobban, Alfred. 1981. A History of Modern France: France of the Republics 1871–1962. 3 vols. Vol. 3. London: Penguin.
Cochet, François. 1997. Histoire économique de la France depuis 1945. Paris: Dunod.
Cohen, Daniel. 2002. Le déclin français: un mythe et une réalité. Le Monde, 9 février, 17.
Collin, Francis, Régine Dhuquois, Pierre-Hubert Goutierre, Antoine Jeammaud, Gérard Lyon-Caen and Albert Roudil, eds. 1980. Le Droit capitaliste du travail, Critique du droit. Grenoble: Presses Universitaires de Grenoble.
Contrepois, Sylvie. 2001. Stratégies et pratiques syndicales au tournant du XXIe siè-cle: une contribution aux théories de l'action collective. Doctorat, Département de sociologie, L'université d'Evry, Paris.
———. 2002. Syndicats, la nouvelle donne. Enquête au cœur d'un bassin industriel. Paris: Syllepse.
Coriat, Benjamin. 1995. France: un fordisme brisé...et sans successeur. In Théorie de la régulation: L'état des savoirs, edited by R. Boyer and Y. Saillard. Paris: La Découverte.
Coupé, Annick and Anne Marchand, eds. 1998. Sud: syndicalement incorrect. Sud-Ptt: une aventure collective. Paris: Syllepse.
Cours-Salies, Pierre. 1988. La CFDT: Un passé porteur d'avenir. Pratiques syndicales et débats stratégiques depuis 1946. Montreuil: La Brèche-PEC.
———. 1998. Un espoir en partie formulé. In Faire mouvement: Novembre-décembre 1995, edited by C. Leneveu and M. Vakaloulis. Paris: Presses Universitaires de France.
Courtois, Gérard. 1999. La scission du Front national fait reculer les idées de l'extrême droite. Le Monde, 4 mai, 8.
———. 2001. L'extrême gauche attire un électorat jeune et populaire. Le Monde, 7 Juin.

Courtois, Gérard and Jérôme Jaffré. 2001. La popularité des mouvement sociaux ne se dément pas depuis 1995. *Le Monde*, 7 Mars, 18.

Coutrot, Thomas. 1996. Les nouveaux modes d'organisation de la production: quels effets sur l'empoi, la formation, l'organisation du travail? In *Données Sociales 1996: La société française*, edited by P. l'Hardy, C. Guével and J. Soleilhavoup. Paris: INSEE.

———. 1998. *L'entreprise néo-libérale, nouvelle utopie capitaliste?* Paris: La Découverte.

———. 2000a. Innovations dans le travail: La pression de la concurrence internationale, l'atoût des qualifications. *Premières synthèses* 09 (2).

———. 2000b. Innovations et gestion de l'emploi. *Premières synthèses* 12 (1).

———. 2001a. Où sont les CHST? *Premières synthèses* 16 (2).

———. 2001b. Une nouvelle période pour la conflictualité sociale? Paris: *ATTAC*.

Coutrot, Thomas and Jean-Luc Paraire. 1996. Le développement récent des politiques de motivation des salariés. In *Relations professionnelles et négociations d'entreprises en 1992*, edited by C. Seibel. Paris: DARES.

Cross, Gary. 1983. *Immigrant Workers in Industrial France: The Making of a New Laboring Class*. Philadelphia: Temple University Press.

Crouch, Colin. 1993. *Industrial Relations and European State Traditions*. Oxford: Clarendon.

Crozier, Michel. 1990. Concept de système comme outil heuristique et comme paradigme du système social. In *Les systèmes de relations professionnelles: Examen critique d'une théorie*, edited by J.-D. Reynaud, F. Eyraud, C. Paradeise and J. Saglio. Paris: Presses du CNRS.

Crozier, Michel and Erhard Friedberg. 1977. *L'acteur et le système: les contraintes de l'action collective*. Paris: Éditions du Seuil.

Daguet, Fabienne. 1996. Le bilan démographique du siècle. In *Données Sociales 1996: La société française*, edited by P. l'Hardy, C. Guével and J. Soleilhavoup. Paris: INSEE.

Dangerfield, Odile and Danièle Prangère. 1999. Les retraites. In *Données Sociales: La société française*, edited by P. l'Hardy, C. Galant, C. Guével and J. Soleilhavoup. Paris: INSEE.

DARES. 2000. *La Négoçiation collective en 1999*. 3 vols. Vol. 1. Paris: Éditions législatives.

Daviet, Jean-Pierre. 1987. Trajectoires d'une grande entreprise privée: Saint-Gobain (1945–1969). In *Le Capitalisme Française XIX–XX Siècle: Blocages et dynamismes d'une croissance*, edited by P. Fridenson and A. Strauss. Paris: Fayard.

Delhoummais, Pierre-Antoine. 1999. Un 'signe de souveraineté monétaire', selon la Banque de France. *Le Monde*, 8 Juillet, 2.

Denis, Jean-Michel. 2001. *Le groupe des dix, un modèle syndical alternatif?* Paris: La documentation Française.

Desjardins, Bernadette, Jean Pélissier, Agnès Roset and Lysiance Tholy. 1998. *Le code du travil annoté*. Paris: Les Publications Fiduciaires.

Dewerpe, Alain. 1989. *Le Monde du Travail en France 1800–1950*. Paris: Armand Collin.

d'Iribarne, Philippe. 1989. *La logique d'honneur*. Paris: Éditions du Seuil.

Dreyfus, Michel. 1995. *Histoire de la c.g.t.* Paris: Éditions complexe.

Duchéneaut, Bernard. 1995. *Enquête sur les PME Françaises: Identités, Contextes, Chiffres*. Paris: Maxima.

———. 1996. *Les dirigeants de PME: Enquête, Chiffres, Analyses pour mieux les connaître*. Paris: Maxima.

Dufour, Christian. 2001. La représentation patronale en mouvement. *Chronique Internationale de l'IRES* (72).

Duménil, Gérard and Dominique Lévy. 2000. *Crise et sortie de crise. Ordre et désordres néolibéraux*. Paris: Presses universitaires de France.

——. 2001. Coûts et avantages du néolibéralisme. Une analyse de classe. Documents pour l'enseignement économique et social (126).

Dunlop, John T. 1958. *Industrial Relations Systems*. Carbondale: Southern Illinois University Press.

Durand, Jean-Pierre. 1996. Le compromis productif change de nature. In *Le syndicalisme au future*, edited by J.-P. Durand. Paris: Syros.

Esping-Andersen, Gosta. 1990. *The Three Worlds of Welfare Capitalism*. Cambridge: Polity Press.

——. 1992. Realignment of Labour Movements and Welfare States. In *the future of Labour Movements*, edited by M. Regini. London: Sage.

Euzéby, Chantal. 1998. *Mutations économiques et sociales en France depuis 1973*. Paris: Dunod.

Fléchaire, Laurent. 2002. La relance de 1981. *Le Monde*, February 5, V.

Fox, Alan. 1966. Industrial sociology and industrial relations: an assessment of the contribution which industrial sociology can make towards understanding and resolving some of the problems now being considered by the Royal Commission. Royal Commission on Trade Unions and Employers' Associations; *Research Paper 3*. London: HMSO.

Frémy, Dominique and Michèle Frémy. 2000. *Quid 2001*. Paris: Robert Laffont.

Frey, Jean-Pierre. 1995. *Le rôle social du patronat: Du paternalisme à l'urbanisme*. Paris: L'Harmattan.

Frickey, Alan and Jean-Luc Primon. 2001. Du diplôme à l'"emploi: des inégalités croissantes. In *Cadres: la grande rupture*, edited by P. Bouffartigue, A. Grelon, G. Groux, J. Laufer and Y.-F. Livian. Paris: La Découverte.

Fridenson, Patrick. 1994. La circulation internationale des modes managériales. In *L'invention de la gestion: histoire et pratiques*, edited by J.-P. Bouilloud and B.-P. Lecuyer. Paris: L'Harmattan.

Fridenson, Patrick and Jean-Louis Robert. 1997. Les ouvriers dans la France de la Second Guerre Mondiale: un bilan. In *Industrialisation et Sociétés d'Europe Occidentale*, edited by P. Fridenson. Paris: Éditions de l'Atelier.

Friez, Adrien. 1999. Les salaires depuis 1950. In *Données Sociales: La société française*, edited by P. l'Hardy, C. Galant, C. Guével, J. Soleilhavoup and S. Tagnani. Paris: INSEE.

Friot, Bernard. 1997. Régime générale et retraites complémentaires entre 1945 et 1967: le paritarisme contre la démocratie sociale. *La Revue de l'IRES* (24).

——. 1998. *Puissances du salariat: Emploi et protection sociale à la française*. Paris: La Dispute.

Garcia, Alexandre and Caroline Monnot. 1999. Les syndicats s'attaquent aux discriminations visant leurs militants. *Le Monde*, 6 avril, 8.

Gemelli, Giuliana. 1994. Pour une analyse comparée du développement des écoles de gestion en Europe: le rôle de la fondation Ford. In *L'invention de la gestion: histoire et pratiques*, edited by J.-P. Bouilloud and B.-P. Lecuyer. Paris: L'Harmattan.

Glyn, Andrew. 2001. *Inequalities of employment and wages in OECD countries*. Oxford: Department of Economics.

Goetschy, Janine and Patrick Rozenblatt. 1992. France: The Industrial Relations System at a Turning Point? In *Industrial Relations in a New Europe*, edited by A. Ferner and R. Hyman. Oxford: Blackwell.

Goff, Jean-Pierre Le. 1995. *Le mythe de l'entreprise*. 2nd ed. Paris: La Découverte.

Goux, Dominique and Eric Maurin. 1996. La mobilité sociale en France. In *Données Sociales 1996: La société française*, edited by P. l'Hardy, C. Guével and J. Soleilhavoup. Paris: INSEE.

Groux, Guy. 1990. Le syndicalisme-cadres de l'après-guerre à nos jours. In *Jean-Daniel Reynaud, François Eyraud, Catherine Paradeise, Jean Saglio*, edited by J.-D. Reynaud, F. Eyraud, C. Paradeise and J. Saglio. Paris: Presses du CNRS.

——. 1996. La CGC: du métier d'ingénieur à l'action collective. In *L'unité syndicale en France*, edited by P. Cours-Salies and R. Mouriaux. Paris: Éditions Syllepse.

Groux, Guy and Cathérine Lévy. 1993. *La possession ouvrière: Du taudis à la propriété (XIXe–XXe siècle)*. Paris: Éditions de l'Atelier/Éditions Ouvrières.

Groux, Guy and Rene Mouriaux. 1989. *La CFDT*. Paris: Economica.

——. 1992. *La CGT: Crises et alternatives*. Paris: Economica.

Guilbert, Madeleine. 1966. *Les femmes et l'organisation syndicale avant 1914*. Paris: CNRS.

Guillén, Mauro F. 1994. *Models of Management: Work, Authority, and Organization in a Comparative Perspective*. Chicago: University of Chicago Press.

Hampden-Turner, Charles and Fons Trompenaars. 1993. *The Seven Cultures of Capitalism: Value systems for creating wealth in the United States, Britain, Japan, Germany, France, Sweden and the Netherlands*. London: Piatkus.

Hancké, Robert C. 2001. State, Market and Firms: Industrial Restructuring in France, 1980–2000. PhD, Political Science, Massachusettes Institute of Technology.

——. 2002. *Large Firms and Institutional Change: Industrial renewal and economic restructuring in France*. Oxford: Oxford University Press.

Henderson, David. 1998. *The Changing Fortunes of Economic Liberalism: Yesterday, Today and Tomorrow*. London: Institute of Economic Affairs.

Hetzel, Anne-Marie, Josette Lefèvre, René Mouriaux and Maurice Tournier. 1998. *le syndicalisme à mots découverts: dictionnaire des fréquences (1971–1990)*. Paris: Éditions Syllepse.

Hofstede, Geert. 1984. *Culture's Consequences: International differences in work-related values*. Abridged ed. London: Sage.

Howell, Chris. 1992. *Regulating Labor: The State and Industrial Relations Reform in Postwar France*. Princeton, New Jersey: Princeton University Press.

Husson, Michel. 2000a. *Le grand bluff capitaliste*. Paris: La Dispute.

——. 2000b. *The viability of redistribution*. Attac 2000.

——. 2002a. Les coordonnées macro-économiques de la nouvelle conflictualité. In *L'année sociale 2002*, edited by R. Mouriaux. Paris: Syllepse.

——. 2002b. Réduction du temps de travail et emploi: une nouvelle évaluation. *Revue de l'IRES* 1 (32).

Hyman, Richard. 1994. Theory and Industrial Relations. *British Journal of Industrial Relations* 32 (2).

——. 1996. Union identities and ideologies in Europe. In *The Lost Perspective? Trade unions between ideology and social action in the New Europe: Significance of Ideology in European Trade Unionism, Vol. 2*, edited by P. Pasture, J. Verberckmoes and H. de Witte. Aldershot: Avebury.

——. 2001. *Understanding European trade unionism: between market, class and society*. London: Sage.

INSEE. 1997. *Les Revenus Sociaux, SYNTHESES*. Paris: INSEE.

——. 2000. *Tableaux de l'économie Française: Edition 2000*. Cdrom edition. Paris: INSEE.

——. 2001a. *Annuaire Statistique de la France*. Edited by P. Champsaur. Paris: INSEE.

——. 2001b. *France, Portrait Social 2001–2002*. Edited by N. Roth, C. Grimler and G. Martin-Houssart. Paris: INSEE.

——. 2001c. *Tableaux de l'Économie Française 2001–2002*. Edited by A. Betton, V. Charpiot, J. Khouri and A. Maillochon. Paris: INSEE.

IRES-DARES. 1998. *Les Comités d'Entreprise: enquête sur les élus, les activités et les moyens*. Paris: Les Éditions de l'Atelier.

Jacquier, Jean-Paul. 1998. *Les Clés du Social en France*. Paris: Editions Liaisons.
Jeanneney, Sylviane G. 1991. L'alternance entre dirigisme et libéralisme monétaires (1950–1990). In *Entre l'État et le marché*, edited by M. Lévy-Leboyer and J.-C. Casanova. Paris: Éditions Gallimard.
Jefferys, Steve. 1986. *Management and Managed: Fifty years of crisis at Chrysler*. Cambridge: Cambridge University Press.
——. 1996a. Down but not out: French Unions after Chirac. *Work, Employment & Society* 10 (3).
——. 1996b. France 1995: the backward march of labour halted? *Capital and Class* (59).
——. 1997. The Exceptional Centenary of the Confédération générale du travail, 1895–1995. *Historical Studies in Industrial Relations* (3).
——. 1999. L'évolution des conditions de travail dans le secteur bancaire et le futur du syndicalisme. Report for CFDT and Unifi. Keele University.
——. 2000. A 'Copernican revolution' in French Industrial Relations: are the times a'changing? *British Journal of Industrial Relations* 38 (2).
Jefferys, Steve and Sylvie Contrepois. 2001. The French State and Wage Determination. Paper read at European Industrial Relations Association, June; Oslo.
Kemp, Tom. 1979. *Industrialization in nineteenth century Europe*. 8th ed. London: Longman.
Kogut, Bruce and David Parkinson. 1993. The Diffusion of American Organizing Principles to Europe. In *Country Competitiveness: Technology and the Organizing of Work*, edited by B. Kogut. Oxford: Oxford University Press.
Kourchid, Olivier and Roland Trempé, eds. 1994. *Cent ans de conventions collectives: Arras, 1891–1991*. Lille: Revue du Nord.
Labbé, Dominique. 1994. *Les élections aux comités d'entreprise (1945–1993)*. Grenoble: CERAT.
Labbé, Dominique and Maurice Croisat. 1992. *La fin des syndicats?*. Paris: L'Harmattan.
Lambert, Yves. 2000. Religion: développement du hors piste et de la randonnée. In *Les valeurs des Français: évolutions de 1980 à 2000*, edited by P. Brèchon. Paris: Armand Colin.
Lane, Christel. 1989. *Management and Labour in Europe: The industrial enterprise in Germany, Britain and France*. Aldershot: Edward Elgar.
Lefebvre, Michel. 2001. 100,000 mineurs en grève contre l'occupant. *Le Monde*, 10–11 Juin, 12.
Lefranc, Georges. 1977. Le socialisme en France: 1919 à 1945. In *Histoire générale du socialisme*, edited by J. Droz. Paris: Presses universitaires de France.
Lévy-Leboyer, Maurice. 1997. Le patronat français a-t-il échappé à la loi des trois générations? In *Industrialisation et Sociétés d'Europe Occidentale*, edited by P. Fridenson. Paris: Éditions de l'Atelier.
Liaisons-Sociales. 2002. Les votes au scrutin présidentiel selon la proximité syndicale. *Liaisons-Sociales Quotidien*, 30 avril, 1.
Linhart, Danièle. 1996. L'approche française de l'évolution du travail et de l'entreprise. In *L'État des Relations Professionnelles: Traditions et perspectives de recherche*, edited by G. Murray, M.-L. Morin and I. d. Costa. Toulouse: Octares.
Lyon-Caen, Antoine. 1990. L'égalité et la loi en droit du travail. *Droit social* (1).
——. 1998. Réduction du temps de travail: rémuneration ou les ombres nécessaires de la loi du 13 Juin 1998. *La Revue juridique d'Ile-de-France* (53).
Lyon-Caen, Gérard, Jean Pélissier and Alain Supiot. 1994. *Droit du travail*. 17th ed. Paris: Dalloz.
Magraw, Roger. 1992. *A History of the French Working Class*. 2 vols. Oxford: Blackwell.

Maier, Charles S. 1970. Between Taylorism and Technocracy: European ideologies and the vision of industrial productivity in the 1920s. *Journal of Contemporary History* (5).

Malan, Anna and Patrick Zouary. 2000. La représentation des salariés: Le point de vue des employeurs. *Premières synthèses* 24 (1).

Marceau, Jane. 1989. France. In *The Capitalist Class: An International Study*, edited by T. Bottomore and R. J. Brym. London: Harvester Wheatsheaf.

Marchand, Olivier. 1999. Population active, emploi et chômage au cours des années quatre-vingt-dix. In *Données Sociales: La société française*, edited by P. l'Hardy, C. Galant, C. Guével, J. Soleilhavoup and S. Tagnani. Paris: INSEE.

Marchand, Olivier and Claude Thélot. 1991. *Deux Siècles de Travail en France*. Insee Études. Paris: INSEE.

———. 1991. Population active et productivité du travail, 1800–1990. In *Entre l'Etat et le Marché*, edited by M. Levy-Leboyer and J.-C. Casanova. Paris: Editions Gallimard.

Maurice, Marc. 1993. Les nouveaux systèmes productifs: entre 'Taylorism' et 'Toyotism'. *Sociologie du Travail* (1).

Menanteau, Jean. 1999. La moitié des 6000 marchés ruraux ne répond pas aux critères de Bruxelles. *Le Monde*, 2 juillet, 12.

Mendras, Henri and Alistair Cole. 1988. *Social Change in Modern France: Towards a Cultural Anthropology of the Fifth Republic*. Paris: Cambridge University Press.

Merlier, Roselyne. 2001. Les licenciements des représentants du personnel en 1999. *Premières synthèses* 47 (1).

———. 2002. Les conflits en 2000: le regain se confirme. *Premières synthèses* 09(1).

Mesrine, Annie. 1999. Les différences de mortalité par milieu social restent fortes. In *Données Sociales 1999: La société française*, edited by P. l'Hardy, C. Galant, C. Guével, J. Soleilhavoup and S. Tagnani. Paris: INSEE.

Milner, Susan. 1991. *The Dilemmas of Internationalism: French Syndicalism and the International Labour Movement, 1990–1914*. Oxford: Berg.

Ministère de l'emploi et de la solidarité. 1994. *Les institutions représentatives du personnel*. Paris: La documentation Française.

Mioche, Philippe. 1987. Le Financement public de la sidérurgie: réalité ou illusion d'un contrôle par l'État (1945–1965)? In *Le Capitalisme Francaise XIX–XX Siècle: Blocages et dynamismes d'une croissance*, edited by P. Fridenson and A. Strauss. Paris: Fayard.

Montalembert, Marc de, ed. 2001. *La protection sociale en France*. Paris: La documentation Française.

Morin, François. 2000. A transformation in the French model of shareholding and management. *Economy and Society* 29 (1).

Morrisson, Christian. 1991. L'inégalité des revenus. In *Entre l'État et le marché*, edited by M. Lévy-Leboyer and J.-C. Casanova. Paris: Éditions Gallimard.

Moss, Bernard H. 1976. The origins of the French labor movement, 1830–1914: the socialism of skilled workers. Berkeley: University of California Press.

———. 1994. Working-class Struggles in France: a Revival of Marxian Historiography? *French Politics & Society* 12 (2 & 3).

Mouriaux, René. 1994. *Le syndicalisme en France depuis 1945*. Paris: La Découverte.

———. 1995. Syndicalisme, questions féminines et féministes (1895–1994). In *La liberté du travail*, edited by R. Mouriaux and P. Cours-Salies. Paris: Syllepse.

———. 1996. *Le syndicalisme enseignant en France, Que sais-je?* Paris: Presses universitaires de France.

———. 1998. Sud-Ptt: une démarche syndicale originale. In *Sud syndicalement incorrect: Sud-Ptt. Une aventure collective*, edited by A. Coupé and A. Marchand. Paris: Syllepse.

——. 2001. L'Année sociale 2000. In *L'année sociale: les faits, les dates, les documents*, edited by R. Mouriaux. Paris: Syllepse.

Noiriel, Gérard. 1986. *Les ouvriers dans la société française: xix–xx siècle*. Paris: Seuil.

Northcutt, Wayne. 1992. *Mitterrand: A Political Biography*. New York: Holmes & Meier.

Notat, Nicole. 1998. *Du bon usage des 35 heures*. Paris: Seuil.

OECD. 1992. Employment Outlook. Paris: OECD.

——. 1996a. Earnings inequality, low-paid employment and earnings. *Employment Outlook* (July).

——. 1996b. Historical Statistics: 1960–1994. Paris: OECD.

——. 1997a. *France 1997*. Paris: OECD.

——. 1997b. Is Job Insecurity on the Increase in OECD countries? *Employment Outlook* (July).

——. 1998a. Employment Outlook. Paris: OECD.

——. 1998b. *National Accounts, Main Aggregates, 1960–1996*. 2 vols. Vol. I. Paris: OECD.

Orange, Martine and Anne-Marie Rocco. 1999. Nationalisations-privatisations: l'État gagnant. *Le Monde*, 17 juillet, 15.

Palier, Bruno and Giuliano Bonoli. 1996. Le modèle français. *Problèmes économiques* (6–13 novembre).

Pichot, E. 1996. *L'Europe des représentants du personnel et de leurs attributions économiques*. Luxembourg: European Commission.

Pigenet, Michel. 1997. L'usine et le village: Rosières (1869–1914). In *Industrialisation et Sociétés d'Europe Occidentale*, edited by P. Fridenson. Paris: Éditions de l'Atelier.

Pigeyre, Frédérique. 2001. Femmes dirigeantes: les chemins du pouvoir. In *Cadres: la grande rupture*, edited by P. Bouffartigue, A. Grelon, G. Groux, J. Laufer and Y.-F. Livian. Paris: La Découverte.

Piketty, Thomas. 2001. *Les hauts revenus en France au XXe siècle: Inégalités et redistributions 1901–1998*. Paris: Grasset.

Pinçon, Michel and Monique Pinçon-Charlot. 2000. *Sociologie de la bourgeoisie*. Paris: La Découverte.

Piotet, Francoise, Marion Correia, C. Lattès and Jean Vincent. 1992. *Le développement de la syndicalisation à la CFDT. Les exemples de la Fédération Interco et de la Fédération nationale des syndicats de Santé et des Services sociaux*. Paris: Centre de sociologie du travail et de l'entreprise.

Pisani-Ferry, Jean. 2001. *La bonne aventure. Le plein emploi, le marché, la gauche*. Paris: La Découverte.

Plaisance, Eric. 1998. Éducation et formation. In *L'état de la France, 98–99*, edited by S. Cordellier and E. Poisson. Paris: La Découverte.

Plihon, Dominique. 1998. *Les banques: nouveaux enjeux, nouvelles stratégies*. Paris: La documentation Française.

Pollet, Gilles and Didier Renard. 1997. Le paritarisme et la protection sociale. Origines et enjeux d'une forme institutionnelle. *La Revue de l'IRES* (24).

Préel, Bernard. 1989. *La société des enfants gâtées*. Paris: La Découverte.

Price, Roger. 1993. *A Concise History of France*. Cambridge: Cambridge University Press.

Quine, Maria S. 1996. *Population Politics in Twentieth-Century Europe: Fascist Dictatorships and Liberal Democracies*. London: Routledge.

Renault, Enguérand. 1998. La Bourse en quête de fonds de pension français. *Le Monde*, 30 novembre.

Reynaud, Jean-Daniel. 1975. *Les syndicats en France*. 2 vols. Paris: Editions du Seuil.

——. 1990. Un paradigm du système social. In *Les systèmes de relations professionnelles*, edited by J.-D. Reynaud, F. Eyraud, C. Paradeise and J. Saglio. Paris: Presses du CNRS.

——. 1993. *Les règles du jeu: L'action collective et la régulation sociale.* 2nd ed. Paris: Armand Colin.

Robert, Jean-Louis. 2000. 1791: liberté du marché et Nation. *Le Monde*, 14 Novembre: X.

——. 2001. Vichy et al Charte du travail. *Le Monde*, 3 Avril: VI.

Roger, Pierre. 2001. Refondation sociale, année zéro. In *L'année sociale: les faits, les dates, les documents*, edited by R. Mouriaux. Paris: Syllepse.

Rollat, Alain. 1985. *Les hommes de l'extrême droite: Le Pen, Marie, Ortiz et les autres.* Paris: Calmann-Lévy.

Rosanvallon, Pierre. 1988. *La question syndicale.* Paris: Hachette.

Rousso, Henry. 1987. Les Paradoxes de Vichy et de l'Occupation: Contraintes, archaismes et modernités. In *Le Capitalisme Française XIX–XX Siècle: Blocages et dynamismes d'une croissance*, edited by P. Fridenson and A. Strauss. Paris: Fayard.

Rozès, Stéphane. 2001. La fin de l'exception idéologique. In *Cadres: la grande rupture*, edited by P. Bouffartigue, A. Grelon, G. Groux, J. Laufer and Y.-F. Livian. Paris: La Découverte.

Ruelland, Nadine. 1999. Les élections aux comités d'entreprise en 1997. *Premières synthèses* 19 (1).

——. 2000. Les élections aux comités d'entreprise en 1998. *Premières synthèses* 41 (1).

——. 2001a. Les élections aux comités d'entreprise en 1999. *Premières synthèses* 49 (1).

——. 2001b. Les institutions représentatives du personnel en 1999. *Premières synthèses* 48 (1).

Saglio, Jean. 1990. Négoçier les décisions téchnologiques, ou seulement leurs effets? In *Les systèmes de relations professionnelles: examen critique d'une théorie*, edited by J.-D. Reynaud, F. Eyraud, C. Paradeise and J. Salgio. Paris: Editions du CNRS.

Sainsaulieu, Renaud. 1988. *L'indentité au travail.* Paris: Presses de Sciences Po.

Savatier, Jean. 1990. La liberté dans le travail. *Droit social* 1 (Janvier):49–58.

Schor, Ralph. 1996. *Histoire de l'immigration en France de la fin du XIXe siècle à nos jours.* Paris: Armand Colin.

Segrestin, Denis. 1992. *Sociologie de l'entreprise.* Paris: Armand Colin.

Sellier, François. 1984. *La confrontation sociale en France: 1936–1981.* Paris: Presses Universitaires de France.

——. 1990. L'évolution des règles sur les salaires dans le système français de relations professionnelles. In *Les systèmes de relations professionnelles: Examen critique d'une théorie*, edited by J.-D. Reynaud, F. Eyraud, C. Paradeise and J. Saglio. Paris: Presses du CNRS.

Servan-Schreiber, Jean-Jacques. 1969. *The American Challenge.* New York: Atheneum.

Shorter, Edward and Charles Tilly. 1974. *Strikes in France 1830–1968.* Cambridge: Cambridge University Press.

Simon, Jacques. 1981. Les conflits du travail en 1981. *Bulletin mensuel des statistiques du travail.* Supplement (95):6.

Sociales-DARES, INSEE-Liaisons. 1998. *Les relations sociales en entreprise.* Paris: Éditions Liaisons.

Sorge, Arndt. 1995. Labour relations, organization and qualifications. In *Comparative Industrial and Employment Relations*, edited by J. v. Ruysseveldt, R. Huiskamp and J. v. Hoof. London: Sage.

Soubiran-Paillet, Francine. 1998. De nouvelles règles du jeu? Le décret d'Allarde (2–17 mars 1791) et la loi Le Chapelier (14–17 juin 1791). In *Deux Siècles de Droit du Travail: L'histoire par les lois*, edited by J.-P. L. Crom. Paris: Les Éditions de l'Atelier.

Stoffaës, Christian. 1991. La restructuration industrielle, 1945–1990. In *Entre l'État et le marché*, edited by M. Lévy-Leboyer and J.-C. Casanova. Paris: Éditions Gallimard.

Supiot, Alain. 2001. La contractualisation de la société. *Le Courrier de l'environnement de l'INRA*, 43 (Mai).

Terrail, Jean-Pierre. 1990. *Destins ouvriers: La fin d'une classe?* Paris: PUF.

Thoemmes, Jens and Gilbert de Terssac. 1997. La négociation du temps de travail et les composantes du référentiel temporal. *Loisir et société*, 20 (1).

Timbart, Odile and Evelyne Serverin. 1995. Les condamnations pour infraction au droit social de 1990 à 1993. Paris: Ministère de la Justice.

Touraine, Alain. 1990. La crise du système des relations professionelles. In *Les systèmes de relations professionnelles: Examen critique d'une théorie*, edited by J.-D. Reynaud, F. Eyraud, C. Paradeise and J. Saglio. Paris: Presses du CNRS.

——. 1993. *La voix et le regard: Sociologie des mouvements sociaux*. 2nd ed. Paris: Seuil.

——. 1996. L'ombre d'un mouvement. In *Le grand refus: Réflexions sur la grève de décembre 1995*, edited by A. Touraine, F. Dubet, D. Lapeyronnie, F. Khosrokhavar and M. Wieviorka. Paris: Fayard.

Touraine, Alaine, Michel Wieviorka and Francois Dubet. 1987. *The Workers' Movement*. Cambridge: Cambridge University Press.

Traxler, Franz. 1994. Collective Bargaining: Levels and Coverage. In *Employment Outlook. July*. Paris: OECD.

Triclin, Alexis. 2001. Le contrat de travail. In *La protection sociale en France*, edited by M. de Montalembert. Paris: La documentation Française.

——. 2001. L'entreprise. In *La protection sociale en France*, edited by M. de Montalembert. Paris: La documentation Française.

Ubbiali, Georges. 2001. Réflexions sur les analyses du syndicalisme et les moyens de sortir de la crise. *Critique Communiste* (162).

Vaslin, Jacques-Marie. 2000. 200 ans de crédit public en France. *Le Monde*, 26 Septembre, VI.

——. 2001. La Troisième voie du chemin du fer. *Le Monde*, 3 Avril, VI.

Vernon, Guy. 2000. The economics of European accident rates. PhD, Economics Department, Warwick University, Warwick.

Verret, Michel. 1992. Où va la classe ouvrière? In *Ouvriers, ouvrières: un continent morcelé et silencieux*, edited by G.-P. Azémar. Paris: Éditions Autrement.

Visser, Jelle. 1999. Industrial Relations and Social Dialogue. Geneva: ILO.

Weber, Henri. 1986. *Le parti des patrons: Le CNPF (1946–1986)*. Paris: Seuil.

Wilsford, David. 1991. The Continuity of Crisis: Patterns of Health Care Policymaking in France. In *The French Welfare State: Surviving Social and Ideological Change*, edited by J. S. Ambler. New York: New York University Press.

Windolf, Paul. 1999. L'évolution du capitalism moderne: La France dans une perspective comparative. *Revue française de sociologie* XL (3).

Winock, Michel. 1995. *La fièvre hexagonale: les grandes crises politiques 1871–1968*. Paris: Seuil.

Zarca, Bernard. 1993. Les patrons dans la statistique officielle française. *Politix* (23).

Zouary, Patrick. 2000. Entre crise et croissance: une évolution des relations professionnelles en entreprise. *Premières synthèses* 49 (1).

——. 2002. Le regard des salariés sur la représentation syndicale. *Premières synthèses* 22 (1).

Index

DATE DUE